Mary Ann's

Cookbook

Mary Ann's

GILLIGAN'S ISLAND

Cookbook

Dawn Wells

Ken Beck and Jim Clark

RUTLEDGE HILL PRESS
Nashville, Tennessee

Several recipes in this book have a tropical flair.
They are garnished with a palm tree.

Published in Nashville, Tennessee by Rutledge Hill Press, 211 Seventh Avenue North, Nashville, Tennessee 37219.
Distributed in Canada by H. B. Fenn and Company Ltd., 1090 Lorimar Drive, Mississauga, Ontario

Design by Harriette Bateman
Typesetting by Stephen Woolverton, Nashville, Tennessee

Library of Congress Cataloging-in-Publication Data

Wells, Dawn
    Mary Ann's Gilligan Island cookbook / Dawn Wells, with Ken Beck and Jim Clark : Foreword by Bob Denver.
        p.   cm.
    Includes index.
    ISBN 1-55853-245-5
    1. Cookery. 2. Menus. 3. Gilligan's Island (Television program) I. Beck, Ken, 1951– : II. Clark, Jim, 1960– . III. Gilligan's Island (Television program) IV. Title
TX714.W34 1993
641.5—dc20   93–32529
                                                                            CIP

Printed in the United States of America
    3 4 5 6 7 8 — 98 97 96 95 94 93

"Gilligan's Island" Cast and History

Gilligan—Bob Denver
Skipper Jonas Grumby—Alan Hale Jr.
Thurston Howell III—Jim Backus
Lovey Howell—Natalie Schafer
Ginger Grant—Tina Louise
Professor Roy Hinkley—Russell Johnson
Mary Ann Summers—Dawn Wells
Creator/Executive Producer—Sherwood Schwartz

"Gilligan's Island" premiered September 26, 1964, on CBS-TV and concluded its prime-time run with ninety-eight episodes on September 3, 1967.

The show spent many weeks in the Top Ten and finished with a ranking of 18th in the Nielsen ratings during its first season and 22nd in its second season, but was bumped from the CBS lineup after its third season to make room for "Gunsmoke." Yet, the series was already in rerun syndication by that time, so in fact "Gilligan's Island" has never been off the air since the first episode was broadcast.

The Castaways returned in animated form in September 1974 on Saturday mornings on ABC-TV in "The New Adventures of Gilligan," which aired for three seasons. Then in September 1983, CBS launched "Gilligan's Planet," which had the cartoon castaways marooned on a remote planet for a year of Saturday mornings.

The original TV series also spawned three TV movies: *Rescue from Gilligan's Island* in 1978, *The Castaways on Gilligan's Island* in 1979, and *The Harlem Globetrotters on Gilligan's Island* in 1981. Could the tide on Gilligan's Island be rising yet again? Don't bet a coconut cream pie against it.

Dedication

This book is dedicated to my wonderful mother, Evelyn G. Wells, without whom this book could not have been done.

Her love, kindness, generosity, tireless efforts, knowledge of what tastes good and what doesn't, years of collecting the best recipes, and her magical hands in the kitchen made this possible.

Thank you, Mama, for this very special time together and for loving me as you do.

A Note From Mom

It has been a great experience and pleasure to help my daughter, Dawn, complete this "Gilligan's Island" cookbook. I am so happy that she asked me to help her compile it. The time we spent together was wonderful and interesting.

When Dawn was growing up, we lived alone. Dawn liked to cook things and make taffy with her friends. We had recipes from both of her grandmothers, and Dawn liked whatever I cooked—except some vegetables, of course.

Dawn has always been a caring and unusually exhilarating person to be with in her many pursuits. For me, this cookbook is another expression of that spirit.

Contents

Foreword by Bob Denver

Dawn and I have been friends for almost thirty years now. We do a couple of personal appearances a year. We've been "rescued" all over this country.

To watch her fans come up and ask for autographs is not only educational but sometimes hilarious. I've seen grown men shaking in their boots with nerves all a-jangle, stuttering, and blushing. Once I saw a man lean over and whisper to her, and later I asked her what he had said. "Thank you for getting me through puberty in the nicest of ways" had been his message.

It's not only the guys who are awestruck. Girls and women thank her for being a role model.

Over the years I've done my own informal survey to find out which of the two girls on the show is more popular. Dawn's "Mary Ann" wins hands down over "Ginger." It doesn't surprise me. Dawn's basic qualities come through the character. She is a warm and caring person with a good sense of humor, and she has energy beyond belief and is smart too. To know her is to like her.

When the history of television is written, "Gilligan's Island" will probably be included, and Dawn's contributions will be understood. All I know is that working with her every week was a joy. When "the powers that be" moved Russell Johnson and her from the end credits to the front with the rest of the cast, justice was done.

Hope you readers enjoy this book, and "Hey, you kids! No pie throwing!"

Bob Denver
"Gilligan"

Introduction

As Kansas farm girl Mary Ann Summers, I was the cook for the three adventurous seasons I enjoyed being shipwrecked on Gilligan's Island with my six fellow Castaways. It seemed you could throw anything—from lobsters and coconuts to papaya and seaweed—at Mary Ann, and in a matter of minutes she could whip up a delicious South Seas banquet ready to spread on the table.

My joy of cooking goes back many years before I was marooned on Gilligan's Island. My own love of cooking and natural comfort in the kitchen came to me from my mom, my grandmothers, and even my great-grandmother.

I was born and raised in Reno, Nevada, and am a fourth-generation Nevadan. My great-great grandfather on my mom's side drove the stagecoach from Reno to Virginia City during the gold rush of 1849. He even drove the founders of the famous Con Chollar gold mine to Promontory Point, Utah, where they witnessed the historic event of driving the famous golden spike celebrating the completion of the first intercontinental railroad.

My Grandmother Wells grew up in Calaveras County (best known for the jumping frog contest), California, where her parents operated the Avery Hotel near Angel's Camp. She was one of nine children. The women all cooked for the public, including a few bandits like a Robin Hood-type desperado named Joaquin Marietta and Black Bart, who robbed the hotel one afternoon and tied up all the women and locked them in the cellar. He stole all the food (they baked about two dozen pies a day), but he left a fifty-dollar gold piece on the table to pay for the imposition. Both of my grandmothers were fabulous cooks, and when my Grandmother Wells moved to Reno, I spent a lot of time eating at her table. My mother's mother, Grammie Rose, is the one who taught my mother many of the wonderful recipes in this book.

Both of my grandmothers and my mom made ravioli from scratch. As my Grandmother Wells used to say, "It takes three whole days to make them and only twenty minutes to eat them."

My father founded a company called Wells Cargo, which included trucking, mining, and road construction. He also was one of the founders of and named the Thunderbird Hotel in Las Vegas. During the last years of his life, he operated the hotel. In fact, he brought the first Broadway show to Las Vegas, *Flower Drum Song,* in about 1962. He was a real pioneer of Nevada.

My parents divorced when I was four, but I felt like I always had two families. I lived with my mom in Reno. My father and stepmother lived in Las Vegas with their two children. So I have a sister, Weslee, and a brother, Joe Carson, and nieces and nephews as well.

I can remember my first experience of cooking by myself. I tried at age eight to give my mother, Evelyn Wells, a surprise birthday party, wanting to do all of the cooking by myself. It's an easy birthday to remember because my mother and I were born on the same day: October 18. I made a banana cake, but I made one little mistake. When I read the recipe, I combined the frosting and cake recipes by putting real cream and whipped cream, mashed bananas and sliced bananas all together. As only a mother can do, she assured me it was great—a little too heavy, but good, she said. (That special ingredient of love always helps the flavor of any food.)

When I was growing up, I made many traditional treats with my mother, like Christmas cookies, fudge, and taffy, but I really didn't get serious about cooking until I was in my early twenties. But I ate everything and still like such foods as liver, beet tops, snow pudding, squash, spinach, asparagus, and lamb.

I learned mostly by just being around my mother. She is a true artist in the kitchen. My dad was a pretty good cook, too. I particularly remember his phenomenal home-made pinto beans. One of the best dishes passed down through the family is my very special "brownstone cake" (Mary Ann's Birthday Cake), based on an old recipe of my mother's Aunt Louise. It's so special that I've never had a birthday without it. My mother makes it for me and even mails it to me if I'm not at home.

Between the two of us, I bet my mother and I have a thousand recipes. With her guidance, I have tried to pick out some of my favorites and very special ones I think you will enjoy. We've also tried to select recipes that represent the kinds of foods the Castaways themselves would enjoy—both on the island and after their rescue. We've had fun with naming the recipes, too.

I'm delighted that we've been able to include recipes that my cast-mates Bob Denver, Russell Johnson, and Tina Louise have so graciously supplied, and the late Alan Hale, Jim Backus, and Natalie Schafer are remembered here with favorite recipes either given to me by them or kindly shared by their families. You'll also find the "Gilligan" heritage of the Harlem Globetrotters represented by delicious recipes from beloved Globetrotter Geese Ausbie.

In addition, there are some wonderful recipes from the dear man who started it all way back in 1964: Sherwood Schwartz, the creator and executive producer of "Gilligan's Island." (Actually, Mildred, his lovely wife, an incredible sculptor in her own right, provided the recipes.) Sherwood's creative genius put us on that fun-filled island, and then he saw to it that we were safely rescued and lived happily ever after. Sherwood's vision, determination, and loving attention to every aspect of "Gilligan's Island" remain the backbone of the show's enormous appeal even after all these years.

Finally, I've gathered some genuine native recipes from an adventure I took to the Solomon Islands with a group of fabulous women from one of my alma maters, Stephens College. So you can enjoy authentic dishes covering a complete range of tastes—from the heartland of Mary Ann's Kansas to the tropics of Gilligan's Isle, as well as from my house and my mom's kitchen. And just as there was never a shortage of coconut cream pies on our island, you'll discover several delicious variations of Mary Ann's famous coconut cream pie here, especially my favorite, my great-grandmother's recipe.

Sprinkled among the recipes are some of my favorite personal anecdotes about the show and the cast, as well as photos, Castaway biographies, trivia quizzes and bits of classic episode dialogue about food and other curiosities of "Gilligan's Island."

I have so many happy memories of my years as a Castaway, and it gives me pleasure to share them with you, along with some of my favorite recipes. I wish you smooth sailing in all your cooking. If you plan to be stranded on an island, bring along this book. It will stick to your ribs as well as tickle your fancy.

Bon voyage and Aloha!

Menus

Deciding which dishes to serve often can be almost as much fun as actually making the recipes. Here are some sample menus and parties to get you sailing in the direction of Gilligan's Island. But as the Castaways themselves found out, you can also have some wonderful adventures by plotting your own course.

Thanksgiving Feast

Ginger Ale Fruit Cocktail
Flaming Passion Cranberry Salad
Mary Ann's Roast Turkey
Howells' Stuffy Stuffing
Mademoiselle Ginger's Mashed Potatoes
Gilligan's Giblet Gravy
Ginger's Sweet Potato Soufflé
Country Club Creamed Onions
Apricot Ahoy Casserole
Ping Pong Popovers or Sea Biscuits
Easy Breezy Pumpkin Pie
Professor's Pecan Pie with Ginger's Top
    Billing
Cinnamon-flavored Coffee
Champagne or Sparkling Cider

Mary Ann's Birthday

Jonathan Kincaid Stalks
Orange You Glad It's Onion Salad
Skinny Mulligan's Shrimp Enchiladas
Richter Scale Green Chile Rice
Scarecrow Screamed Spinach
Mary Ann's Birthday Cake
Tropic Port Lemonade

Mary Ann's Favorite Kansas Supper

Summers Farm Cauliflower and Radish
    Salad
Howell Stake
Ponce de Leon Potatoes and Cucumbers
Community Hut Corn Sauce

Atomic Corn Bread
Mary Ann's Favorite Butterscotch Tapioca
    Pudding
Mint-flavored Iced Tea

Mary Ann's Pancake Breakfast

Mary Ann's Pancakes
Professor's Pancakes
Gilligan's Pancakes
Lovey's Pancakes
Fried Ham, Bacon, or Sausage
Sliced Oranges Sprinkled with Coconut
Hot Coffee or Tea
Cold Milk

Columbus Day Landing Feast

Mary Ann's Marinated Mushrooms
Surfin' Salami Canapes
Moolah Mozzarella Marinara
Operation Orchid Onion and Bean Salad
Seance Ham Salad
Howell's Sour Dough Bread
Great Raftini Fettuccini and Chicken
    Livers
Weenie Linguine
Bikini Fried Zucchini or Cary Grant
    Eggplant
Balboa Broccoli Casserole
Little Spuddy Gnocchi
Java Gelatin
Professor's Apples Archimedes
Cappuccino or Espresso with Orange Slice

Lovey's New Year's Day Siesta Brunch

Guadalcanal Guacamole
Enrico Rodriguez Huevos Rancheros
Jack and the Beanstalk Bean Pot
Lovey's Margaritas
Cinnamon-flavored Coffee

Mrs. Howell's Garden Club Luncheon

Mrs. Howell's Tea Sandwiches
Skipper's Dream Sandwich
Maritime Marmalade Bread
Fiji Fruit Salad
Lovey's Lady Baltimore Cake
Hot Coffee or Hazelnut-flavored Tea
Champagne with Dash of Crème de Cassis

Harvard Club Brunch

Ship Shrimp Dip
Mushroom Cheese Mosquito Bites
Cranberry Pear Corsage
A Howell's Pheasant Under Glass
New World New Potatoes
Mary Ann's Carrots
Thurston's Lord Baltimore Cake
Champagne and Peach Juice
Vanilla-flavored Coffee

Mary Ann's Fourth of July Picnic

Horner's Corners Potato Salad
Sinbad's Five-Pepper Slaw
Mary Ann's Fried Chicken
Kona Banana Bread
Fireworks Celebration Cake
Watermelon
Tropic Port Lemonade
Iced Coffee

Sinko de Minnow

Guadalcanal Guacamole
Pearly White Gazpacho
Pancho Tortilla Soup
Three-hour Tour Fruit Salad
High Tide Tamale Bake

Gang Plank Flank Steak
Double-Vision Banana Cream Pie
Pineapple Knockout Drop Cookies
Lovey's Margaritas
Tropic Port Lemonade (limeade version)

Thurston Howell III's Income Tax Day Lunch

Peanut Butter and Sliced Banana
  Sandwiches
Non-fat Milk

Einstein's Birthday Bash

Orange You Glad It's Onion Salad
Apricot Spear Ribs (with dumplings
  instead of rice)
Dreamy Potato Dumplings
Kansas Fried Cabbage
Yale Man Yogurt Bread
Old Family Recipe Prune Cake
Professor's M.I. Tea

Island Christmas Dinner

Captain Grumby's Roquefort Logs
Flaming Passion Cranberry Salad
Eva's Duckling
Mamasita Howell's Famous Duck Gravy
Longitude and Latitude Wild Rice
Squish Squash
Dow Jones Green Beans and Sour Cream
Sea biscuits
Grandma's Carrot Pudding
Howell's Grog

Crate Arrival Surprise Beach Party

Avocado Grenade Soup
Mission Control Marinated Shrimp
Aloha Fruit Bowl
Compass Points Potato Casserole
Skipper's Goodbye Ribeye
Coral Cornmeal Cakes
Uncharted Cherry Cake
Papaya Nut Pie
Norbett Sherbet Punch

Professor's Labor Day Picnic

Southampton Tomato and Avocado Soup
Professor's Miracle Rescue Slaw
Vandenberg Air Force Basil Shrimp
Cheery Daytime Baked Tuna Sandwich
Skipper's Dream Sandwich
Professor's Apples Archimedes
Thursty's Iced Mint Tea

Hurricane Party

Jet Pack Pepperoni Squares
Spinnaker Spinach Salad
Grandma's Ham Loaf
Maritime Marmalade Bread
Mr. Howell's Gold Bars
Tsunami Punch

Mary Ann's Valentine Party

Mr. Howell's Wall Street Walnut Cake
Lovey's Vanilla Ice Cream
Geiger Counter Berry Glace
Ginger's Star Sugar Cookies
Ginger Snaps
Cheery Cherry Cream Cheesecake
Papuan Punch
Keptibora Punch

Gilligan's Fish Fry

Island Fish
Something Fishy
Don't Rock the Boat Rockfish
Cinderella Corn
New World Potatoes
Skipper's Skillet Bread
Little Buddy Coconut Crunch Pie
Propeller Piña Colada

Gilligan's Lunch

First Mate Potato Salad
Ark-tic Pea Salad
Giant Gilligan Burger
Bikini Fried Zucchini
Rudder Peanut Butter Pie
Chocolate Milk

Lovey's Ice Cream Social

Lovey's Vanilla Ice Cream
Indigo Mob Mocha Cheesecake
Thurston's Denver Mint Ice Cream
Chocolate Tree Parfait
Ginger's Star Sugar Cookies
Marooned Macaroons
Champagne with Strawberry Juice

Ginger's Academy Award Banquet

Ginger's Hawaiian Ginger Beets
Mary Ann and Ginger's Sweet and Sour
    Pork
Bird of Paradise
Shrimp Tahiti
Curried Treasure Fruit
Karate Pinky Carrots (add Ginger)
Gorgeous Gingerbread and Banana
    Shortcake
Ginger's Top Billing
Ginger Tea

Boris Balinkoff's Halloween Meal

Corny Hamlet Chowder
Winfield Winter Vegetable Salad
Lovey's Luncheon Loaf
Periscope Persimmon Cake
Hot Apple Cider (spiced)

Alaskan Supper (April Fool's)

Hut Pizza
Watubi Chicken and Yams
Lovey's Broccoli Brooches
Coral Chocolate Sponge Cake
Cuckoo Cooler

St. Patrick's Day Dinner
Everything's green

Professor's Avocado-stuffed Eggheads
Jonathan Kincaid Stalks
Leaky Ship Watercress Soup
Mighty Sailor Man Meat Loaf
Regatta Risotto
Ho-Ho-Ho Potato Hoe Cakes

Gilligan's Island's Best Key Lime Pie
Tropic Port Limeade with Scoop of Lime
   Sherbet
Irish Coffee

Skipper's All-Vegetable Dinner

Sea Chest Stuffed Mushrooms
Egads Lovey Eggplant
Howell Empire Onion Pie
Hilarious Asparagus Soup
Santa Lucia Linguine
Jungle Zoo-chini
Twenty Trunk Chocolate Trifle
Carrot Juice

Island Easter Dinner

Juicy Fruit Soup
Sinbad's Five-Pepper Slaw
Yummy Ham Mummy
Compass Points Potato Casserole
Mr. Howell's Swiss Bank Chard
Mary Ann's Famous Coconut Cream Pie
Uncharted Cherry Cake
Iced Tea with Lemon and Lime

Mary Ann's Winfield Winner

Sea Saw Blue Cheese Slaw
Wrongway Feldman's Pork Turnover
Capsized Baked Potato
Scarecrow Screamed Spinach
Grandma's Shortcake with Ginger's Top
   Billing
Iced Tea and Coffee

Mary Ann's 4-H Club Dinner

Slice and Dice Salad
Rain Dance Dressing
Luxury Liner Liver
Drum Beet Tops
Jungle Zoo-chini
Mary Ann's Favorite Butterscotch Tapioca
   Pudding
Iced Tea and Coffee

Mary Ann's Intercontinental Meal

Home Sweet Hut Pineapple Cheese Ball
Mobster Lobster Bisque
Grass Skirt Green Bean Salad
Radioactive Ravioli with Machete
   Spaghetti Sauce
Mud Bog Pie
Vanilla-flavored Coffee

Skipper's Rescue Luau

Home Sweet Hut Pineapple Cheese Ball
Three-hour Tour Fruit Salad
Mission Control Marinated Shrimp
Apricot Ahoy Casserole
Great Fire God Spare Ribs
Summers Sour Cream Apple Pie
Sailor's Rum Cake
Millionaire's Mango Daiquiri

Mary Ann's Meat Loaf Meal

Orange You Glad It's Onion Salad
Mom's Meat Loaf Ramoo
Uncle Ramsey's Rice and Raisins
Curried Treasure Fruit
Gilligan's Island Best Key Lime Pie
Orange Spiced Tea

Simple Mainland Meal

Ark-tic Pea Salad
Easy Turkey Tortilla Casserole
Plan B Green Beans with Basil
Coral Chocolate Sponge Cake
Iced Tea and Coffee

Gilligan's Every Day Diet
(recipes from Bob Denver's wife, Dreama)

Poo-Poo-Pee-Doo Dip
Tiny Ship Tossed Salad
Chicken Dijon Gillianna
Signal Fire Vegetables
Headhunter Cheddar Herb Bread
Honeybees Oatmeal Cake
Herbal Tea

Mary Ann's

GILLIGAN'S ISLAND

Cookbook

Mrs. Lovey Howell

The world is Mrs. Howell's oyster. And her world is the Oyster Bay Yacht Club and the Sunnybrook Yacht Club and the Newport Country Club.

Life has always been dreamy for Lovey—even before she was voted Pitted Prune Queen and was a sorority sister at Vassar, which is probably where (other than four-star restaurant menus) she picked up most of the Italian and French she knows.

About the only weight on Mrs. Howell's shoulders are her necklaces (including a 48-carat diamond brooch) and her assortment of furs (though watch out for fur from cats; she's allergic). Her one-pound diamond engagement ring is about her only other burden.

Mrs. Howell seems to adapt to primitive island life quite well. It's true she misses her homes in Newport, New York, Palm Beach, Paris, and everywhere else. Yet somehow she makes do without hairdresser Rodney and chauffeur Charles, though surely she misses friends like Princess Grace and Prince Rainier.

And while Mrs. Howell is a member of the DAR and even has been a nurse's aid, most of all she is devoted Lovey to husband Thurston. Together they swoon in the Howell manner.

Appetizers

Ship Shrimp Dip

1 8-ounce can frozen cream of shrimp
  soup, thawed
An equal amount mashed shrimp

½ cup sour cream
1 tablespoon horseradish
¼ teaspoon Worcestershire sauce

In a serving bowl combine all of the ingredients. Refrigerate for 1 hour. Serve with crackers, etc. Makes about 3 cups.

———————— **"** ————————

Howell Etiquette:
Mr. Howell: The Duke's first day. We must have him for cocktails.
Mrs. Howell: Oh, Thurston, always the right saying at the right time. No
  wonder you're always sitting on the host's right hand.
Gilligan: Isn't that kind of uncomfortable?

———————— **"** ————————

Guadalcanal Guacamole

2 ripe avocados, peeled, pitted, and
  mashed
2 cloves garlic, minced
½ cup finely chopped onion
2 tablespoons lemon or lime juice

Couple generous dashes Tabasco sauce
1 cup sour cream
½ cup mayonnaise
Chips

In a large bowl combine all of the ingredients except the chips. Serve the guacamole with the chips. Makes about 3 cups of guacamole.
From Natalie Schafer.

Poo-Poo-Pee-Doo Dip

1 8-ounce can pineapple tidbits
2 8-ounce packages cream cheese, soft-ened
1 8-ounce can water chestnuts, drained and chopped
3 tablespoons chopped fresh chives

1 teaspoon seasoned salt
¼ teaspoon pepper
1 cup chopped pecans
Fresh parsley
Assorted crackers

Drain the pineapple, reserving 1 tablespoon of juice. In a small bowl combine the pineapple, cream cheese, water chestnuts, chives, salt, pepper, and pecans. Stir in the reserved juice, mixing well. Garnish with parsley. Cover and chill.

Serve with crackers. Makes about 3 ½ cups of dip.

From Dreama and Bob Denver.

———————— ❝ ————————

Gilligan: I didn't drink rum. I drank nitro.

Mrs. Howell: Oh, mixed drinks are even worse.

———————— ❞ ————————

Sea Chest Stuffed Mushrooms

12 to 16 fresh medium mushrooms
½ cup butter or margarine
1 clove garlic, mashed
3 tablespoons finely chopped green pep-per
3 tablespoons finely chopped onion

1 ½ cups fresh ¼-inch bread cubes (or bread crumbs)
½ teaspoon salt
⅛ teaspoon pepper
½ cup Parmesan cheese
Finely chopped crab or shrimp (optional)

Wipe the mushrooms, and remove and finely chop the stems. In a large skillet heat 3 tablespoons of butter. Sauté the bottom side of the caps for 2 to 3 minutes. Arrange the caps in a shallow pan, rounded side down. Heat the remaining butter and sauté the mushroom stems, garlic, green pepper, and onion for about 5 minutes, until tender. Remove the pan from the heat and stir in the bread cubes and season-ings. Fill the caps, mounding the filling mixture in the center. Bake at 350° for 15 minutes. Makes 6 to 8 servings.

Mary Ann's Marinated Mushrooms

1 ½ pounds mushrooms
½ cup olive oil
⅓ cup lemon juice or ¼ cup wine
   vinegar
¼ teaspoon dry mustard
¼ teaspoon salt

¼ teaspoon garlic salt
1 clove garlic, crushed
¼ teaspoon dried basil
⅛ teaspoon pepper
2 cups thinly sliced celery

Wash the mushrooms, and cut the stems into thin slices. In a small bowl combine the olive oil, lemon juice, dry mustard, salt, garlic salt, garlic, basil, and pepper. Stir to blend. In a medium bowl combine the mushrooms and celery, and pour the marinade over them. Cover and refrigerate overnight.

Arrange the marinated vegetables on a shallow platter and decorate with parsley. Makes about 6 servings.

Note: Serve a platter of marinated vegetables instead of a salad.

The Tennessean

Just hanging around

Please, Don't Ask

The question I'm asked most often is, "Where'd you get all those clothes?" I just say, "Thank goodness for the Howells and all of those trunks!" (And Mary Ann's good home-ec training for remaking Lovey's outfits.)

Mushroom-Cheese Mosquito Bites

Easy and good.

½ of a 17 ½-ounce package frozen puff
 pastry
1 tablespoon margarine
¾ pound thinly sliced mushrooms

1 teaspoon dried thyme
Salt and pepper to taste
1 tablespoon beaten egg
1 cup shredded Swiss cheese

Let the pastry stand for 20 to 30 minutes at room temperature.

In a skillet heat the margarine and sauté the mushrooms and thyme for about 8 to 10 minutes until brown. Add salt and pepper to taste. Let the mushrooms cool or chill.

Unfold the pastry in a lightly greased 15x10-inch baking pan. Brush the pastry with the beaten egg. Prick all over with a fork. Scatter the mushrooms and cheese evenly over the pastry. Bake at 425° for about 20 minutes, until richly browned. Serve hot or warm in wedges. Makes 10 to 12 servings.

The Tennessean

The ship set ground on the shore of this uncharted desert isle

Professor's Avocado-Stuffed Eggheads

4 hard-boiled eggs
1 avocado
Lemon juice
2 teaspoons prepared horseradish mustard
1 teaspoon lemon juice
1 teaspoon salt
2 tablespoons butter or margarine

1 tablespoon finely chopped onion
2 tablespoons all-purpose flour
1 teaspoon instant chicken bouillon granules
1 teaspoon dried parsley flakes
½ cup milk
½ cup water
¼ cup chopped fully cooked ham

Peel the eggs and halve them lengthwise. Remove the yolks and set the whites aside.

Halve the avocado lengthwise and rub lemon juice over the cut edges. Peel and mash half of the avocado. Store the remaining half for another use. Combine the mashed avocado with the egg yolks, mustard, 1 teaspoon of lemon juice, and salt. Mix well. Fill the halved egg whites with the avocado mixture, and arrange the stuffed eggs in 2 casseroles.

In a small saucepan melt the butter and cook the onion until tender but not brown. Stir in the flour, bouillon granules, and parsley. Combine the milk and water, and add it all at once to the flour. Cook, stirring constantly, until smooth. Pour the sauce over the eggs. Sprinkle ham over the sauce. Bake at 350° for 20 to 25 minutes. Makes 4 servings.

———————— " ————————

Skipper: Wow, what a brilliant idea!
Professor: Well, frankly, Skipper, I think it's my most brilliant idea. There's only one thing I'm not certain of.
Skipper: Oh, what's that?
Professor: If it will work.

———————— " ————————

Jonathan Kincaid Stalks

Cream cheese, softened
Apricot brandy

Crushed pineapple, drained
Celery cut into 2-inch pieces

In a mixing bowl combine the cream cheese, apricot brandy, and crushed pineapple. Fill the pieces of celery with the cream cheese mixture. Chill.

Egad Lovey Eggplant

1 1-pound eggplant
2 cloves garlic, minced
¾ cup lemon juice
6 tablespoons sesame seed butter

(tahini)
½ cup minced fresh parsley
Salt and freshly ground pepper to taste
Sliced toasted pita bread or crackers

Trim off the stem end of the eggplant, and pierce all over with a fork. Roast the eggplant at 500° until the eggplant is tender and the skin is wrinkled. Let it cool for 1 hour. Scrape out the pulp and mash it with the garlic, lemon juice, sesame butter, and parsley. Season with salt and pepper. Refrigerate for at least 1 hour.
Serve with sliced toasted pita bread or crackers. Makes 6 to 8 servings.

―――――― 66 ――――――

Mrs. Howell: I always did hear that the way to a man's stomach is through the kitchen.

―――――― 99 ――――――

Hut Pizza

3 ½ cups crisp rice cereal, crushed
6 tablespoons butter, melted
1 tablespoon sugar
2 3-ounce packages cream cheese, softened
1 14-ounce can sweetened condensed
milk

⅓ cup lemon juice
1 teaspoon vanilla extract
1 20-ounce can crushed pineapple
1 tablespoon cornstarch
¼ cup toasted chopped pecans
Toasted pecan halves

In a mixing bowl combine the cereal, butter, and sugar. Press the mixture into the bottom of a 12-inch pizza pan. Bake at 350° for 10 minutes. Cool.
In a small mixer bowl beat the cream cheese, sweetened condensed milk, lemon juice, and vanilla with an electric mixer on low speed until smooth. Spread the filling over the crust. Cover and chill.
In a saucepan combine the undrained pineapple and cornstarch. Cook and stir until bubbly, then cook and stir 2 minutes more. Cool. Spread the pineapple mixture over the cheese layer. Sprinkle chopped pecans in the center and trim the edges with pecan halves. Cover and chill. Makes 10 servings.

Surfin' Salami Canapes

½ pound hard salami, finely chopped
1 pimiento, finely chopped
⅓ cup chopped green pepper
3 tablespoons chopped ripe olives

½ cup mayonnaise
½ cup butter, softened
32 2-inch bread rounds (white or whole
wheat)

In a small bowl combine all of the ingredients except the bread rounds. Spread the mixture on the bread and arrange on a serving platter. Makes 32 canapes.

"

Gilligan: Me! An officer? That's impossible!
Skipper: Why?
Gilligan: I'm too busy being the whole crew.

"

Trivia Quiz

Mary Ann's Taste Testers

1. What is Gilligan's favorite candy?

   Licorice

2. How does the Skipper like his steak prepared?

   Rare—with onions and fried potatoes

3. What does Gilligan always eat at the movies?

   Popcorn

4. What food does Leo the lion enjoy most?

   Corned beef

5. What does Mr. Howell use as a golf ball?

   Avocado pit

Blue Moon Blue Cheese Spread

½ cup soft butter
½ pound blue cheese, crumbled
2 tablespoons lemon juice

1 cup coarsely chopped walnuts
½ pint whipping cream

In a medium bowl cream together the butter and blue cheese until well blended and smooth. Add the lemon juice and nuts. Set the mixture aside.

Just before serving, whip the cream and fold it into the butter mixture. Place the spread in a serving bowl and garnish with walnut or pecan halves. Makes 4 cups of spread.

The Set

Because of intense fog at Zuma Beach, CBS was forced to build a lagoon on the studio lot, but we shared it with other shows. Our show would shoot Monday and Tuesday, and then they'd take away all our palm trees and tropical plants. In would come the tumbleweeds, the willows, and the pine trees and, presto, it would be Dodge City and ready for "Gunsmoke." I always loved the fact that you could change the landscape the way you changed furniture. Oh, the magic of show biz.

The lagoon had all these incredibly beautiful plants. They had three or four greensmen who took care of the flowers, trees, and all our plants.

On the indoor soundstage, the tropical setting was beautiful. We had plants, trees, and flowers. It was always pretty. The huts had their own permanent spots. It was a small studio—very intimate and very lovely. (Talk about disillusionment, I think they shoot "Roseanne" there today.)

Lagoon Dip

1 8-ounce carton whipped cream cheese
2 cups shredded cheddar cheese
¼ cup milk
3 tablespoons port wine (or grape juice)

1 teaspoon Worcestershire sauce
½ teaspoon salt
½ teaspoon dry mustard
1 ripe sweet pineapple

In a medium bowl beat together the cheeses, milk, wine, Worcestershire sauce, salt, and dry mustard. Cut the pineapple in half crosswise and cut the pineapple meat out of the bottom half of the shell and cut into cubes. Fill the shell with cheese mixture and refrigerate until ready to serve. Cut the crown off the top half of the pineapple and cut off the rind. Cut into quarters, cut away the core, and cut the meat into chunks. Refrigerate. Let the cheese-stuffed pineapple stand at room temperature for 15 minutes to soften before serving. Serve with the pineapple chunks. Makes 6 to 8 servings.

Natalie, a crew member, and I take a break during the first day of filming the first episode of "Gilligan's Island." A historic day, I'd say.

Puffed Ham and Cheese Pith Helmet

1 6-serving size package chicken flavor or corn bread stuffing mix

8 ounces cheddar cheese, shredded or cut in ½-inch cubes

4 ounces (about 1 cup) slivered boiled ham

3 tablespoons all-purpose flour

3 tablespoons butter or margarine, melted

4 eggs, slightly beaten

3 ½ cups whole milk (or reconstituted nonfat dry)

1 teaspoon seasoned salt

Pour the stuffing crumbs into a greased 2-quart baking dish. Top with cheese and ham. Sprinkle with flour and drizzle evenly with butter. In a medium bowl combine the eggs, milk, and seasoned salt, mixing well. Pour the filling over the crumb mixture. Bake uncovered at 350° for 1 hour. Makes 2 quarts or 8 to 10 servings.

The smell of success?

Moolah Mozzarella Marinara

¼ cup olive oil
1 clove garlic, minced
1 tablespoon minced parsley
½ teaspoon dried basil
½ teaspoon dried oregano
2 cups canned tomatoes, chopped

Salt and pepper to taste
Oil
2 pounds Mozzarella cheese, cut in cubes
2 eggs, beaten
2 cups seasoned bread crumbs

In a saucepan heat the oil and sauté the garlic until golden brown. Add the parsley, basil, oregano, tomatoes, and salt and pepper to taste. Simmer the marinara sauce over low heat for 1 hour.

In a saucepan heat 2 inches of oil to 350°. Dip each cheese cube into the beaten eggs, then coat with the seasoned crumbs. Fry 4 or 5 pieces at a time until golden brown. Drain on paper towels. Serve accompanied by marinara sauce. Makes 6 to 8 servings.

Howell Empire Onion Pie

1 ½ cups Ritz Cracker crumbs
¼ cup soft margarine
2 tablespoons margarine
5 large onions, diced
½ cup sliced mushrooms

Parsley
4 eggs
1 tablespoon sour cream
Salt and pepper to taste

In a small bowl combine the cracker crumbs and ¼ cup of margarine. Mix until blended. Press the mixture into a 9-inch pie pan. Bake the crust at 300° for 10 minutes. Cool before filling.

In a sauté pan melt 2 tablespoons of margarine and cook the onions, mushrooms, and a small amount of parsley until golden. Cool. Place the mixture in a blender and add the eggs, sour cream, salt, and pepper. Mix until blended. Turn into the cracker crust. Bake at 350° for 30 minutes or until set. Makes 8 to 10 servings.

——————— **"** ———————

Skipper: Now folks, let's stop complaining and face up to the fact. We have to stay on these rations for a while. One string bean, one olive and one cup of soup per person.
Mr. Howell: Ginger, I'll give you $500 for your olive.
Mrs. Howell: Oh, Thurston, that's not fair.
Mr. Howell: You're right, dear. Make it a thousand.
Mary Ann: Imagine. A thousand dollars for an olive.
Ginger: Without a martini?

——————— **"** ———————

Home Sweet Hut Pineapple Cheese Ball

2 8-ounce packages cream cheese, soft-
    ened
1 8 ½-ounce can crushed pineapple,
    drained
2 cups chopped pecans
¼ cup finely chopped green pepper

2 tablespoons finely chopped onion
1 tablespoon seasoned salt
Pineapple slices for garnish
Maraschino cherries for garnish
Parsley for garnish

In a bowl beat the cheese with a fork until smooth. Gradually stir in the pineapple, 1 cup of pecans, green pepper, onion, and seasoned salt. Shape into a ball. Roll the ball in the remaining pecans. Wrap the ball in plastic or foil and refrigerate for 6 to 8 hours or overnight.

Garnish with pineapple slices, maraschino cherries, and parsley. Surround with crackers. Makes 40 servings.

Mary Ann searches for wild berries

Guava Cheese Pie

½ cup guava paste
½ cup cream
3 eggs
1 pound sieved cottage cheese

1 tablespoon lime juice
Pinch salt
1 8-inch graham cracker crust
Dash mace

Chop the guava paste into small cubes. In a saucepan heat the guava paste and cream over the lowest heat possible until the paste partially melts but tiny blobs remain. In a small bowl beat the eggs until fluffy and lemon-colored. In a large bowl combine the cottage cheese, beaten eggs, guava mixture, lime juice, and salt. Pour the filling into the crust and sprinkle with mace. Bake at 350° for 45 to 55 minutes. Makes 1 8-inch pie.

I was raised with love, morals, values, principles, and a sound work ethic. I was taught to be kind, considerate, and loving to other people, as well as to share responsibilities. Mary Ann is the same way.

She is practical, kind, loving, and hard working. So I think Mary Ann is a very good role model for young girls today. All the basics are within her—she has principles and sticks to them and the ability to share and give, as well as a positive outlook.

Mary Ann has been part of my life since 1964, almost three decades ago, so I know her quite well. I know how she would react to things and what her attitudes and opinions would be. She has really become a part of me. And I think I'm somewhat similar to Mary Ann. At least I've tried to live my life by the same kind of high standards that Mary Ann follows.

Captain Grumby's Roquefort Logs

1 ½ cups crumbled Roquefort cheese
1 8-ounce package cream cheese,
 softened
1 cup grated cheddar cheese

2 tablespoons heavy cream
⅓ cup minced walnuts
1 cup toasted coconut

In a medium bowl combine the cheeses until well blended. Add the cream. Mix in the nuts. Chill the mixture for 1 hour.

Shape into 1 ½-inch logs, and roll in coconut. Chill for 3 hours. Makes about 32 logs.

Jet Pack Pepperoni Squares

2 cups Bisquick
2 hard-boiled eggs, chopped
½ cup chopped pepperoni
½ cup chopped onion

1 teaspoon dried oregano leaves
⅛ teaspoon pepper
⅔ cup milk
Softened butter

In a medium bowl mix together the Bisquick, eggs, pepperoni, onion, oregano, pepper, and milk. Spread the dough in a greased 9-inch square pan. Spread with softened butter. Bake at 450° for 15 to 20 minutes. Cut into squares. Makes 9 to 12 servings.

The Creator

I was very naive and new to Hollywood when I auditioned for the role of Mary Ann, and Sherwood Schwartz was the first person I met when I interviewed for the role. I was very green and knew almost nothing about how the business worked. I didn't know any of the ins or outs, but Sherwood was very kind and witty and made me feel comfortable. He was warm and personable and helpful. I also think my training at Stephens College gave me a sense of confidence. I was never nervous, and with the great stage training I had there and at the University of Washington in Seattle, I was prepared plus I'd also had a lot of actual stage experience.

Working with Sherwood was like being in a family. He was extremely professional, but lighthearted. You always knew you were in competent hands. Sherwood instinctively knows what's right and what's wrong, what's funny and what isn't. His tenacity to stick to what he believed in is what got "Gilligan's Island" on the air in the first place, and his talent drew the high ratings.

Not only is Sherwood immensely talented and just plain funny, but he has a wonderful family too. He and his wife, Mildred, who is a terrific sculptor, have been married for over fifty years and have four great, successful children (Ross, Lloyd, Hope, and Donald). Through the years they have remained a very close, delightful family, which is rare in Hollywood.

I can remember Lloyd and Hope visiting the "Gilligan" set when they were little. Lloyd has become a writer and producer (he even played my fiancé in · the *Rescue* special!), and Hope has become an outstanding composer. I am so proud to have known them all this time.

Sherwood is such a kind, good soul. He was always positive and optimistic. When the show was cancelled by CBS, he called to say he had some bad news—the network had decided not to renew the show. We were all quite shocked, but somehow it was easier hearing it from Sherwood.

Schwartz 'n' Eggers

2 tablespoons butter	2 tablespoons green pepper
2 tablespoons all-purpose flour	1 ¼ cups canned tomatoes
1 cup milk	1 clove garlic, minced
Butter	½ teaspoon chili powder
2 tablespoons onion	10 hard-boiled eggs, sliced

In a saucepan melt 2 tablespoons of butter and blend in the flour. Gradually add the milk, stirring constantly until thick and smooth. Set the cream sauce aside.

In a skillet melt a small amount of butter and sauté the onion and green pepper. Add the tomatoes, garlic, and chili powder, and cook until thick. Add the tomato mixture to the cream sauce. In a greased pan alternate layer of eggs and sauce. Top with cracker crumbs and grated cheese. Bake 15 minutes. Makes 6 servings

From Mildred and Sherwood Schwartz.

Mrs. Howell's Imported Caviar Pie

1 dozen hard-boiled eggs, finely
  chopped
1 medium onion, finely chopped
Mayonnaise

¼ cup sour cream
4 ounces caviar (black or red or both),
  rinsed well
Wafer crackers

In a large bowl combine the eggs and onion, and add mayonnaise to hold the mixture together. Spread the filling into a 10-inch pie plate. Spread with a very thin layer of sour cream. Spread the caviar over the pie with a spoon.

Serve with table wafer crackers, and provide butter knives for guests to help themselves. Makes about 10 to 12 servings.

Note: If using lump caviar, rinse and drain well. If using any other caviar, it is not necessary to rinse and drain. Or do a design with black and red caviar.

———————— **"** ————————

Mr. Howell: Uh-ho, I'm simply famished.

Mrs. Howell: I'm so hungry, I could eat *domestic* caviar.

———————— **"** ————————

Dawn Wells collection

This is a recent picture of me with my favorite TV producer of all time, Sherwood Schwartz. Besides "Gilligan's Island," Sherwood also created "The Brady Bunch." This photograph was taken at the opening of *The Brady Bunch* at the Westwood Playhouse in 1992.

The Tennessean

Mr. Howell

Thurston Howell III speaks the universal language: money. That's no surprise since he had proper training at Harvard and SMU (Super Millionaires University). And there's no question about his favorite herb: mint.

But there's more to the Wizard (and Wolf) of Wall Street than his enormous wealth. (Egads, man! Bite your tongue!) There's his lovely Lovey, his wife for 20-odd years. And there's his comfort during bear markets, his Teddy.

The Howell empire covers every imaginable sort of business venture—from a movie studio and Howell Aircraft to a sugar plantation and the Tahatchapookoo Oil and Mining Company in Dustbowl, Oklahoma. That's not to mention the catch-all parent company of Howell Industries.

An avid golfer, Mr. Howell is a member of many clubs, such as Winged Foot, Pebble Beach, and his beloved Harvard Club. But his favorite club is the New York Stock Exchange. He also enjoys playing polo at West Brookdale with steeds Bruce and Sea Biscuit.

Mr. Howell likewise has plenty of time for reading. In fact, he doesn't mind reading the same edition of *The Wall Street Journal* day after day on the island. He also keeps a copy of *A Million Ways to Make a Million* handy, though he probably knows it by heart. Still, his most preferred reading is the Social Register.

Even though a Howell was the first passenger on the Mayflower and the first to land at Plymouth Rock, life has not aways been smooth sailing for the Howells. Tragedy struck his family during the stock market crash in '29, when a young Mr. Howell himself became "just a millionaire." But not all of his tastes are expensive. He says he doesn't like caviar, and he admits that he has a strong yen for Perry Mason mysteries.

Though he may seem somewhat defenseless at times, Mr. Howell claims both to have been the captain of the boxing team at Vassar and to have a black belt in karate earned in Japan.

More than his fortune, Mr. Howell says the real mark of a Howell and the thing he's proudest of is his modesty. However, that's one Howell commodity that you might have trouble taking to the bank.

Beverages

Cuckoo Cooler

¼ cup instant coffee
⅓ cup sugar
1 cup milk

3 6 ½-ounce bottles Coca-Cola, chilled
1 cup softened vanilla ice cream

In a punch bowl combine the instant coffee, sugar, and milk. Add the Coca-Cola and stir in the softened ice cream. Makes 5 to 6 servings.

"

A Little Drinky:
Mr. Howell: How's your drink, my dear?
Mrs. Howell: Very nice, thank you.
Mr. Howell: Would you care for another one?
Mrs. Howell: Thank you, dear. This time would you give me a little mint?
Mr. Howell: Which little mint would you prefer? The one in Denver or the one in San Francisco?

"

Howell's Grog

3 cups lowfat milk
½ cup rum
2 ripe bananas in chunks

3 tablespoons sugar
Nutmeg

In a blender combine the milk, rum, bananas, and sugar. Chill. Before serving, sprinkle on nutmeg. Makes 8 servings.

Keptibora Punch

2 tablespoons instant tea
1 6-ounce package strawberry gelatin
⅓ cup sugar
2 cups boiling water
¼ cup lemon juice
6 cups cold water

2 cups rosé wine, chilled
1 quart lemon-lime carbonated
   beverage, chilled
1 10-ounce package frozen sliced strawberries, slightly thawed

In a large mixing bowl combine the tea, gelatin, and sugar. Pour the boiling water over the mixture and stir until the gelatin is dissolved. Add the lemon juice, cold water, and wine. Chill.

At serving time, pour the punch over ice cubes in a punch bowl. Add the carbonated beverage and strawberries. Makes about 40 servings.

Dawn Wells collection

In *The Harlem Globetrotters on Gilligan's Island,* Bob Denver's wife, Dreama (bottom right), joined us as a cheerleader. Notice also that by this time it had become O.K. to show my belly button.

Cool Choco Java

4 cups (32 ounces) extra-strong coffee
8 ice cubes
2 tablespoons sugar

½ cup chocolate syrup
1 pint coffee ice cream
Chocolate shavings

Brew the coffee using 4 measuring cups of water to 8 approved coffee measures of coffee. Cool to room temperature.

In a blender combine 2 cups of coffee with the ice cubes and sugar, and blend at medium speed. Pour into 8 glasses, about 3 ounces in each. Place the remaining coffee in the blender, add the chocolate syrup and ice cream, and blend at high speed. Fill the glasses with the chocolate mixture and garnish with shaved chocolate, if desired. Makes 8 servings.

Double Dribble

While filming *The Harlem Globetrotters on Gilligan's Island,* it was difficult to find cheerleader outfits that would look good on all four of the women. So we only had one outfit each. We were told by the wardrobe designers not to eat, drink, or do anything while in these costumes.

I was sitting in my chair drinking coffee with cream from a styrofoam cup when one of the Globetrotters came up behind me and asked for an autograph. I put the styrofoam cup between my teeth as I took the pen and paper to sign my autograph. When I finished writing, I said, "Here," and tilted my head back with the coffee cup in my teeth as I handed him the autograph over my shoulder. As I leaned back, the coffee spilled from the cup and ran all down the front of my costume.

They had to take me into the washroom and wash me and the costume, then try to dry me off with a hair dryer so I wouldn't hold up the filming. Talk about embarassed! Of course, if I wanted to do that again as a comedy bit, I could never repeat it, I'm sure.

Ginger's Raspberry-Lemon Thaw

1 10-ounce package frozen raspberries
1 pint lemon sherbet, softened

1 quart milk

Thaw the raspberries. In a large mixing bowl beat the sherbet and raspberries, adding milk gradually. Serve in chilled glasses. Makes about 6 cups.

Hot Ginger Lemonade

4 cups water
¾ cup frozen lemonade concentrate,
   undiluted

3 to 4 tablespoons slivered candied
   ginger
lemon slices for garnish

In a saucepan combine the water, lemonade concentrate, and ginger. Heat until simmering. To serve, stir well, pour into serving cups, and garnish with lemon slices. Makes 6 to 8 servings.

Dawn Wells today

Norbett Sherbet Punch

1 46-ounce can pineapple juice, chilled
1 pint orange juice, chilled
¼ cup lemon juice, chilled

1 quart ginger ale, chilled
1 quart pineapple sherbet

In a punch bowl blend the juices. Add the ginger ale and sherbet, stirring until the sherbet is softened and partially dissolved. Garnish the punch bowl with an ice ring. Makes about 4 quarts.

Red Black Blox Beaver Blink Drink

1 pint cranberry juice cocktail
1 ½ cups fresh lemon juice
1 cup sugar

2 28-ounce bottles chilled ginger ale
1 pint raspberry sherbet

Combine the cranberry juice cocktail, fresh lemon juice, and sugar, blending well. Chill. To serve, pour the cranberry juice mixture over ice in a punch bowl. Add the chilled ginger ale and sherbet. Stir to partially dissolve the sherbet. Serve at once, lacing each serving with rum, if desired. Makes 24 punch cup servings.

Bola Bola Serum

1 quart apple juice
¼ cup honey
1 cup blanched, whole almonds
1 cup raisins
Peel from 2 oranges, chopped
12 whole cloves

1 cinnamon stick
2 pints cranberry juice cocktail
10 7-ounce bottles lemon-lime carbonated beverage
2 trays ice cubes

In a saucepan combine the first seven ingredients. Simmer for 30 minutes. Set the mixture aside for 1 hour. Strain. Return the almonds to the apple juice and chill. In a punch bowl combine the apple juice and cranberry juice. Slowly add the chilled lemon-lime carbonated beverage. Add the ice cubes. Makes nearly 1 gallon.

Shipwreck Punch

2 46-ounce cans pineapple juice
1 pint orange juice
1 12-ounce can papaya nectar
¼ cup lemon juice

1 pint dark rum
½ pint brandy
1 large bottle champagne (about 26 ounces)

In a large bowl combine all of the ingredients except the champagne. Cover and refrigerate for 24 hours to allow the flavors to mellow. Pour over ice in a punch bowl. Add the chilled champagne just before serving. Makes about 1 gallon.

Lovey's Margaritas

1 cup tequila
½ cup Triple Sec

½ cup pineapple juice
½ cup lime juice

Stir or shake with a lot of crushed ice, strain and serve. (Usually the glasses are coated with a thin layer of salt on the rim, but Natalie didn't like excess salt. Still delicious...and potent!) Makes 4 margaritas.
From Natalie Schafer.

Thursty's Iced Mint Tea

Lemon slices
Orange slices

Fresh mint
1 quart iced tea, sweetened to taste

Place some of the lemon slices, orange slices, and fresh mint in the pitcher. Pound and twist some of the mint and add it to the tea pitcher. Garnish glasses with lemon slices and mint sprigs. Makes 1 quart.

My Dear Mrs. Howell

Natalie Schafer was a lovely lady and my dear friend with a one-of-a-kind personality. There was a special bond between us. She didn't have a daughter and as the years passed, we grew closer and closer.

Once she came to visit me at my home in Florida. We went to the beach, and it caused such a sensation because people saw Mary Ann and Mrs. Howell at the same time. Of course, she always wore a "Lovey" hat.

I remember dropping her off at the airport. She had this darling chihuahua named Lovey, which she carried in her handbag. She tried to sneak Lovey onto the plane in her custom-made bag with air holes in each end. However, that day the airline discovered it and would not allow her to take Lovey on board.

Fortunately, after tears and tantrums another airline gave them a seat, and when Natalie got back to Los Angeles, she called me and said, "Darling, I will never come back to Florida unless, of course, I can walk." She had a love for life and a zest for the unusual. She loved to shock you and to say things that would make your hair stand up—just to see your reaction. She would ask you very personal questions and before you knew it, you'd answered her and told her more than you intended. She was fun, utterly feminine, seemingly helpless, and as sharp as a fox.

Tropic Port Lemonade

½ cup lemon juice
1 ¾ cups sugar syrup
2 cups pineapple juice

1 cup grapefruit juice
¾ cup orange juice
2 cups soda water

In a glass combine the lemon juice, sugar syrup, and pineapple juice. Stir well. Add or substitute any of the optional ingredients, as desired. Decorate with maraschino cherries and/or fresh mint sprigs. Makes 4 servings.

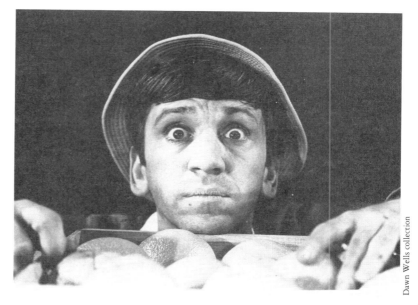

Dawn Wells collection

Vitamin C as far as the eye can see.

Millionaire's Mango Daiquiri

2 ounces lemon or lime juice
½ cup water
Sugar

6 ounces light rum
1 mango, peeled and seeded

In a pitcher mix the lemon juice and water, and add sugar to taste. Add the rum and mix well. In a blender purée the mango and blend until smooth. Add rum mixture and blend. Add crushed ice and mix thoroughly. Serve in chilled cocktail glasses or pour over additional crushed ice. Makes 2 servings.

Ginger Tea

1 large ginger root, peeled　　　　　　**Sugar**
1 gallon water

In a stock pot place the ginger root in the water. Bring the water to a boil, reduce the heat, and simmer for 30 minutes. Strain and sweeten to taste. Makes 1 gallon.

――――――― ❝ ―――――――

Skipper: Mr. Howell, I gotta take my hat off to you. Beneath that rough exterior, there lies a heart of gold.
Mr. Howell: No, if that were true, I'da had it removed and minted years ago.

――――――― ❞ ―――――――

Professor's M.I. Tea

1 cup Tang powder　　　　　　**1 teaspoon ground cinnamon**
1 cup instant tea　　　　　　**1 teaspoon ground cloves**
1 cup sugar　　　　　　**1 10-ounce package lemonade mix**

In a large bowl combine all of the ingredients. Store the mixture in a jar. To make beverage add 2 or 3 teaspoons to 1 cup boiling water. Makes about 68 servings.

Propeller Piña Colada

¼ cup unsweetened pineapple juice　　　　**1 cup ice cubes**
2 to 3 ounces dark rum　　　　**Spears of fresh pineapple for garnish**
2 to 3 tablespoons coconut cream

In a blender purée the pineapple juice, rum, coconut cream, and ice until frothy. Pour immediately into an iced goblet, and garnish with pineapple. Serve. Makes 1 serving.

Tsunami Punch

1 16-ounce can peaches, undrained
⅓ cup orange juice
3 tablespoons lime juice
3 sprigs fresh mint, leaves only
⅛ teaspoon grated lime rind

⅛ teaspoon grated orange rind
1 quart ginger ale, chilled
Champagne to taste
Mint for garnish

In a blender, whirl the peaches with their syrup until puréed. Add the orange juice, lime juice, mint leaves, lime and orange rinds. Pour the mixture into a pitcher and refrigerate until chilled.

Just before serving add the ginger ale and champagne. Garnish with mint sprigs. Makes about 20 to 30 servings.

Wrongway Feldman wakes up to island life:
Wrongway: That's awful! What is that?!
Ginger: It's coffee.
Wrongway: Coffee?
Ginger: We make it from fish. I mean, the instant's not as good as the regular, but...

Papuan Punch

This is great served over ice in a scooped-out watermelon.

1 fifth Midori melon liqueur
1 fifth light rum
12 ounces crème de banane
1 46-ounce can unsweetened pineapple
  juice

12 ounces Rose's lime juice
1 ½ quarts chilled club soda
1 lime, thinly sliced
1 pint strawberries, sliced

In a large punch bowl combine all of the ingredients except the fruit slices, stirring to blend. Add a large block of ice and garnish with the sliced fruit. Makes about 60 servings.

Gilligan's Staying Power

I think "Gilligan's Island" is a wonderful half-hour escape. It's clean, funny, lighthearted, and melts your troubles away. It's also timeless. There are no cars or clothes that date it.

We had a phenomenal cast with a splendid variety of comedians. Everybody was a little larger than life, and everybody physically fit their roles so well. We were a family. Truthfully, the person most unlike his character was Bob Denver.

And the comedy still holds up. When I watch the show now, many episodes still make me laugh. It's nonsensical, but it's good. I think it's also a pretty show to look at. We were one of the first to take the sitcom out of the living room. It was pre-"Fantasy Island" and it was beautiful. Kids still come up to me and say you were my family after school.

Soups

Hilarious Asparagus Soup

¼ cup margarine
2 large leeks (1 cup), white only, chopped
3 teaspoons instant chicken bouillon granules
3 cups water

2 10-ounce packages frozen asparagus pieces (or 2 ½ cups fresh)
¼ cup all-purpose flour
1 teaspoon salt
⅛ teaspoon pepper
2 cups light cream

In a stock pot melt the butter and sauté the leeks until soft. In a separate stock pot combine the bouillon granules and water, and bring the mixture to a boil. Add the asparagus and cook for 5 minutes. Remove the asparagus with a slotted spoon, and add it to the leeks. Add the flour to the vegetables, stirring until absorbed. Gradually add the chicken broth, stirring until smooth. Add the salt and pepper, and simmer for 3 minutes. In a blender purée part of the soup at a time. Pour the soup into a bowl, add the cream, and stir to blend. Cover. Chill for at least 4 hours. Garnish with cream if desired. Makes 6 to 8 servings.

Avocado Grenade Soup

4 cups thin white sauce
1 cup finely mashed avocado
⅛ teaspoon ginger
Pinch salt

Grated rind of 1 orange
2 tablespoons whipped cream
Pinch paprika
1 avocado, thinly sliced

In a saucepan combine the white sauce, mashed avocado, ginger, salt, and orange rind. Beat until well blended. Heat the soup through. Just before serving add the whipped cream, paprika, and slices of avocado. Makes 6 servings.

———————— *((* ————————

Professor: I have a B.A. from USC, a B.S. from UCLA, an M.A. from SMU and a Ph.D. from TCU.
Mr. Howell: Well, I don't know anything about your education, but it sounds like a marvelous recipe for alphabet soup.

———————— *))* ————————

Leaky Ship Watercress Soup

6 tablespoons margarine or butter
1 large bunch watercress (2 cups),
 washed and stems removed
4 large leeks (2 cups), chopped, white
 part only
3 tablespoons all-purpose flour
1 teaspoon salt
3 teaspoons instant chicken bouillon
 granules
2 teaspoons fresh basil (or 1 teaspoon
 dried)
3 cups water
1 cup heavy cream
1 cup plain yogurt (or half and half)
Watercress and sliced radishes
 for garnish

In a heavy pot melt the margarine and sauté the watercress and leeks, cooking until tender but not brown. Stir in the flour, chicken bouillon, salt, and basil. Cook for about 1 minute, stirring constantly until the mixture bubbles. Slowly add the water, stirring constantly until smooth. Heat slowly to boiling. Reduce the heat, cover, and simmer for 15 minutes. Remove the soup from the heat and allow it to cool. Pour part of the soup at a time into the blender and whirl until smooth. Pour the soup into a large bowl, and stir in the heavy cream and yogurt. Garnish with watercress and sliced radishes. Makes 6 servings.

Dawn Wells collection

Not in Kansas anymore

Pearly White Gazpacho

1 pound cucumbers, peeled and seeded
2 cups plain yogurt
2 tablespoons lemon juice
1 clove garlic, peeled
2 cups chicken broth
2 tablespoons fresh cilantro

1 cup water
2 tablespoons thinly sliced green onions
  for garnish
Cucumber spears for garnish
6 whole green onions for garnish

In a blender combine the cucumber, yogurt, lemon juice, garlic, and ½ cup of chicken broth. Blend until smooth. Add the remaining chicken broth, cilantro, and water. Chill up to 1 day. Serve in tall glasses with sliced green onions, cucumber spears, and whole green onions for garnish. Makes 4 servings.

Soup du jour à la Gilligan

Gilligan: What's soup du jour?

Skipper: Gilligan, everybody knows what soup du jour is. For goodness sake, they're the simplest words in the world.

Gilligan: You don't know either.

Skipper: I do too, Gilligan, but I didn't want to show off. Now tell him what it is, Professor.

Professor: Soup of the day!

Skipper: What is it?

Mr. Howell: Well, it's a combination of the magnificent cuisines form the master chef.

Skipper: Never mind all that static, Mr. Howell. What is it?

Mr. Howell: Seaweed soup.

Southampton Tomato and Avocado Soup

6 tomatoes, chopped
6 green onions, minced
1 clove garlic, minced
1 bay leaf
¼ teaspoon salt

2 teaspoons fresh basil (chopped)
1 cup cold water
2 cups hot water
1 peeled and diced avocado
1 cup heavy cream (or half and half)

In a stock pot combine the tomatoes, onion, garlic, bay leaf, salt, basil, and cold water. Simmer for 20 to 30 minutes. Add the hot water and simmer for 15 minutes more. Remove the soup from the heat and allow it to cool. Remove the bay leaf. In a blender purée the soup with the avocado. Pour the soup into a bowl and add the cream. Stir well. Refrigerate until chilled. Makes 6 servings.

Gilligan stew

Gonzalez Gazpacho

2 ½ pounds ripe tomatoes
¼ cup wine vinegar
2 tablespoons olive oil
Salt
4 ripe tomato slices
1 small firm-ripe avocado
1 tablespoon lime juice

⅔ cup thinly sliced cucumber
⅓ to ½ cup sour cream
⅓ cup chopped red or white onion
⅓ cup chopped fresh cilantro
1 to 2 tablespoons minced fresh hot chili
  (such as jalapeño)
Lime wedges

Dip 2 or 3 tomatoes at a time in boiling water to cover for 20 to 30 seconds, lift out, then peel and core. If the tomatoes are juicy, cut them in half crosswise and squeeze gently to push out and discard seed pockets. Cut the tomatoes into 1-inch chunks. In a blender or food processor purée the tomatoes a portion at a time. In a large bowl mix the puréed tomatoes, vinegar, olive oil, and salt to taste. Cover and chill until cold, at least 1 hour or overnight.

In each of 4 shallow bowls, pour equal portions of tomato mixture. Lay 1 tomato slice on top. Peel, pit, and thinly slice the avocado. Brush the avocado slices with lime juice. Offer avocado, cucumber, sour cream, onion, cilantro, chili, and lime wedges to add to each bowl to taste. Serve cold. Makes 4 servings.

Suave Vichyssoise

My mom has often made this for us. Delicious.

6 or 7 leeks
¼ cup butter
1 quart (4 cups) chicken broth
3 medium potatoes, peeled and diced

1 cup heavy cream (or 1 cup sour cream)
Salt
Dash nutmeg
Chopped chives as garnish

Split the leeks, remove the outer leaves, and wash them well to rinse out sand. Trim off the green tops, leaving only the white part. Slice the leeks rather fine. In a skillet melt the butter and sauté the leeks until tender. In a pot combine the leeks with the chicken broth and potatoes. Bring the broth to a boil, reduce the heat, and simmer covered until the potatoes are well cooked, about 30 to 35 minutes.

Strain and reserve the broth. In a blender purée the vegetables. Add the broth and blend until smooth. Chill the soup for 24 hours.

About 1 hour before serving, stir in 1 cup heavy cream, salt to taste, and a dash of nutmeg, and chill again. Serve with finely chopped chives on top. Makes 4 to 6 servings.

——————— **"** ———————

Professor: I'll get Mr. Howell and we'll reconnoiter.
Skipper: All right, we'll get Mr. Howell and we'll reconnoiter.
Gilligan: O.K. But I think we oughta scout it out a bit first.

——————— **"** ———————

Juicy Fruit Soup

1 cup apricots (canned or fresh)
1 cup peaches (canned or fresh)
½ cup prunes (canned) or plums
¼ cup sugar (more for fresh fruit)
3 tablespoons tapioca

½ cup red raspberry syrup
1 stick cinnamon
3 teaspoons grated orange peel
1 cup half and half

In a stock pot combine the apricots, peaches, prunes, sugar, tapioca, red raspberry syrup, cinnamon stick, orange peel, and the juice from the canned fruit. When soft, purée the fruit in a blender until smooth. Refrigerate the soup until chilled. When cold, add the half and half. Makes 4 to 6 servings.

Egads! Good help is so hard to find these days.

Cool Million Cucumber Soup

¼ cup butter or margarine
4 cups chopped, peeled cucumbers
1 cup chopped green onions
¼ cup all-purpose flour

4 cups chicken broth
Salt and pepper to taste
½ cup half and half
Cucumber slices for garnish

In a large skillet over medium heat melt the butter. Sauté the cucumbers and green onions until tender, about 5 minutes. Stir in the flour until well blended. Gradually add the chicken broth, stirring constantly, until the mixture thickens slightly and begins to boil. Add salt and pepper to taste. Reduce the heat, cover, and simmer for 10 minutes, stirring occasionally.

Pour about 2 cups of mixture into the blender container. Blend at medium speed until puréed. Strain the mixture into a large bowl, and discard the seeds. Repeat with the remaining mixture. Stir in the half and half, cover, and refrigerate for several hours.

Garnish the soup with cucumber slices. Makes about 4 cups or 8 first-course servings.

Roomus Igloomus Bisque

1 pound small mushrooms
4 cups chicken broth
¼ cup butter or margarine
3 tablespoons all-purpose flour
¼ teaspoon dry mustard

Dash nutmeg
¼ cup sherry
½ cup half and half
Whipped cream for garnish
Paprika

Wash the mushrooms and remove the stems. Finely chop the stems. In a stock pot combine the chopped stems and chicken broth, and simmer for 30 minutes. Strain. In a saucepan melt the butter and sauté the mushroom caps until lightly browned. Sprinkle the flour, mustard, and nutmeg over the mushrooms and stir well. Gradually add the broth and cook, stirring constantly, until the mixture thickens slightly. Cook over low heat for 10 minutes. Stir in the sherry and half and half, and heat to serving temperature. Top with whipped cream and sprinkle with paprika. Makes 6 to 8 servings.

——————— **"** ———————

A definition from the Professor, as revealed in Mary Ann's dream:
Professor: "Igloomus" is from the Eskimo word "igloo" meaning mush. "Roomus" is from the Latin word motel, meaning vacancy or, in the layman's tongue, room. Therefore, roomus igloomus—mushroom.

——————— **"** ———————

Harvard Club Clam Bisque

2 ½ quarts clams
½ cup cold water
3 ½ cups boiling water
3 tablespoons butter or margarine
3 tablespoons all-purpose flour
1 ½ cups half and half

Salt and white pepper
Nutmeg
Thyme
3 egg yolks, beaten
Paprika

Wash clams in shells in several changes of cold water. Place the clams in a kettle and add ½ cup cold water. Cover tightly and steam until the shells open. Remove and reserve the clams. Strain the liquid through a fine cloth into another saucepan. Add the boiling water and keep hot.

In a skillet melt the butter and blend in the flour. Gradually stir in the hot clam liquid. Bring the liquid to a boil and cook for 3 to 4 minutes. Stir in the half and half. Season to taste with salt, pepper, and a pinch of nutmeg and thyme. Bring the soup to a boil. Remove the pan from heat. Add the egg yolks gradually, stirring constantly. Add the reserved clams. Sprinkle with paprika. Makes 6 to 8 servings.

Chicken Chowder Consolidated

2 tablespoons butter or margarine
¼ cup chopped onion
¼ cup sliced mushrooms
1 10 ¾-ounce can cream of celery soup
1 ½ soup cans water
1 cup diced, cooked chicken

¼ cup cooked corn
¼ cup chopped canned tomatoes
⅛ teaspoon thyme
Dash pepper
Crumbled cooked bacon

In a stock pot melt the butter and sauté the onion and mushrooms until tender. Add the soup, water, chicken, corn, tomatoes, thyme, and pepper. Heat, stirring often. Garnish with crisp crumbled bacon if desired. Makes 4 servings.

Wrong Message in a Bottle

I used to wear caps on my two front teeth while filming. The caps were just temporary, so whenever we weren't shooting, I would carry them around in a little glass jar that I kept in my cleavage. When filming started for my scenes, I would simply turn away from the camera and anybody watching, remove the jar, and slip the caps on.

Well, when we were shooting the *Rescue* special, one of the assistant directors came over and said, "Would you please put your teeth on in front of the crowd? They think you're doing cocaine." So for the rest of the shoot, I made sure I put the caps on where everybody could see what I was and wasn't doing.

But you won't see me doing that these days because I've had braces to correct the teeth, so now the smile is all mine.

Mary Ann's Cream of Carrot Soup

1 ¼ cups milk
1 ½ teaspoons all-purpose flour
½ teaspoon salt

Dash pepper
¾ cup diced cooked carrots
2 tablespoons peanut butter

In a blender combine the milk, flour, salt, pepper, carrots, and peanut butter. Blend at low speed for about 2 minutes, until the carrots are puréed. Pour the mixture into a saucepan and bring the mixture to a boil. Boil, stirring constantly, for about 1 minute. Makes 4 servings.

Mobster Lobster Bisque

3 6-ounce lobster tails
½ cup butter or margarine
2 tablespoons minced onion
2 tablespoons diced celery
2 tablespoons all-purpose flour

1 teaspoon salt
1¼ teaspoon paprika, or to taste
Dash white pepper
1 quart milk
Parsley

In a large kettle bring salted water to a boil. Cook the lobster tails for about 9 minutes, until the shells are bright red and the flesh is opaque and shrinks slightly from the shells. Remove the shells and finely chop, grind, or flake the meat in a blender, using a little of the milk called for to facilitate flaking of meat. In a skillet melt the butter and cook the onion and celery in butter until tender but not browned. Stir in the flour, salt, paprika, and pepper. Gradually add the milk and cook, stirring constantly, until smooth and slightly thickened. Add the lobster meat and heat. Serve in heated bowls and sprinkle with parsley or garnish with a thin slice of lobster. Makes 6 servings.

Dressed to kill

Corny Hamlet Chowder

1 tablespoon butter or margarine
1 small onion, chopped
1 cup diced ham
2 ½ cups water
1 cup cubed potato
½ teaspoon salt

⅛ teaspoon pepper
2 tablespoons all-purpose flour
Water
1 cup half and half
2 cups cooked corn cut off the cob

In a large saucepan melt the butter and cook the onion and ham until the onion is tender but not browned. Add 2 ½ cups of water, the potato, salt, and pepper. Cover and simmer for 15 minutes or until the potato is tender. Blend the flour with a little water to make a smooth paste. Stir the paste into the potato mixture and cook, stirring constantly, until the mixture comes to a boil. Stir in the half and half and corn. Heat just to a boil, stirring often. If the soup is too thick, thin it with milk or more half and half and reheat. Serve in warm bowls. Makes 4 to 6 servings.

Shipwrecked

High IQ Wild Rice Soup

1 medium onion, thinly sliced
3 tablespoons butter
4 ounces fresh mushrooms, sliced
¼ cup all-purpose flour
4 cups chicken stock

1 cup half and half
¼ cup dry sherry
1 ½ cups cooked wild rice
Chopped parsley

Cut the sliced onion into quarters. In a stock pot melt the butter and sauté the onion and mushrooms until the onion is transparent. Add the flour and cook for 2 to 3 minutes, stirring often. Slowly add the stock, and cook for 10 minutes, until smooth. Add the half and half, sherry, and rice. Stir until hot. Garnish with parsley. Makes 8 servings.

Bingo Bango Bongo Black Bean Soup

½ cup olive oil
½ pound salt pork or bacon, diced
½ pound Westphalian, Black Forest, or prosciutto ham, diced
8 large onions, chopped
8 cloves garlic, minced or pressed
6 large stalks celery, including leaves, chopped

2 pounds dried black beans, sorted for debris and rinsed
½ teaspoon cayenne pepper
4 teaspoons ground cumin
6 quarts regular-strength chicken broth
¼ cup wine vinegar
1 cup dry sherry
Toppings (see below)

In a 10- to 12-quart kettle heat the oil and add the salt pork, ham, onion, garlic, and celery. Cook over medium-high heat, stirring occasionally, until the vegetables are soft and lightly browned, and all juices have evaporated, about 40 minutes.

Add the beans, cayenne, cumin, and broth to the kettle. Bring the soup to a boil over high heat. Reduce the heat, cover, and simmer gently for 2 ½ to 3 hours or until the beans mash very easily. Let the soup cool to lukewarm.

In a blender or food processor whirl a portion of the soup at a time until smooth. Return the soup to the kettle and reheat it or cover it and refrigerate for up to 3 days. Heat over medium-low heat, stirring occasionally, until heated to serving temperature, about 45 minutes. Blend in the vinegar and sherry. Ladle the soup into bowls and embellish as desired with soup additions. Makes 20 to 24 servings.

Toppings: In separate containers serve warm Polish kielbasa or garlic sausages (about 3 pounds) cut in ½-inch slices; hot cooked rice (4 to 6 cups); finely chopped green or red onion (2 cups); 8 hard-cooked eggs, finely chopped and dusted with paprika; 4 unpeeled lemons, cut in wedges or paper-thin slices; sweet pickle relish (1 ½ cups); and chopped green chilies (2 7-ounce cans).

Baywatch Lentil Soup

½ cup margarine
2 cups chopped onions
1 pound dry lentils, washed and picked
  over
10 cups water

2 tablespoons chopped parsley
2 teaspoons salt
¼ teaspoon pepper
2 bay leaves

In a stock pot melt the margarine and sauté the onions for 5 minutes or until tender. Stir in the lentils, water, parsley, salt, pepper, and bay leaves. Bring to a boil, cover, and reduce the heat. Simmer for 1 ½ to 2 hours, until the lentils are tender. Remove the bay leaves. In a blender purée the soup. Makes 12 servings.

——————— " ———————

Hard times on the island:
Mr. Howell: Thurston Howell III in a soup line. I'll be drummed out of the
  social register!

——————— " ———————

S.S. Minnow Strewn

¾ cup great northern white beans
1 teaspoon salt
⅛ pound salt pork
6 sprigs parsley
½ cup chopped celery, plus leaves
  from 1 celery stalk
2 tablespoons olive oil
½ large onion, chopped
½ teaspoon dried thyme
2 tomatoes, peeled and chopped
1 carrot, diced

1 potato, diced
3 stalks celery, diced
1 13 ¾-ounce can beef broth
2 cups coarsely chopped cabbage
2 zucchini, coarsely chopped
1 teaspoon fresh basil
½ bulb garlic, minced
Salt and pepper to taste
1 cup cooked pasta (optional)
Grated Parmesan cheese

In a stock pot soak the great northern white beans overnight. Drain, add water to cover, and bring the water to a boil. Remove the pan from the heat, and let the beans stand for 1 hour.

Return the beans to the heat, add the salt, and simmer until tender, about 1 ½ hours. Cool. In a blender purée the soup until smooth.

Mince the salt pork, parsley, and celery. In the stock pot heat the olive oil and slowly sauté the onion and thyme. Add the tomatoes, carrot, potato, and celery. Add the beef broth and the bean purée, cover, and simmer for 15 minutes. Add the cabbage, zucchini, basil, and minced garlic. Add more broth if too thick. Cook the soup 20 minutes longer. Season to taste and add the pasta if desired. Serve with grated Parmesan and bread. Makes 12 servings.

Blaze of Noon Chicken Soup

Really good and easy.

1 4- to 5-pound stewing chicken
6 cups cold water
1 bay leaf
8 to 10 peppercorns
1 tablespoon salt
¼ cup margarine
2 large onions, chopped
3 celery stalks, diced
3 carrots, diced
2 cloves garlic, minced

1 10-ounce package frozen corn
1 4-ounce can diced green chilies, drained
1 10-ounce can garbanzos, drained
1 4-ounce jar pimientos, drained
¼ cup parsley, chopped
1 teaspoon dried sage
1 teaspoon salt
½ teaspoon pepper
Sliced olives (optional)

In a large stock pot cover the chicken with cold water, and add the bay leaf, peppercorns, and salt, and simmer uncovered for 30 minutes or until tender. When cooled, discard the bay leaf and peppercorns. Remove the chicken from the bones, and cut it into 1 inch pieces. Return the chicken to the broth and set the pot aside. In a skillet melt the margarine and sauté the onions, celery, carrots, and garlic for 10 minutes. Transfer the sautéed mixture to the chicken and broth, and add the corn, green chilies, garbanzos, pimientos, parsley, and sage. Simmer the soup for 30 minutes. Season with salt and pepper if needed. Ladle the soup into bowls, and sprinkle on sliced olives.

This is a full meal with bread and salad. Makes 10 to 12 servings.

Pancho Tortilla Soup

Vegetable oil
8 corn tortillas
3 tablespoons vegetable oil
½ cup chopped onion
1 minced garlic
1 cup chopped tomato

6 cups chicken broth
4 sprigs cilantro (or parsley)
2 tablespoons minced green chilies
Salt and pepper to taste
Grated cheddar cheese (optional)

Cut the corn tortillas into ¾ inch strips. In a skillet heat a small amount of oil. Fry the strips until just crisp, a third at a time. Drain on paper towels.

In a stock pot heat 3 tablespoons of vegetable oil. Sauté the onion and garlic for 2 to 3 minutes, but do not brown. Add the chopped tomatoes and cook for 2 minutes. Stir in the chicken broth, and add the cilantro and green chilies. Simmer for 10 minutes. Remove the cilantro, and season with salt and pepper if necessary. Add the tortilla strips, and simmer for 3 to 4 minutes. Top with grated cheddar if desired. Makes 6 servings.

Zucchini Watercress Soup Nyet

¼ cup butter
2 cups finely chopped yellow onions
3 cups chicken stock
4 medium-size zucchini (about 2 pounds)

1 bunch watercress
Salt and ground pepper
Fresh lemon juice to taste

In a stock pot melt the butter and add the onion. Cover and cook over low heat, stirring occasionally, until the onions are tender and lightly colored, about 25 minutes. Add the stock and bring it to a boil. Scrub the zucchini, trim the ends, and chop it coarsely. Drop the zucchini into the stock and return to a boil. Reduce the heat, cover, and simmer for about 20 minutes. Meanwhile, pull the leaves and small stem off the watercress, and rinse well. Remove the soup from the heat and add the watercress. Cover, and let the soup stand for 5 minutes.

Pour the soup through a strainer, reserving the broth. In a food processor or mill purée the solids. Add 1 cup of liquid, and process until smooth. Return the puréed soup to the pot and add additional 2 cups of cooking liquid. Season to taste with salt, pepper, and lemon juice. If desired, substitute 1 cup of heavy cream for ½ or 1 cup of cooking liquid. Makes 6 servings.

From Mildred and Sherwood Schwartz.

---- " ----

Mr. Howell: This is a very difficult instrument [the triangle]. It's easy to play a wind instrument.
Skipper: Yeah, especially for you with all that hot air.
Mr. Howell: Heavens to Toscanini! I've been insulted.

---- " ----

Skipper's Navy Bean Soup

2 cups navy beans
3 quarts water
1 pound smoked pork
1 tablespoon minced onion
½ teaspoon celery salt

2 teaspoons salt
⅛ teaspoon pepper
¼ teaspoon dry mustard
1 teaspoon brown sugar
Parsley

Soak the beans overnight in water to cover. Drain.

In a stock pot combine the beans, 3 quarts of water, the pork, onion, and celery salt, and cook until the beans are very soft. Remove and discard the pork, and press the mixture through a coarse sieve. Add salt, pepper, mustard, and sugar. Return the mixture to the pot and cook for 5 minutes. Garnish with parsley. Makes 8 to 10 servings.

Thurston's Heavens To Fort Knox Chili

My husband, Jimmy, tried cooking exactly once. When we were first married, I became ill with the flu and the doctor suggested that he boil me an egg—which he did, with no water in the pot! Just an egg, a pot, and a flame! The explosion was violent; the aroma was no aid to my condition; and the expense of scraping, scrubbing, and painting the kitchen was so great that he was barred from that part of the house ever after. This penalty never upset him.

Anyway, this was his favorite dish. It bears no resemblance to Mexican or Texas chili. It's fast, easy, and a great solution to false hunger the morning after.

Henny Backus

3 tablespoons bacon fat
1 medium onion, chopped
1 large green pepper, chopped
2 cloves garlic, run through a press
1 pound ground round
1 ½ 20-ounce cans whole tomatoes
1 ½ 20-ounce cans kidney beans, drained and liquid reserved
1 ½ teaspoons salt

3 whole cloves
1 bay leaf
3 tablespoons good, strong, fresh chili powder
Leftover stew meat
Toasted saltines
Sour cream
Cooked rice

In a stock pot heat the bacon fat and sauté the onion, chopped peppers, garlic, and meat until brown and crumbly. Add the tomatoes, beans, salt, cloves, bay leaf, and chili powder. Bring the mixture to a boil. Reduce the heat and cook over a very low flame for about 2 ½ hours, stirring occasionally. To thicken (we like it soupy so we can dunk), leave the lid off until it reaches thickness desired. Remove the bay leaf.

If desired, add leftover stew meat (or cook some especially for this dish). Serve with toasted saltines, sour cream (lots of it mixed in and heated to boiling). If you use all of these, it is a marvelous party dish, which we then serve over rice. If you don't think it tastes like chili, you're probably right. But I've never been able to come up with a better description for it. Makes 6 servings.

From Henny and Jim Backus.

The Millionaire Gets the Tab

Jim Backus would always ask Natalie Schafer and me to lunch when we were shooting the show. I bet he took us to lunch at least a dozen times, but somehow he never had his wallet with him. He always forgot his money.

Finally one day, Natalie said with a laugh, "This is it!" She marched up to Jim with a typed-up invoice, handed it to him, and said, "You owe me $124 for lunch." Egads, Lovey!

The Professor

The Professor is so identified with his work that everybody seems to forget that his name is Roy Hinkley. But that's easy to understand since just keeping track of his six degrees is enough for anybody to try to remember.

There's no doubt that the Professor is extremely intelligent. He earned a Ph.D. at age 25 and was the top chess player on his team. His master's degree in psychology certainly serves him well in helping the Castaways survive on the island. (The good fortune of his being a well-known scoutmaster doesn't hurt either.)

And despite the occasional glaring oversight or loophole in his logic, the Professor's vast and varied knowledge bails the Castaways out of many a sticky situation. Perhaps more than any other Castaway, it is the Professor who breathes continuous life into their hopes for eventual rescue.

The Castaways can be thankful that the Professor happened to bring along a diverse selection of useful books for his three-hour tour aboard the Minnow. Particularly handy is his *World of Facts,* which is the book he consults most often in search of vital information. At the same time, his volume of *Integrated Calculus* by Zimmerman likely serves him well in calibrating his various island inventions.

The Professor has book ideas of his own, too. When published, his study of ferns should be destined for fame. But his dream book is still *Rust—The Real Red Menace.* As much as the left-handed Professor writes in his log, he likely has the makings of some fascinating memoirs as well.

While stuck on the island, the Professor makes the most of his experience as a research scientist, and his fellow Castaways make good students and sometimes guinea pigs. Most important of all, the Professor keeps the Castaways in touch with outside communication by fixing the radio and by being able to translate virtually any language of the region, whether it be Polynesian, Papoo Papoo, or ancient hieroglyphics.

About the only language the Professor (arguably the island's most eligible bachelor) has difficulty understanding is that of the desperate female hunter (a.k.a. Ginger). She may be a sizzling star in Hollywood, but the only hot star the claustrophobic Professor is interested in is Alpha Centauri.

It just goes to show you that even the Professor has a lot to learn.

Salads

Winfield Winter Vegetable Salad

1 10-ounce package frozen baby lima
  beans
2 cups cauliflowerets
2 hard-boiled eggs, chopped

½ cup thinly sliced green onion
1 cup thinly sliced celery
Salt to taste
Dill Dressing (see below)

In a saucepan bring 1 inch of salted water to a boil. Add the limas, cover, and cook for 8 minutes. Add the cauliflower, replace the cover, and continue cooking for about 5 minutes (until barely tender). Rinse well with cold water.

In a salad bowl combine the limas, cauliflower, eggs, green onion, and celery. Season with salt to taste. Cover and chill well. Prepare the dressing. Makes 6 to 8 servings.

Dill Dressing

⅔ cup sour cream
2 ½ teaspoons prepared horseradish
1 teaspoon dillweed (or 2 teaspoons
  fresh dill)

2 ounces drained anchovy fillets (optional)
Salt and pepper to taste

Combine the sour cream, prepared horseradish, and dillweed. Add the anchovies if desired. Stir and add salt and pepper to taste. Pour the dressing over the salad. Makes about ¼ cup.

———— **“** ————

Professor: There is something rotten in Denmark.
Gilligan: What do we care? We don't live anywhere near Denmark.
Professor: I propose we send the boat out first with a dummy aboard.
Gilligan: Oh-no, oh-no, I'm not going out there alone.
They make seven dummies to put on the boat, which eventually explodes.

———— **”** ————

First Mate Potato Salad

10 to 12 medium potatoes
1 cup chopped onion
½ teaspoon celery seed
2 teaspoons salt
⅛ teaspoon pepper

6 slices bacon, diced
½ cup vinegar (apple or white)
2 tablespoons sugar
3 tablespoons water
2 tablespoons minced parsley

In boiling salted water cook the potatoes until tender. Cool slightly. Peel and thinly slice into a large bowl. Add the onions, celery seed, salt, and pepper, and mix lightly. Keep warm.

In a small skillet cook the bacon until crisp. Drain on a paper towel. In the skillet with the bacon drippings mix the vinegar, sugar, and water. Heat to simmering. Pour the dressing over the potatoes, and sprinkle with bacon and parsley. Serve warm. Makes 8 servings.

The Tennessean

Gilligan gets an earful of news from civilization

Horner's Corners Potato Salad

4 cups warm cooked potatoes, peeled
   and sliced or cubed
¼ cup clear French dressing
1 cup chopped celery
1 medium onion, chopped
4 hard-boiled eggs, sliced

1 ½ teaspoons salt
1 ½ teaspoons pepper
1 teaspoon celery seed
½ cup mayonnaise
¼ cup chopped parsley

In a large bowl pour the French dressing over the warm potatoes. Chill for 2 hours. Add the celery, onion, eggs, salt, pepper, and celery seed. Add the mayonnaise and mix carefully. Chill 4 hours. Sprinkle with parsley. Makes 8 servings.

Variations: Trim the bowl with tiny tomatoes. Add 1 cup of cooked shrimp. Sprinkle with ¼ cup chopped chives or green peppers. Add more mayonnaise if desired. Use cooked salad dressing instead of mayonnaise if desired. Add chopped radishes.

Street Scene

One of my favorite stories took place on a street corner in Los Angeles. I was in my sweats, had my hair in a ponytail, and was wearing sunglasses while riding in the passenger seat of a car. We stopped to give a homeless man some money. He looked in the window, smiled, and said, "Mary Ann, lookin' good, babe." You just never know the impact that show has made on so many lives.

Knock Knockwurst Salad

8 slices bacon
½ cup chopped onion
4 ½ teaspoons all-purpose flour
4 ½ teaspoons sugar
1 teaspoon MSG
1 teaspoon salt
¼ teaspoon pepper

⅔ cup vinegar
⅔ cup water
4 medium potatoes, cooked and peeled
3 knockwurst or 6 frankfurters, cut into
   ½-inch slices
2 cups shredded lettuce, optional

In a large skillet cook the bacon until lightly browned. Remove and crumble the bacon. Pour off half of the drippings. Heat the remaining drippings, and cook the onion until tender. Blend in the flour and cook for 1 or 2 minutes. Add the sugar, MSG, salt, pepper, vinegar, and water. Stir over medium heat until the sauce boils and thickens slightly. Cut the potatoes into ¼ inch slices. Add potatoes and knockwurst to the skillet, mix well, and heat through. Stir in the lettuce and crumbled bacon. Makes 4 main-dish servings.

Operation Orchid Onion
and Bean Salad

1 large onion
1 teaspoon salt
1/4 cup olive oil
2 tablespoons wine vinegar
1/4 teaspoon oregano
Dash pepper
Romaine lettuce

1 green pepper, sliced in rings
1 tomato, cut in wedges
1 8 3/4-ounce can garbanzo beans, drained
Green and ripe olives
Parsley, chopped
Parsley sprigs

Peel and thinly slice the onion. Separate it into rings. In a medium bowl cover the onion with ice water. Add salt and a few ice cubes. Let the onion stand for 30 minutes. Drain on paper towels.

In a separate bowl combine the oil, vinegar, oregano, and pepper. Pour the dressing mixture over the onions and chill. To serve, place the onion rings on a platter lined with Romaine lettuce. Arrange the green pepper rings, tomato wedges, beans, and olives around the onions. Sprinkle the onions with chopped parsley and garnish with parsley sprigs. Makes 6 servings.

Dawn Wells collection

Island girl

Sinbad's Five-Pepper Slaw

1 red bell pepper, cut in julienne strips
1 orange bell pepper, cut in julienne strips
1 green bell pepper, cut in julienne strips
1 purple bell pepper, cut in julienne strips
1 yellow bell pepper, cut in julienne strips
1 red onion, cut in strips
2 tablespoons tarragon vinegar

1 tablespoon Dijon mustard
2 teaspoons sugar
1 teaspoon salt
¼ teaspoon Tabasco sauce
1 jalapeño pepper, minced
Freshly ground pepper
¼ cup vegetable oil
2 tablespoons peanut oil
1 tablespoon caraway seeds
2 tablespoons grated lime rind

In a large bowl combine the peppers and onion. In a separate bowl whisk together the vinegar, mustard, sugar, salt, Tabasco, jalapeño, pepper, and oils until smooth and thick. Toss the dressing with the vegetables, and add the caraway seeds and lime rind. Makes 12 servings.

——————— **"** ———————

Mr. Howell: Sometimes I think a woman's place is in the hut.

——————— **"** ———————

Grass Skirt Green Bean Salad

4 to 6 cups green beans
2 sprigs fresh dill
Coarse salt
Oil/vinegar dressing
1 shallot, minced

1 tablespoon olive oil
2 tablespoons butter
1 crushed garlic clove
2 slices stale French bread
1 lettuce heart

Wash the beans, and snip off the ends. French-cut them down the middle. Drop the beans into 3 cups rapidly boiling lightly salted water. Add the dill sprigs, and boil rapidly for 6 to 8 minutes, uncovered. Test for doneness, cooking longer if you like. Drain and shake over low heat to dry. Grind a little coarse salt over the beans. Add the shallot to the dressing, and pour it over the hot beans. Cook uncovered for 2 to 4 minutes. Turn the mixture into a glass bowl, cover, and chill.

Before serving, in a small skillet heat the oil and butter, and brown the garlic. Remove the garlic. Fry the bread slices until golden, flipping over to absorb the butter.

Grate the lettuce heart. Toss the lettuce bits into the beans. Crumble and add the fried bread. Garnish with dill. Makes 6 to 8 servings.

Ark-tic Pea Salad

1 10-ounce package frozen peas, thawed
Chopped green onion

Sour cream
Crumbled cooked bacon

In a medium bowl toss the peas with chopped green onion, sour cream, and crumbled bacon. Makes 4 to 6 servings.

Variation: Add chopped water chestnuts if desired.

Seance Ham Salad

½ cup red wine vinegar
½ cup oil
¼ cup water
½ pound peppered ham, cubed
½ pound prosciutto, cubed

3 stalks celery, sliced diagonally
1 medium green pepper, cut in strips
½ medium onion, chopped
4 hot cherry peppers
Boston lettuce, torn

In a small bowl combine the vinegar, oil, and water. In a glass bowl combine the remaining ingredients. Pour the dressing over the salad. Makes 4 to 6 servings.

Willy Gilligan's Chilly Curried Rice Salad

1 tablespoon olive oil
1 teaspoon curry powder
1 13 ¾-ounce can chicken broth
1 cup chopped celery
1 tablespoon chopped onion
1 cup raw converted rice (not instant)

½ cup water
½ cup slivered toasted almonds
⅔ cup raisins
⅓ cup mayonnaise
⅔ cup coconut (or more)
Parsley or tomato wedges

In a saucepan heat the oil. Add the curry and heat gently for 1 minute. Add the broth, celery, rice, and water, and heat to boiling. Reduce the heat, cover, and simmer for 20 to 25 minutes, until the liquid is absorbed. Chill 6 hours or more.

Stir in almonds, raisins, mayonnaise, and coconut. Garnish with parsley and/or tomato wedges. Makes 6 to 8 servings.

The girl next door

Sea Saw Blue Cheese Slaw

2 Red Delicious apples (6 ounces each),
   cored and thinly sliced
¼ cup thinly sliced red onion
3 tablespoons chopped parsley
¼ cup finely shredded carrot

½ cup finely shredded cabbage
1 tablespoon lemon juice
¼ cup sour cream
¼ cup mayonnaise
1 ounce crumbled blue cheese

In a glass bowl combine all of the ingredients. Let the mixture sit for 6 hours or overnight. Makes 4 servings.

Flaming Passion Cranberry Salad

1 16-ounce can whole cranberry sauce
1 cup boiling water
1 3-ounce package gelatin (red, orange,
   or yellow)
1/4 teaspoon salt

1 tablespoon lemon juice
1/2 cup mayonnaise
1 apple or orange, peeled and diced
1/4 cup chopped walnuts

In a saucepan heat the cranberries. Strain the juice into a bowl and add the boiling water and gelatin. Add the salt and lemon juice. Chill until thick enough to mound when dropped from a spoon. Beat in the mayonnaise with a rotary beater until light and fluffy. Fold in the cranberries, apple, and walnuts. Pour into 8 6-ounce fruit juice cans and chill until firm.

Cut birthday candles in half to shorten. Place the candles in the gelatin after unmolding and light. Makes 8 servings.

Mary Ann: Well, Professor, I'll bet you never thought you'd be coaching a beauty contest.

Professor: Mary Ann, the combination of your natural attributes and my scientific approach will prove unbeatable. Look! Seawood shampoo for lustrous hair, crushed blackberries for darkening the lashes, powdered hibiscus for ruby lips, and coconut oil for baby-soft skin.

Mary Ann: Just add a little vinegar and I can enter the contest as a Caesar salad.

Professor's Miracle Rescue Slaw

1 small head green cabbage, diced into
   1/4-inch dice (about 4 to 5 cups)
3 or 4 green onions including tops,
   chopped into 1/4-inch dice
1/2 cup cucumber, finely diced
6 radishes, finely chopped

1 small carrot, finely chopped
Salt to taste
Pepper to taste
1 cup salad dressing
Milk

In a large bowl combine the cabbage, onions, cucumber, radishes, carrot, salt, and pepper. In a separate bowl thin the salad dressing with a little milk. Toss the dressing into the salad. Chill for a couple of hours. Makes 8 to 10 servings.
From Connie and Russell Johnson.

Skipper's steak out

Ginger Ale Fruit Cocktail

1 21-ounce can fruit cocktail
1 21-ounce can grapefruit sections
  (or fresh)

1 20-ounce can pineapple tidbits
2 bananas, sliced
Ginger ale

In a serving bowl combine the fruit and add ginger ale. Makes 10 to 12 servings.

Fiji Fruit Salad

1 cantaloupe, diced
2 bananas, sliced
1 cup miniature marshmallows

½ cup pecan halves
½ cup mayonnaise
1 ½ ounces crème de banane

In a serving bowl combine the cantaloupe, bananas, marshmallows, and pecans. In a separate bowl blend the mayonnaise and crème de banana together. Toss the dressing with the fruit. Makes 4 to 6 servings.

51

Three-Hour Tour Fruit Salad

1 6-ounce package lemon gelatin
1 ½ teaspoons salt
2 cups boiling water
1 20-ounce can crushed pineapple with syrup
½ cup sliced pimiento-stuffed olives

1 cup chopped celery
1 cup mashed avocado
½ cup chopped onion
Cherry tomatoes
Dillweed
Mayonnaise

In a bowl dissolve the gelatin and salt in boiling water. Add the pineapple with syrup and chill until slightly thickened. Add the olives, celery, avocado, and onion, and pour the mixture into a 2-quart ring mold or individual molds. Chill until firm, 3 to 4 hours.

Unmold onto lettuce. Fill the center of the ring with cherry tomatoes sprinkled with dillweed. Garnish with a dollop of mayonnaise. Makes 8 to 10 servings.

———————— **66** ————————

Professor: Well, Gilligan, this is where we're going to spend the rest of our lives.
Gilligan: Well, maybe we won't live that long.

———————— **99** ————————

Aloha Fruit Bowl

2 pears
2 apples, cored and cubed
1 banana, sliced
1 cup red seedless grapes

½ cup celery, sliced
½ cup raisins
Hula Dressing (see below)
Lettuce leaves

Halve, core, and slice pears crosswise into crescents. In a large bowl combine the pears, apples, banana, grapes, celery, and raisins. Coat with a small amount of Hula Dressing and toss gently. Place in a lettuce-lined bowl. Serve with additional dressing. Makes 6 servings.

Hula Dressing

¾ cup oil
⅓ cup honey
¼ cup lime juice
2 tablespoons lemon juice

1 teaspoon grated lime or lemon peel
½ teaspoon dry mustard
½ teaspoon salt

In a small bowl combine the oil, honey, lime and lemon juices, peel, mustard, and salt and beat with a rotary beater. Chill. Makes 1 ⅓ cups.

Cranberry Pear Corsage

2 cups diced pears
¾ cup chopped celery
½ cup coarsely chopped walnuts

Mayonnaise
Jellied cranberry sauce
Lettuce

In a medium bowl combine the pears, celery, and walnuts. Add mayonnaise to moisten. Serve over slices of cranberry sauce on lettuce lined plates. Makes 4 to 6 servings.

Orange You Glad It's Onion Salad

One of my mom's favorites.

4 large oranges
1 large red onion
½ cup salad oil
¼ cup white wine vinegar

2 tablespoons sugar
¾ teaspoon paprika
½ teaspoon salt
½ teaspoon dry mustard

Cut and peel the white membrane from the oranges. Thinly slice crosswise and place in a shallow bowl. Thinly slice the onion crosswise, and separate into rings. Tuck the onion slices in among the orange slices.

In a separate bowl blend together the oil, vinegar, sugar, paprika, salt, and dry mustard. Pour the dressing over the onion and oranges. Refrigerate for at least 2 hours. Makes 6 to 8 servings.

The Tennessean

Ginger Grant

Cosmonaut Coconut Chicken Salad

1 cup chopped cooked chicken
1 cup diced celery
½ cup grated coconut
½ cup green seedless grapes
¼ cup chopped pecans or walnuts
Salt

1 tablespoon pimiento
½ cup mayonnaise
Cream
1 ripe avocado
Lime juice

In a medium bowl combine the chicken, celery, coconut, grapes, and pecans. Season with salt to taste. In a separate bowl combine the pimiento and mayonnaise, thinning a little with cream. Turn the dressing into the salad. Chill.

Cut the avocado in half, and rub lime on the avocado to prevent darkening. Fill each half with chicken. The chicken salad may be served without avocado. Makes 2 servings.

——————— **"** ———————

After seeing a bald Gilligan:
Professor: What'd you say we all go and have some breakfast?
Mrs. Howell: That's a lovely idea. I'll have a boiled egg.

——————— **"** ———————

Mars Chicken Salad

⅓ cup white wine vinegar
1 tablespoon Dijon mustard
5 teaspoons sugar
2 cloves garlic, minced
¼ teaspoon salt
½ cup vegetable oil
1 head romaine lettuce

3 cups shredded, cooked chicken
¾ cup California ripe olives, halved
⅓ cup sunflower seeds, shelled
¼ pound whole green beans, steamed
Cherry tomatoes for garnish
Hard-boiled eggs for garnish
Sunflower seeds for garnish

In a blender combine the vinegar, mustard, sugar, garlic, and salt, and blend until smooth. While blending, slowly add the oil until well blended and the dressing is thickened. Makes 1 cup of mustard dressing.

Line a bowl with lettuce leaves. Shred the remaining lettuce to measure 1 quart and place it in the bowl. In a separate bowl combine the chicken, olives, sunflower seeds, and ½ cup of mustard dressing. Heap the chicken salad over the lettuce, and arrange the green beans on top. Garnish with cherry tomatoes, ripe olives, sieved hard-boiled eggs, and sunflower seeds. Serve with extra dressing. Makes 4 servings.

Howell Cotillion Cantaloupe Chicken Salad

2 pounds chicken breasts
2 cups thinly sliced celery
5 ounces slivered almonds
2 11-ounce cans mandarin orange sections, drained
3 medium cantaloupes, cut into bite-size chunks

¾ cup sour cream
¾ cup mayonnaise
3 tablespoons minced candied ginger
2 tablespoons lemon juice
½ teaspoon salt
1 teaspoon grated orange peel
Dash nutmeg

In a stock pot simmer the chicken in salted water for 20 to 25 minutes. Drain, cool, and cut into bite-size cubes. In a large bowl combine the chicken, celery, almonds, and oranges. Add the cantaloupe. In a separate bowl combine the sour cream, mayonnaise, ginger, lemon juice, salt, orange peel, and nutmeg. Pour just enough dressing over the chicken mixture to blend. Makes 10 to 12 servings.

Dawn Wells collection

Hard-boiled egghead

Russell, Bob, and I continue to make personal appearances together and we remain the best of friends.

Dawn Wells collection

Erika Tiffany Smith's Chicken Salad

1 whole large chicken breast, boned,
  cooked, skinned, and cut in strips
1 medium orange, sectioned
½ cup seedless grapes, halved
1 tablespoon honey

1 tablespoon lemon juice
Salt to taste
2 tablespoons salad oil
1 cup chow mein noodles

In a medium bowl toss together the chicken, orange, and grapes. In a jar combine the honey, lemon juice, and a dash of salt. Add the oil and shake well. Drizzle over the chicken mixture, and toss to coat. Spoon the salad into a container, and chill overnight or up to 2 days. Mix with noodles just before serving. Makes 2 servings.

Summer's Farm Cauliflower and Radish Salad

One of my favorite salads. Really refreshing.

2 cups thinly sliced cauliflower
1 cup thinly cut radishes
¼ cup chopped green onion (tops too)
Salt and pepper to taste
½ teaspoon sugar

1 teaspoon lemon juice
½ cup mayonnaise
½ cup sour cream
½ teaspoon celery seeds

In a large bowl combine the cauliflower, radishes, onions, salt, pepper, sugar, and lemon juice. In a separate bowl combine the mayonnaise, sour cream, and celery seeds. Turn the dressing into the salad, tossing to coat. Refrigerate for 1 hour.
Adjust the seasonings if desired. Makes 4 to 6 servings.

Here's an early publicity shot of me as Mary Ann with just a 'hint' of navel showing. I got away with mine, Jeannie. Did you?

Dawn Wells collection

Island Cottage Vegetable Salad

Crisp lettuce leaves
2 tomatoes
1 ½ cups cottage cheese
½ teaspoon grated onion

¼ teaspoon salt
Dash paprika
Dressing (any kind desired)

Line a salad bowl with lettuce. Peel the tomatoes and cut them into wedges. Place the tomato wedges around the edge of the bowl. In a separate bowl mix the cottage cheese with the onion, salt, and paprika. Pile the cottage cheese mixture in the center of the bowl. Add dressing. Makes 4 to 6 servings.

Grandmother's Salad Dressings

3 tablespoons sugar
1 teaspoon salt
1 tablespoon prepared mustard
1 ½ tablespoons flour

1 egg
¾ cup milk
¼ cup vinegar
1 tablespoon butter

In the top of a double boiler over hot water mix the sugar, salt, mustard, flour, egg, milk, and vinegar. Cook, stirring constantly, until thickened. Add the butter and blend well. Cool.

Variations: To the above add any of the following:

Coleslaw: 2 tablespoons of mustard sauce.

Hawaiian: 3 tablespoons of orange juice and 3 tablespoons of pineapple juice.

Manhattan: ½ cup of sandwich spread.

Peanut Butter: ¼ cup of peanut butter.

Savory: ¼ cup of India relish.

Whipped Cream: ¾ cup of whipped cream.

----------- **"** -----------

Professor: Excuse me, folks, you've given me food for thought.

Mrs. Howell: What an odd time to get hungry.

----------- **"** -----------

Tiny Ship Tossed Salad

1 head leaf lettuce, torn
3 stalks of celery, thinly sliced
1 11-ounce can mandarin oranges,
    drained
¼ cup vegetable oil
2 tablespoons sugar

1 tablespoon white vinegar
½ teaspoon salt
¼ teaspoon pepper
5 drops hot sauce
¼ cup slivered almonds
2 tablespoons sugar

In a salad bowl combine the lettuce, celery, and oranges. Cover and chill for up to 3 hours if desired.

In a separate bowl combine the oil, sugar, vinegar, salt, pepper, and hot sauce. Chill. Stir well before serving. Makes ⅓ cup of dressing.

In a heavy saucepan combine the almonds and sugar. Cook over medium heat, stirring constantly, until golden. Pour on waxed paper and cool. Break into pieces and store in an airtight container.

Just before serving, toss with the vinaigrette dressing and sprinkle with caramelized almonds. Makes 6 to 8 servings.

From Dreama and Bob Denver.

Spinnaker Spinach Salad

1 pound spinach
½ pound bacon
¼ cup bacon drippings
2 tablespoons wine vinegar
2 teaspoons Dijon mustard

½ teaspoon sugar
1 teaspoon Worcestershire sauce
3 tablespoons chili sauce
1 ½ tablespoons lemon juice

Clean the spinach well. Break off the stems, drain well, wrap in a towel, and chill. Cut the bacon into ½-inch lengths. In a skillet cook the bacon until brown and crisp. Remove the bacon. Drain and discard all but ¼ cup of drippings. Heat the drippings until hot, then stir in the vinegar, mustard, sugar, and Worcestershire. Boil until the liquid has mostly evaporated. Blend in the chili sauce and lemon juice. Bring to a rolling boil, then pour over the spinach. Mix quickly, and invert the pan over the spinach for 1 to 2 minutes to warm it lightly. Stir in the bacon. Makes 4 to 6 servings.

―――――――― **"** ――――――――

Professor: Perhaps we should investigate this?

Mr. Howell: Before lunch! Not even Perry Mason investigates on an empty stomach.

Gilligan: Mr. Howell, aren't you coming?

Mr. Howell: No, Gilligan, there are two things I detest—one is investigating a mystery before lunch

Gilligan: And the other?

Mr. Howell: Any sort of danger.

―――――――― **"** ――――――――

Lovey's Lemon Poppy Dressing

2 tablespoons poppy seeds
¼ cup honey
½ cup salad oil
½ teaspoon cinnamon

¼ teaspoon coriander
¾ teaspoon salt
⅓ cup fresh lemon juice
Fruit salad

In a blender blend the poppy seeds on high speed for 1 minute, until the seeds are crushed. Add the honey, oil, cinnamon, coriander, and salt. Blend until well mixed. Add the lemon juice and blend until creamy. Store in a tightly covered jar in the refrigerator until ready to use.

To serve, shake the dressing and spoon over fruit salad. Makes 1 cup dressing.

Mary Ann's Mayonnaise Dressings

1 cup mayonnaise

Add the following ingredients to the above for these variations:

Celery: ¼ cup of finely chopped celery and 2 tablespoons of chopped green pepper.

Club: 2 tablespoons of chopped currants, 2 tablespoons of chopped raisins, and 1 tablespoon of chopped nuts (Waldorf salad).

Different: 1 chopped hard-boiled egg, 1 tablespoon of chopped pimiento, and 2 tablespoons India relish (molded salad).

Fruit Topping: ½ cup of whipped cream, and minced crystalized ginger.

Horseradish: Mix 2 tablespoons of horseradish with ¼ cup of cold water. Let the mixture stand for 10 minutes, then add the mayonnaise.

Indian: ¼ cup of chow-chow pickle (string bean or spinach salads).

Russian: ½ cup chili sauce (bean or ham salad).

Thousand Island: ¼ cup of chili sauce, 2 tablespoons of chopped green pepper, 2 tablespoons of chopped stuffed olives (watercress, fish salads).

Italian: Herbs and/or Parmesan cheese.

Marie Antoinette's French Dressings

½ teaspoon salt

1 teaspoon sugar

⅛ teaspoon paprika

¼ cup vinegar

½ cup olive oil

Add the following ingredients to the above for these variations:

Anchovy: 2 tablespoons of finely chopped anchovies.

Chiffonade: 2 tablespoons of chopped parsley, 2 teaspoons of chopped onion, 1 hard-boiled egg, chopped, ¼ cup of chopped cooked beets.

Curry: ⅛ teaspoon of curry powder, 2 hard boiled eggs, sieved.

Catsup: ¼ cup of catsup.

Mustard: 2 tablespoons of prepared mustard.

Piquante: ½ teaspoon of mustard, ⅛ teaspoon of Worcestershire sauce, ½ teaspoon of onion juice, 2 drops of Tabasco sauce.

Roquefort: ¼ cup crumbled Roquefort (or blue cheese)

Summer (fruits): Use 1 tablespoon less of vinegar, add 3 tablespoons of pineapple juice, 3 tablespoons of orange juice, 1 teaspoon of sugar.

Parisian: 2 tablespoons of chopped green pepper, 2 tablespoons of chopped red pepper, 2 tablespoons of chopped celery, 1 ½ teaspoons of chopped onion, 1 ½ teaspoons of chopped parsley.

Note: Put a clove of garlic in the jar for green salads. Add fresh herbs or Parmesan cheese to the basic dressing.

Mary Ann in the floating hut in *Rescue from Gilligan's Island*

Avocado Lava Dressing

1 large ripe avocado
½ cup water
¼ cup olive oil

1 ½ teaspoons seasoning salt
¼ cup garlic red wine vinegar

Peel, seed, and cut the avocado into chunks. In a blender combine the avocado and remaining ingredients. Blend for about 1 minute, until smooth. Makes 1 ½ cups.

Midrift Mushroom Dressing

½ pound fresh mushrooms
½ cup olive oil
½ cup white wine vinegar
2 teaspoons seasoning salt

1 teaspoon Italian herbs
½ teaspoon cracked black pepper
¼ teaspoon garlic powder

Brush the mushrooms very well. Slice thinly and place in a large bowl. In a pint jar combine the oil, vinegar, seasoning salt, Italian herbs, cracked pepper, and garlic powder. Shake well to blend. Pour the dressing over the sliced mushrooms, tossing well to coat. Cover tightly and marinate overnight to allow the mushrooms to absorb the flavor.

Serve on tossed mixed greens, or sliced tomatoes and avocados, or use as an hors d'oeuvre on toothpicks or crackers. Makes about 1 pint.

Working up an appetite with a jungle jog

Favorite Episode

My favorite episode is *And Then There Were None*, where I play a Cockney girl in the dream sequence. It was always fun to play another character, and doing the accent was a bonus. Another of my favorites was the Sherlock Holmes-Dracula episode (*Up at Bat*). I loved being the old hag.

Also, it was fun being hit on the head and imagining I was Ginger in one episode (*The Second Ginger Grant*). Tina was a great sport to allow me to try to mimic her voice. That experience also came in handy several years later when I got to furnish the voices of both Mary Ann and Ginger in the "Gilligan's Planet" cartoon series.

Breads

Howell's Yorkshire Pudding

2 tablespoons beef drippings
6 large eggs
2 cups milk
Meat drippings

2 cups all-purpose flour
½ teaspoon salt
¼ teaspoon garlic powder
¼ teaspoon pepper

Generously grease 8 to 10 deep muffin cups with 2 tablespoons of beef drippings. In a large bowl beat the eggs with an electric mixer at medium speed for about 1 minute, until frothy. Beat in the milk and meat drippings. At low speed add the flour, salt, garlic powder, and pepper. Fill the muffin cups ½ full. Place the pan on a cookie sheet. Bake at 375° for 50 minutes. Make a slit in the top of each popover to release the steam. Bake for 10 more minutes.

Serve immediately with roast beef. Makes 8 to 10 servings.

“

Gilligan: I'm so hungry I could kiss the ground. (He does it.) This island tastes terrible.

”

Chicken Soup Coops

2 cups sifted all-purpose flour
3 teaspoons baking powder
1 tablespoon sugar
½ teaspoon salt

1 10 ¾-ounce can cream of chicken soup
1 egg, beaten
¼ cup shortening, melted

Grease 12 large muffin cups. In a large bowl sift together the flour, baking powder, sugar, and salt. In a separate bowl combine the soup, egg, and melted shortening. Add the soup mixture to the dry ingredients and stir gently just until mixed. Fill greased muffin cups ⅔ full. Bake at 400° 20 minutes. Makes 12 large muffins.

Ping Pong Popovers

My mom made these a lot when we lived in Reno.

2 eggs
1 cup milk
1 cup sifted all-purpose flour

½ teaspoon salt
1 tablespoon salad oil

Grease 6 to 8 muffin cups. In a mixing bowl combine the eggs, milk, flour, and salt. Beat with an electric mixer at low speed for 1 ½ minutes. Add the oil and beat for 1 ½ minutes. Do not overbeat. Fill the muffin cups ½ full. Bake at 475° for 15 minutes. Reduce the heat to 350° and bake for 25 to 30 minutes or until brown and firm. A few minutes before the popovers are done, prick each woth a fork to allow the steam to escape. Makes 6 to 8 popovers.

Sea Biscuits

2 cups sifted all-purpose flour
4 teaspoons baking powder
½ teaspoon salt
½ teaspoon cream of tartar

2 teaspoons sugar
½ cup shortening (Crisco)
⅔ cup milk

In a medium bowl sift together the flour, baking powder, salt, cream of tartar, and sugar. Cut in the shortening until the mixture resembles coarse crumbs. Add the milk all at once, and stir only until the dough follows a fork around the bowl. Turn onto a lightly floured surface, and knead gently for ½ minute. Pat or roll out to ½-inch thickness and cut with a biscuit cutter. Bake on an ungreased cookie sheet at 450° for 10 to 12 minutes. Makes 16 medium biscuits.

Variations: Put melted butter on ½ of them, then top with another biscuit. Add ¼ cup grated cheese or the grated rind of 1 orange and part orange juice instead of milk.

Atomic Corn Bread

1 ½ cups self-rising cornmeal
1 cup all-purpose flour
½ cup oil
1 cup sour cream

1 16-ounce can creamed corn
1 ½ cups grated Velveeta cheese
2 eggs
½ to ¾ cup jalapeño green sauce

In a medium bowl combine all of the ingredients, blending well. Pour the batter into a hot, greased pan. Bake at 400° for 30 minutes. Makes 12 servings.

Alan, Tina, and I have more fun than a wheelbar-
row full of Gilligans as we pose for a publicity
shot with Bob in front of the lagoon.

Dawn Wells collection

Coral Cornmeal Cakes

1 ½ cups all-purpose flour
½ cup cornmeal
½ teaspoon salt
3 teaspoons baking powder
2 tablespoons sugar

2 tablespoons melted shortening
   or margarine
½ cup water
Oil for frying

In a medium bowl sift together the dry ingredients. Add the melted shortening
and blend thoroughly. Add the water gradually until a pliable dough is formed. If
necessary add a little more water. Turn the dough onto a floured board and knead
gently. Pull off portions of the dough, shape into balls, and press the balls flat. In a
skillet heat some oil and fry the cakes until brown. Turn and allow the other side to
brown. Remove the cakes from the oil and drain on absorbent paper. Good hot or
cold. Makes 6 servings.

Mr. Howell: If it weren't for the money, I'd rather be poor.

Mr. Howell's Left Bank French Toast

¼ cup butter or margarine
2 tablespoons sugar
¼ teaspoon cinnamon
3 eggs, slightly beaten

¾ cup orange juice
8 or 9 slices firm-type bread
Maple syrup

In a 15 x 10-inch jelly-roll pan melt the butter in a 425° oven. Sprinkle with mixture of sugar and cinnamon. In a shallow bowl mix the eggs and orange juice, and dip the bread slices in the mixture until well soaked but not falling apart. Arrange close together in the prepared pan. Bake at 425° for 20 minutes, or until set. With a pancake turner invert the toast onto serving plates. Serve with maple syrup.

Variations: For Sesame toast, sprinkle melted butter with 2 tablespoons sesame seeds.

Good ol' Golden Rule days

Cuckoo Coconut Toast and Pineapple

6 slices firm white bread
2 eggs
½ cup light cream or milk
1 tablespoon sugar
1 teaspoon ginger
½ cup corn flakes, finely crushed

½ cup shredded coconut, finely chopped
Butter or margarine
1 8-ounce can crushed pineapple
Sour cream
Brown sugar

Trim the crusts from the bread slices. In a shallow bowl beat the eggs with the cream or milk, sugar, and ginger. In a separate bowl combine the corn flakes and coconut. Heat a griddle or large frying pan over medium heat. Coat the griddle with butter or margarine. Dip each slice of bread into the egg mixture until well saturated, remove, and drain briefly. Dip the egg-soaked bread in the coconut mixture to coat both sides and place on the griddle. Cook slowly until browned on each side. Remove to warm plates and serve immediately, or place in a warm oven until all are browned. At the table serve bowls of the pineapple, sour cream, and brown sugar for toppings. Makes 3 servings.

Gilligan's Aisle

I boarded an airplane coming back from Disney World several years ago, and when I began to walk down the aisle to my seat, the entire group of passengers and airline attendants burst out in the "Gilligan's Island" theme song. That can't help but brighten your day.

Kansas Tornado Toast

2 ripe bananas (or peaches)
¼ cup milk
3 eggs
1 tablespoon sugar
2 teaspoons maple syrup or honey

½ teaspoon vanilla extract
Pinch salt
10 bread slices
Butter

Peel and slice the fruit into a blender. Add the milk, eggs, sugar, syrup or honey, vanilla, and salt. Blend well. Pour the mixture into a shallow bowl. In a skillet melt a small amount of butter. Dip the bread into the liquid mixture, and fry until browned. Turn and brown on the other side. Makes 10 slices.

Skipper's Skillet Bread

2 tablespoons butter or margarine
1 ⅓ cups yellow cornmeal
2 tablespoons sugar
1 teaspoon baking soda
1 teaspoon salt

⅓ cup sifted all-purpose flour
2 cups milk
2 eggs, beaten
1 cup buttermilk

In a 9-inch skillet or baking pan melt the butter in a 400° oven while mixing the batter. In a medium bowl sift together the cornmeal, sugar, soda, salt, and flour. Stir in 1 cup of milk, the eggs, and buttermilk, and mix well. Pour the batter into the skillet, then pour 1 cup of milk over the top of the batter. Do not stir. The milk will settle to the middle of the bread to form a custard layer in the center. Bake at 400° for 35 minutes or until the bread is done. Do not overbake. Cut into wedges and serve hot with butter and honey, molasses, or maple syrup. Makes 8 to 10 servings.

Dawn Wells collection

Brave and Sure—The Skipper, Alan Hale, actually operated his own restaurant, The Lobster Barrel, for many years in Los Angeles, where he was a congenial and popular host.

Howells's Stuffy Stuffing

Butter
1 medium onion, finely chopped
2 large cloves garlic, minced
¾ cup chopped fresh parsley
Chopped celery to taste (optional)
Giblets, cooked and finely chopped
6 cups dry French bread crumbs
3 eggs, beaten

6 tablespoons cooked spinach, mashed
and drained
½ cup melted butter
Parmesan cheese
Italian herbs
Salt and pepper to taste
Broth

In a skillet melt a small amount of butter and sauté the onion, garlic, and parsley. In a large bowl combine all of the ingredients, adding broth as needed. Makes enough stuffing for a 14-pound turkey.

Little Spuddy Gnocchi

2 cups unseasoned mashed potatoes
2 egg yolks
1 teaspoon salt

1 cup sifted all-purpose flour
½ cup grated Parmesan cheese

In a large bowl mix the potatoes, egg yolks, and salt well. Gradually blend in the flour to make a smooth, stiff dough. Stir in the cheese. Shape into small balls, and mark with the tines of a fork, or shape into long rolls and cut into ¼-inch pieces. Drop a few gnocchi at a time into boiling water, and cook until they rise to the top. Makes 6 servings.

Gilligan's Green Chile
Grilled Cheese Sandwich

3 tablespoons margarine, softened (or
butter)
8 slices white bread (Italian or French)

8 slices cheddar cheese
1 4-ounce can whole green chilies, slit,
seeded, and opened up

Butter 4 slices of bread on one side. Place the bread buttered-side down in a skillet. On the unbuttered side of each place one cheese slice and one whole chile, opened flat. Then add another cheese slice, and top with the remaining bread slice. Butter the top of the bread. Grill on both sides over medium heat, until golden. Serve at once. Makes 4 servings.

Bird brain

Mrs. Howell's Tea Sandwiches

This recipe reminds me of Natalie Schafer.

4 ounces soft cream cheese
¼ cup chopped watercress

6 slices date-nut bread,
½-inch thick

In a small bowl blend the cream cheese and chopped watercress. Spread evenly over the bread slices. Cut each slice into 4 triangles. Garnish with sprigs of watercress. Makes 24 finger sandwiches.

4 ounces cream cheese
⅓ cup thinly sliced cucumber

4 slices square whole grain bread (crusts off)

Spread the cream cheese on the bread. Arrange sliced cucumbers on 2 slices. Cover with other 2 slices of bread. Cut into triangles. Makes 8 finger sandwiches.

Skipper's Dream Sandwich

¾ cup sour cream
2 tablespoons onion soup mix
2 tablespoons horseradish cream
Salt and pepper to taste
12 slices thinly sliced roast beef

8 slices thinly sliced French bread
Butter or margarine
4 lettuce leaves
4 slices garlic dill pickles

In a medium bowl mix the sour cream, onion soup mix, horseradish, salt, and pepper together. Lightly toss half of the cream mixture with the thinly sliced beef. Spread the bread with butter or margarine. Lay 3 slices of beef on each of 4 buttered bread slices. Top with a crisp lettuce leaf and a tablespoonful of sour cream dressing, then cover with a second slice of buttered bread. Cut diagonally and place on a plate. Garnish each sandwich with a slice of garlic dill pickle. Makes 4 sandwiches.

―――――――――― 66 ――――――――――

Skipper: Now, I want you to go to the top of that hill and keep a sharp look out for icebergs.
Gilligan: Aye, aye, icebergs? Skipper, we're in the tropics.
Skipper: I know. That's why they're hard to find.

―――――――――― 99 ――――――――――

Cheery Daytime Baked Tuna Sandwich

1 10 ¾-ounce can cream of mushroom
  soup
¾ 10 ¾-ounce can cream of celery soup
1 6-ounce can chopped water chestnuts
2 tablespoons grated onion
1 9 ¼-ounce can drained tuna

2 tablespoons pimientos
10 slices bread, crusts removed
4 eggs
2 to 3 tablespoons milk
Potato chips

In a medium bowl mix together the mushroom soup, celery soup, water chestnuts, onion, tuna, and pimientos. Spread the tuna mixture between slices of bread. Wrap individually in foil and freeze overnight or longer.
   Remove the sandwiches from freezer. Beat the eggs with the milk. Dip each sandwich in the egg mixture, and roll in crushed potato chips. Bake at 350° for 1 hour. Makes 5 sandwiches.

Lovey's Luncheon Loaf

1 loaf French bread
1 cup butter or margarine
¼ pound ham
¼ pound corned beef
2 hard-boiled eggs

1 tablespoon green bell pepper
¼ cup sliced pimiento-stuffed olives
1 teaspoon Worcestershire sauce
Salt and pepper to taste

Cut the bread in half lengthwise, and hollow out the inside of the top and bottom, leaving a 1-inch shell. In blender or grinder make crumbs of the bread scraps.

In a medium bowl cream the butter until smooth. Stir in the ham, corned beef, eggs, green pepper, olives, and Worcestershire sauce. Season with salt and pepper to taste. Stir in the bread crumbs until evenly distributed. Mound the filling on the bottom half of the bread, and replace the top. Gently press the loaf together. Wrap in foil, and refrigerate until ready to serve. Cut into 1-inch slices. Makes about 12 slices.

——— ❝ ———

Ginger: Gilligan can help you with the pancakes.
Gilligan: Pancakes!
Mary Ann: Sure, I mashed it from breadfruit, put in coconut milk and wild duck eggs. How's it taste?
Gilligan: Like breadfruit, coconut milk, and wild duck eggs.

——— ❞ ———

Mary Ann's Pancakes

3 eggs
1 cup sifted all-purpose flour
3 teaspoons baking powder
½ teaspoon salt

2 teaspoons sugar
1 teaspoon light brown sugar
½ cup buttermilk
2 tablespoons butter, melted

In a medium bowl beat the eggs with an electric mixer at high speed for about 2 minutes. Sift the flour with the baking powder, salt, and sugar. Add the brown sugar, and beat until smooth. Fold in the flour mixture. Stir in the buttermilk and butter until combined, but do not overbeat. Grease and slowly heat the griddle, and pour ¼ cup of batter for each pancake. Cook until bubbles form and the edges are dry. Turn and cook for 2 minutes longer, or until browned. Makes 8 to 10 pancakes.

Variations: For blueberry pancakes gently add 1 ¼ cups of fresh blueberries. Be careful not to break the berries while stirring. For cornmeal pancakes reduce the flour to ¾ cup, and blend in ¼ cup of cornmeal.

Hat Slap Flapjacks

1 cup cottage cheese
6 eggs, well beaten

6 tablespoons all-purpose flour
6 tablespoons melted butter

In a medium bowl beat the cottage cheese with a hand beater until smooth. Add the remaining ingredients and beat until well blended. Pour about ¼ cup of batter for each pancake onto a hot greased griddle. Cook, turning once, until done. Makes about 4 to 6 servings.

Skipper's Pancakes

½ cup 100% bran cereal
½ cup pancake mix
⅔ cup milk

1 egg
1 tablespoon vegetable oil

In a medium bowl combine the cereal and pancake mix. Stir in the milk, egg, and oil. Let the mixture stand for 5 minutes. Use a scant ¼ cup batter for each pancake. Cook on a hot greased griddle. Makes 10 pancakes.

Dawn Wells collection

The Skipper and his favorite cook on the island

This is a shot of John Rich, probably my favorite director, during the run of the series, with Jim. This photo was taken on the first day of 'Gilligan' filming on the beach at Malibu.

Howell Pancakes

½ cup pancake mix
1 ¼ cups milk
1 egg
2 tablespoons butter
2 teaspoons almond extract

2 teaspoons confectioners' sugar
1 cup flaked coconut
1 15 ¼-ounce can pineapple tidbits, sliced a bit

In a medium bowl combine the pancake mix, milk, egg, butter, almond extract, sugar, and ⅓ cup of coconut. Beat until fairly smooth. Cook on a lightly greased griddle until bubbles form and the edges are cooked. Turn and cook until the undersides are golden. Serve warm with pineapple and the remaining coconut. Makes about 8 pancakes.

Ginger's Pancake

4 eggs
½ cup all-purpose flour
½ teaspoon salt
½ cup milk

2 tablespoons soft butter
Confectioners' sugar
Jam

In a medium bowl beat the eggs. In a separate bowl sift together the flour and salt. Add the flour mixture to the eggs alternately with the milk to make a smooth batter. Spread the butter into a cold iron skillet. Pour the batter over the bottom and sides of the prepared skillet. Bake at 400° for 20 to 25 minutes, reducing the heat gradually to 350°. The pancake should puff up at the sides and be crisp and brown. Sprinkle with sugar and jam. Fold like an omelet or cut into wedges, and serve hot. Makes 4 servings.

Professor's Pancakes

¾ cup all-purpose flour
1 teaspoon baking powder
½ teaspoon salt
½ teaspoon cinnamon

¼ cup sugar
1 cup very thinly sliced apples, cut in pieces
1 egg, beaten until light
1 tablespoon butter

In a medium bowl sift together the flour, baking powder, salt, cinnamon, and sugar. In a separate bowl combine the apples, egg, and butter. Add the apple mixture to the dry ingredients. Mix well. Use a scant ¼ cup batter for each pancake. Cook on a hot greased griddle. Makes about 8 pancakes.

Gilligan's Pancakes

¾ cup flour
1 teaspoon baking powder
½ teaspoon salt

1 cup banana pulp
1 egg, beaten until light
1 tablespoon butter, melted

In a medium bowl sift together the flour, baking powder, and salt. In a separate bowl combine the banana, egg, and butter. Add the banana mixture to the dry ingredients. Mix well. Use a scant ¼ cup batter for each pancake. Cook on a hot greased griddle. Makes about 8 pancakes.

Ho-Ho-Ho Potato Hoe Cakes

1 ½ pounds potatoes (4 medium), pared
1 small onion, grated
1 egg
¼ teaspoon Tabasco sauce
2 tablespoons all-purpose flour

½ teaspoon Ac'cent
½ teaspoon salt
⅛ teaspoon nutmeg
3 tablespoons soft-type margarine
Sour cream or applesauce

On a medium grater grate the potatoes. Drain well. In a medium bowl combine the grated potatoes and onion. Add the egg, Tabasco, and flour. Sprinkle with Ac'cent, salt, and nutmeg, and mix thoroughly. In a skillet heat 1 tablespoon of margarine over medium heat. Drop the potato mixture by rounded tablespoonfuls into the skillet. Spread into flat cakes. Fry until golden brown on the bottom side. Turn and brown the other side. Add additional margarine as needed. Serve with sour cream or applesauce. Makes 12 pancakes.

Headhunter Cheddar Herb Bread

4 cups all-purpose flour
¼ cup sugar
2 tablespoons baking powder
1 ½ teaspoons dried thyme
½ teaspoon celery seed
⅛ teaspoon black pepper

Pinch allspice
3 cups coarsely crumbled cheddar
  cheese
1 bunch scallions, including green tops
1 egg
1 ¾ cups milk

In a large bowl combine and mix the flour, sugar, baking powder, and seasonings. Add the cheddar and scallions, and toss to coat. In a separate bowl beat the egg with the milk. Pour the liquids into the dry ingredients. Mix until just blended. The batter will be stiff. Spoon into 2 greased 9 x 5-inch loaf pans and let the dough rise for 20 to 30 minutes. Bake at 375° for 45 minutes or until a toothpick inserted in the center comes out clean. The coarsely crumbled cheddar cheese leaves pockets of melted cheese in the finished loaves. Makes 2 loaves.

From Dreama and Bob Denver.

Dawn Wells collection

Los Angeles Rams quarterback Roman Gabriel played a native warrior in the episode titled *Topsy-Turvy*. He can hunt my head any day.

Yale Man Yogurt Bread

1 cup all-purpose flour
1 cup whole wheat flour
⅔ cup firmly packed brown sugar
¼ cup whole bran cereal
1 teaspoon baking soda
½ teaspoon cinnamon

¼ teaspoon salt
1 beaten egg
1 6-ounce carton yogurt with fruits, raisins, grains
¼ cup milk
¼ cup oil

In a mixing bowl stir together the flours, sugar, cereal, baking soda, cinnamon, and salt. Make a well in the center. In a small bowl combine the egg, yogurt, milk, and oil. Add all at once to the well in the flour mixture. Stir only until moistened. Pour into a greased 8 x 4 x 2-inch loaf pan. Bake at 350° for about 50 minutes or until a wooden pick inserted near the center comes out clean. Cool in a pan for 10 minutes. Serve warm or cool. Makes 1 loaf.

Dawn Wells collection

Marry Ann?—I almost tied the knot with my boyfriend Herbert in Kansas in *Rescue From Gilligan's Island.* But Gilligan and the Skipper came to my rescue. Standing in for Herbert was Lloyd Schwartz, son of Sherwood, and a writer and producer in his own right.

Maritime Marmalade Bread

3 cups sifted all-purpose flour
3 teaspoons baking powder
½ teaspoon salt
¼ cup sugar
½ cup walnuts (or pecans)

1 tablespoon grated orange rind
½ cup orange marmalade
1 cup milk
1 egg, beaten

In a large bowl combine the flour, baking powder, salt, sugar, nuts, and orange rind. In a separate bowl blend together the marmalade, milk, and egg. Add the liquid ingredients to the dry mixture, blending well. Turn into 2 well-greased pans. Let the batter stand for 10 minutes. Bake at 350° for 45 minutes to 1 hour. Makes good sandwiches with cream cheese. Makes 2 loaves.

Howell's Sour Dough Starter

2 cups whole milk　　　　　　　　　**2 cups all-purpose flour**

In a glass jar or crock let the milk stand, covered, in a warm place for about 24 hours or until it sours. Stir in the flour, cover, and let the mixture stand in the same warm place until bubbly and sour, from 2 to 5 days. If any black mold forms, just wipe it away. Store covered in the refrigerator.

Note: Maintain about 3 cups of starter. Immediately after measuring the amount for a recipe, stir enough milk and flour back into the starter to replenish the original amount. The starter should be used and replenished every 2 to 4 weeks.

———————— ❝ ————————

Ginger: Once you've tasted my lips, you'll never be satisfied with bread and water again.

———————— ❞ ————————

Howell's Sour Dough Wheat Bread

1 package dry yeast
1 ½ cups warm water (110°)
3 cups whole-wheat flour
1 cup sourdough starter (see recipe
　　above)
¼ cup dark molasses

3 tablespoons butter, softened
2 teaspoons salt
2 ½ to 3 cups unbleached flour or all-
　　purpose flour
½ teaspoon baking soda

In a large mixing bowl soften the yeast in warm water. Blend in the whole-wheat flour, sourdough starter, molasses, butter, and salt. Combine 1 cup of unbleached flour with the baking soda, and stir it into the the yeast mixture. Add enough remaining flour to make a moderately stiff dough. Turn onto a floured surface and knead for 5 to 8 minutes, until smooth. Shape the dough into a ball. Place the dough in a greased bowl, turning once. Cover with a cloth and set the bowl in a warm place. Let the dough rise for 1 ½ to 2 hours, or until doubled in bulk.

Punch down, and divide in half. Let the dough rest for 10 minutes. Shape into 2 loaves, and place them in 2 greased loaf pans. Cover. Let the loaves rise for 1 hour or until doubled in bulk. Bake at 375° for 35 to 40 minutes. Remove the loaves from the pan and cool on a rack. Makes 2 loaves.

Kona Banana Bread

½ cup shortening
1 cup sugar
2 eggs
¾ cup ripe bananas, mashed

1 ¼ cups sifted cake flour
¾ teaspoon baking soda
½ teaspoon salt
¼ cup chopped nuts (optional)

In a medium bowl cream the shortening and sugar until light. Add the eggs one at a time, beating well after each addition. Stir in the bananas. In a separate bowl stir together the flour, baking soda, salt, and nuts. Add the dry ingredients to the banana mixture, stirring until well blended. Pour into a greased 9-inch square pan. Bake at 350° for 30 to 35 minutes. Cut in squares. Makes 12 servings.

Java Can Bread

1 ½ cups raisins
2 teaspoons baking soda
1 cup boiling water
1 cup sugar
3 tablespoons butter or margarine

1 egg
¼ teaspoon salt
2 cups all-purpose flour
½ cup chopped walnuts or pecans

Grease 2 tall 1-pound coffee cans. Place a round of greased waxed paper in the bottom of each. Measure the raisins into a mixing bowl. Sprinkle on the baking soda, then pour the boiling water over the raisins. Cool. Meanwhile, cream together the sugar and butter, then beat in the egg and salt. Add the mixture to the raisins and mix, then add the flour and mix well. Stir in the walnuts. Turn the batter into the coffee cans. Bake at 350° for 1 hour. Remove the bread from the oven and let it stand for 5 minutes. Turn the bread out of the cans and cool on racks. Makes 2 loaves.

——————— 66 ———————

Mary Ann: I can never get over this jungle supermarket. The only thing missing is trading stamps.

——————— 99 ———————

The Tennessean

The Skipper

No one on the island is more patient than the brave Skipper, Jonas Grumby. Though he is a towering figure at 6-3 and around 221 pounds, the Skipper is really all heart.

Now, sometimes the Skipper does have to stay after Gilligan, and he has been known to swat at his little buddy with his cap a time or two. But most of the time, the Skipper is actually pretty easy going.

That's not to say that the Skipper isn't excitable. In fact, he's probably the most superstitious of the Castaways. After his many years touring the South Pacific in the Navy, the Skipper is well versed in voodoo, witchcraft, and native superstitions, and he often gets the creepy crawlies.

And though the Skipper is a rugged seaman (plus in football he wasn't just a lineman; he *was* the line), he has his tender side. That may be because his Navy duties included being a cook on an aircraft carrier and leading the Navy band on a destroyer for five years. The Skipper also dabbles in poetry when he's bitten by the love bug.

The literature-loving Skipper has read *Four-Masted Schooners I Have Known,* which it would not be going out on a limb to say is more to his liking than the book the Professor once gave him— *The History of Tree Surgery.*

As often as not, the Skipper is smitten with thoughts of food, his first love. He dreams of thick, juicy steaks and the occasional lamb chop. Mary Ann's cooking keeps him happy on the island, but everybody knows his first meal once rescued won't be papayas and tuna.

Entrées

Radioactive Ravioli

A specialty of my Great-Grandmother Avery.

2 big bunches fresh spinach, cooked
6 eggs
1 cup parsley, chopped
4 cloves garlic, minced
¼ cup oil

2 sets brains, cleaned, cooked, and
   chopped (or 2 cups of ground veal)
1 cup grated Romano cheese
Bread crumbs if needed
1 tablespoon Italian seasoning

Press the spinach and strain out the water. Finely chop the spinach. In a large bowl combine the spinach, eggs, parsley, and garlic. Add ¼ cup oil, meat, and cheese. If the filling is too thin, add some bread crumbs. Then add the Italian seasoning.

4 cups sifted all-purpose flour
1 egg
1 to 2 teaspoons salt

1 ½ teaspoons oil
2 ½ cups warm water

On a floured board mix the flour and salt. Make a well in the center, and put the egg, water, and oil in the middle. Mix the ingredients well, and pat the dough into a round. Knead the dough until bubbles appear. Cut off a piece of dough at a time, and leave the rest of the dough covered. Roll the piece of dough out thin enough to see light through faintly.

Place spoonfuls of filling down the dough, folding the dough over to cover the filling. Cut the ravioli with a small glass. Boil the ravioli in salted water for 15 to 20 minutes. Test in 15 minutes. Don't cook too many at a time.

Serve with Mary Ann's Machete Spaghetti Sauce (see recipe, page 167). Makes 6 to 8 servings.

──────── **"** ────────

Skipper: The first thing I'm going to do when I get back—I'm going to have a thick, juicy steak. ... I think I'll have a nice cold beer too!

──────── **"** ────────

Three-Putt Pasta

6 slices bacon
10 ounces spaghetti or other pasta
1 10-ounce package frozen chopped
   spinach

2 cloves garlic, minced
1/8 teaspoon pepper
1/2 cup cream-style cottage cheese
1/3 cup grated Parmesan cheese

In an 8-inch skillet cook the bacon until crisp. Drain, reserving 2 tablespoons of drippings. Crumble the bacon and set it aside. Cook the pasta in a large stock pot of boiling salted water with a little oil for 10 to 12 minutes, until tender but firm.

Meanwhile, in a medium saucepan cook the spinach according to the package directions. In a blender or food processor combine the undrained spinach, reserved bacon drippings, garlic, and pepper. Blend until smooth. Add the cottage cheese, cover, and blend until smooth. Drain the pasta and turn it onto a large platter. Pour the spinach mixture over the pasta and toss. Sprinkle the individual servings with bacon and Parmesan cheese. Serve immediately. Makes 10 to 12 side-dish servings.

———————— 66 ————————

Conversation while operating the Professor's pedal-powered telegraph invention:
Mary Ann: Oh-h, my legs feel like spaghetti!
Ginger: They're stiff as breadsticks!
Gilligan: Spaghetti and breadsticks—must be Italian bikes.

———————— 99 ————————

Great Raftini Fettucini
and Chicken Livers

1/2 pound fettucini or egg noodles
1 pound chicken livers
3 tablespoons butter
1/4 pound fresh mushrooms, sliced
1/2 teaspoon salt
Dash pepper

1/4 cup Brolio Chianti wine
2 tablespoons water
1/4 cup butter
1/2 cup grated Parmesan cheese
1/4 cup light cream
2 eggs, lightly beaten

In a large pot cook the noodles in salted water until tender. Drain, and keep the pasta warm.

In a skillet sauté the chicken livers in 3 tablespoons of butter until well browned. Add the mushrooms, and cook for a minute. Season with salt and pepper, and add the wine and water. Reduce the heat and simmer for a minute. To the drained noodles add 1/4 cup of butter, the Parmesan, and cream. Add the eggs and toss. Arrange the noodles around the edge of the platter, and place the chicken livers in center. Makes 6 servings.

Santa Lucia Linguine

16 ounces linguine, drained
2 cups packed fresh basil (or parsley)
3 cloves minced garlic
1 teaspoon salt

¼ teaspoon pepper
3 tablespoons chopped walnuts
1 cup olive oil
½ cup grated Parmesan cheese

In a blender combine the basil, garlic, salt, pepper, and walnuts. Cover and process. While running, slowly add the oil. Blend 3 to 5 minutes until smooth. Stir in the Parmesan. Toss with linguine. Makes 8 servings.

Note: In summer use basil. In winter use parsley.

The beat of a different drummer

The Tennessean

Weenie Linguine

One of my favorites. A real wiener!

1 pound Italian sausage, skin removed
½ cup butter
1 clove garlic, chopped
1 medium onion, chopped
½ teaspoon oregano
1 teaspoon basil
½ teaspoon tarragon

¼ cup parsley
2 cups sliced mushrooms
8 ounces linguine, cooked al dente and kept warm
1 cup heavy cream
Parmesan cheese
Pepper

In a skillet sauté the sausage until cooked. In a separate pan melt the butter and sauté the garlic, onion, oregano, basil, tarragon, parsley, and mushrooms. Add the sausage and heat through. Toss in the linguine, and add the heavy cream, Parmesan, and pepper. Mix well. Makes 4 to 6 servings.

Lagoon Lasagna

1 cup cooked spinach, drained well
2 cups skim ricotta cheese
2 large eggs
Dash garlic powder
⅓ cup grated fresh Parmesan

¼ teaspoon pepper
⅛ teaspoon nutmeg
1 large jar chunky spaghetti sauce
½ pound uncooked lasagna noodles
¾ pound shredded mozzarella

In a mixing bowl mix together the spinach, ricotta, eggs, garlic powder, Parmesan, pepper, and nutmeg. In the bottom of a greased 9 x 13-inch glass casserole spread ¼ of the spaghetti sauce. Arrange ⅓ of the uncooked noodles over the sauce. Sprinkle with ⅓ of the spinach mixture. Repeat the layers, ending with sauce. Sprinkle with mozzarella cheese. Cover tightly with foil. The lasagna may be refrigerated overnight at this point. Bake at 375° for 1 hour, or 1 ½ hours if chilled.

Let the lasagna stand for 10 minutes before cutting. Makes 6 servings.

———— **"** ————

Skipper: You know what I want for Christmas? A nice, thick, juicy steak.

———— **"** ————

De-Magnetized Meteor Meatballs

1 pound ground chuck
1 beaten egg
2 cloves minced garlic
1 tablespoon chopped parsley
1 teaspoon salt
½ teaspoon pepper
½ teaspoon basil

½ teaspoon oregano
1 cup soft bread crumbs
½ cup grated cheddar and Parmesan, mixed
2 tablespoons fat
Mary Ann's Machete Spaghetti Sauce (see recipe, page 167) or canned

In a mixing bowl combine all of the ingredients except the fat and the spaghetti sauce. Shape into 8 2-inch balls. In a skillet heat the fat and brown the meatballs quickly. Add the meatballs and drippings to Mary Ann's Machete Spaghetti Sauce 30 minutes before the sauce is done. Makes 8 meatballs.

Note: If using sauce from a jar, heat the sauce for 30 minutes, then add the meatballs and drippings, and cook for 30 more minutes. Be careful not to break the meatballs.

Natalie's Rose Bush

When Natalie passed away, I asked the people handling the estate if I could have something living of hers, something from her yard that she loved to see bloom. I knew her favorite rose bush was just outside her living room window.

They said, "Sure, come and get some roses." My mother and two friends of mine went over and dug up several of her rose bushes. While it was not the best time of the year for transplanting rose bushes, nevertheless, every single one of those plants bloomed.

Last year her favorite bush was the first one to bloom. When I walk by it now, I always say, "Hi, Nat."

Easy Turkey Tortilla Casserole

4 cups cooked turkey chunks
2 10 ¾-ounce cans cream of mushroom soup
1 10 ¾-ounce can cream of chicken soup
1 10 ¾-ounce can cheddar cheese soup
1 4-ounce can chopped chilies

1 5 ¾-ounce can chopped ripe olives
1 bunch green onions, chopped
2 dozen corn tortillas, broken into small pieces
1 pound sharp cheddar, grated

In a large bowl mix together all of the ingredients except the tortillas and cheese. In a casserole dish layer half of the tortillas and cheese, then half of the soup mixture. Repeat the layers, ending with cheese on top. Bake at 350° for 30 minutes. Makes 8 to 10 servings.

Zombie Tamale Pie

1 teaspoon salt
1 ½ pounds lean ground beef
1 large onion, chopped
2 cloves garlic, minced
¼ teaspoon pepper
1 cup yellow cornmeal
1 12-ounce can whole kernel corn,
   drained

2 6-ounce cans tomato paste
1 10-ounce can enchilada sauce
1 4-ounce can diced green chilies, drain
1 tablespoon chili powder
1 6-ounce can pitted olives, drained
1 cup milk
1 ½ cups shredded cheddar

In a wide frying pan sprinkle the salt in the bottom and cook the beef over medium heat until browned and crumbly. Stir in the onion and garlic, and cook until the onions are soft. Remove the pan from the heat and discard the excess fat. Stir in the pepper, cornmeal, corn, tomato paste, enchilada sauce, chilies, chili powder, olives, and milk. Pour the mixture into a greased shallow 3-quart casserole. Bake uncovered at 350° for 30 minutes. Sprinkle the cheese evenly over the top and bake for 5 to 10 more minutes, until the cheese is bubbly. Makes 6 to 8 servings.

----------- " -----------

Gilligan: I guess being a zombie kind of takes your appetite away.

----------- " -----------

Kalani's Crab Enchiladas

6 tortillas
Oil
1 ½ cups crab meat (can use imitation
   or canned)
6 tablespoons minced onion
Salsa de tomatillos

Grated Monterey Jack cheese
Sour cream
Pitted ripe olives
Avocado slices
Sliced tomatoes

Heat the tortillas until soft in oil. Place ¼ cup of crab in the center of each, sprinkle with 1 tablespoon onion, and spread a little salsa on top. Roll up the enchiladas and place them seam-side down in a shallow pan or baking dish. Cover with salsa and sprinkle with cheese. Bake at 400° for about 10 minutes, until the cheese is melted.

Serve with a dollop of sour cream. Garnish with olives, avocado, and tomato. Makes 6 enchiladas.

Rescue hula

Rockery Hudpeck's Exotic Enchiladas

2 tablespoons shortening
1 ½ pounds ground beef
2 cloves garlic, minced
½ cup all-purpose flour
3 tablespoons chili powder
1 ½ teaspoons salt
¼ teaspoon pepper

1 12-ounce can or bottle beer
2 cups water
12 tortillas
Oil
1 ½ cups chopped onion
2 cups shredded longhorn or cheddar
    cheese (approximately 8 ounces)

In a large skillet melt the shortening and brown the beef and garlic. Stir in the flour, chili powder, salt, and pepper. Add the beer and water and bring the mixture to a boil. Simmer uncovered for about 15 minutes, stirring several times. In a separate skillet heat a small amount of oil and cook the tortillas until crisp. Divide the onion, cheese, and meat mixture in half.

Place 1 tortilla in the bottom of a shallow 2-quart casserole. Divide half of the onion, cheese, and meat into sixths. Layer the tortilla with ⅙ of the onion, cheese, and meat. Repeat 5 times. Make a second stack in the same way using the remaining ingredients. Bake at 375° for about 25 minutes, until hot and bubbly. Makes 6 servings.

Mary Ann Summers

Skinny Mulligan's Shrimp Enchiladas

3 pints sour cream
1 cup half and half
Garlic salt
Pepper
All-purpose flour (about 3 tablespoons)
16 corn tortillas

4 cups grated cheddar cheese
2 pounds small boiled shrimp
1 4-ounce can Ortega chilies, cut in
  strips
½ cup chopped green onions

In a saucepan gently mix the sour cream and half and half. Add the garlic salt, pepper, and flour to thicken. Cook, stirring constantly, over low heat until the mixture reaches the boiling point, but do not boil. Dip the tortillas in warm oil or butter for 5 seconds each side to soften. Place a little of the cheese and some of the shrimp on the center of each tortilla, and roll up to make an enchilada. Reserve some cheese and shrimp for topping. Place the enchiladas in a Pyrex baking pan. Spread 2 strips of chilies on each, and arrange additional shrimp over all. Cover with cream sauce, and top with the remaining cheese. Bake at 350° for 10 to 15 minutes, until bubbly and the cheese melts. Sprinkle with green onions before serving. Makes 16 enchiladas.

Porthole Enchiladas

1 tablespoon oil
1 clove garlic, minced
1 small onion, chopped
2 tablespoons all-purpose flour
2 cups bouillon
1 cup chopped, peeled tomatoes (or
   drained canned)

1 4-ounce can diced green chilies
12 corn tortillas
4 cups shredded Monterey Jack
1 avocado, peeled and diced
1 cup chopped green onion
Sour cream

In a saucepan heat the oil and sauté the garlic and onion until tender but not browned. Stir in the flour, then slowly add the bouillon. Cook, stirring constantly, until smooth and thickened. Add the chilies and tomatoes and simmer for 5 to 10 minutes.

Dip the tortillas one at a time into the simmering sauce. Place a large spoonful of cheese on each and top with a little sauce. Roll and place in a shallow 9 x 13-inch baking dish seam-side down. Pour the remaining sauce around the enchiladas. Bake at 350° for 15 minutes or until cheese filling begins to melt. Garnish with diced avocado, green onion, and a dab of sour cream. Makes 12 enchiladas.

Everybody's Little Buddy

Bob Denver is a gentle soul. He's bright, almost shy, and very funny and very kind. I think he has that "magic" about him—especially where children are concerned.

I remember going to the mall on a weekend after filming an episode, and there Bob was with ten or twelve kids. He was like the Pied Piper, with the children all following along behind him. Some days he'd be sleepy at work, and once he explained, "We built this spider farm last night and couldn't go to bed until we named all the spiders." He has the soul of a child, combined with the wisdom of an adult. I think he is one of the biggest reasons "Gilligan's Island" remains so popular. Bob has a magic that kids understand and trust.

Enrico Rodriguez Huevos Rancheros

1 tablespoon butter or margarine
1 tablespoon all-purpose flour
1 6-ounce can green chile salsa
¼ cup water
8 pitted ripe olives, halved

4 eggs
¼ cup shredded cheddar cheese
4 slices buttered toast
Salt and pepper to taste

In a skillet with a lid melt the butter. Stir in the flour, and add the salsa, water, and olives. Simmer, stirring constantly, until thickened. Break the eggs into the sauce, then slip a spoon under each so that the eggs will sink into sauce. Top with cheese. Cover. Simmer until the eggs are set, 10 to 20 minutes or to the desired doneness. Serve on buttered toast. Season with salt and pepper to taste. Makes 4 servings.

---------------- ❝ ----------------

Hunger pains:
Mary Ann: Gilligan, you've had breakfast.
Gilligan: Then I'll have lunch.
Mary Ann: But this is breakfast.
Gilligan: I'll fake it.

---------------- ❞ ----------------

Equarico Cheese Enchiladas

1 ½ cups shredded Monterey Jack
  cheese
1 ½ cups shredded cheddar cheese
1 3-ounce package cream cheese, softened
1 cup picante sauce or mild salsa
1 medium red or green pepper, diced

½ cup sliced green onion
1 teaspoon crushed cumin
8 flour tortillas (each 7 - 8 inches)
Shredded lettuce
Chopped tomato
Sliced black olives (optional)

Combine the Monterey Jack, cheddar, cream cheese, picante sauce or salsa, red pepper, onions, and cumin. Mix well. Spoon ¼ cup of the cheese mixture down the center of each tortilla. Roll up into enchiladas and place them seam-side down in a 13 x 9-inch baking dish. Spoon the remaining picante or salsa evenly over the enchiladas. Cover with the remaining cheese mixture. Bake at 350° for 20 minutes or until hot.

Top with lettuce, tomato, and olives. Serve with additional salsa and sour cream, if desired. Makes 4 servings.
From Dreama and Bob Denver.

The Tennessean

Looking good

———— " ————

Wrongway Feldman steers into the thick of things:

Skipper: Oh, but you don't want to eat pineapple and coconuts for the rest of your life!

Wrongway: Oh, but it's better than what I et in New York. Oh-hoh! What a restaurant that was! They couldn't even get a simple little order straight. All I asked for was a plain T-bone steak.

Gilligan: Steak?!

Wrongway: Yeah, a T-bone. And what do they bring me? The filet— that thick (indicating a three-inch gap between thumb and index finger).

Skipper: That *thick?!*

Wrongway: And I like mine well done, you see. And this one was all red and juicy inside. So I sent it back. And they bring me another. And this one was well done all right. But they put on a lot of mushrooms and that bernaise sauce. Heh! And I couldn't even get the waitress' eye. She was busy with some glutton with the French pastry tray with all that chocolate and custard and whipped cream.

Skipper: *That* thick?!

———— " ————

Skipper's Goodbye Ribeye

1 5- to 8-pound beef ribeye roast, first
  cut or small end with or without bone
½ cup coarsely cracked pepper
½ teaspoon ground cardamom
1 tablespoon tomato paste

1 teaspoon paprika
½ teaspoon garlic powder
1 cup soy sauce
¾ cup vinegar

Trim the excess fat from the meat. Combine the pepper and cardamom, and rub the mixture all over the meat. Press the seasonings into the roast. Place the meat in a shallow baking dish. In a bowl combine a small amount of the vinegar and tomato paste and mix well. Gradually add the paprika, garlic powder, soy sauce, and remaining vinegar. Carefully pour the mixture over the meat, and marinate the roast in the refrigerator overnight. Baste several times while marinating.

Remove the meat from the marinade. Let the roast stand at room temperature for 1 hour.

Using a meat thermometer as a guide, place the roast on a rotisserie, centered and balanced. Cook to 135° for rare (approximately 1 ½ hours on a Farberware rotisserie). Makes 8 to 10 servings.

Note: Cooking will be quicker on a gas grill.

Alternate Cooking Method: Wrap the meat in foil and place it in a shallow pan. Roast at 300° for 2 hours for medium-rare. Open the foil; ladle out and reserve the drippings. Brown the roast, uncovered, at 350° while making gravy.

Gravy: Strain the pan drippings, skimming off the excess fat. To 1 cup of meat juices add 1 cup water, and bring the mixture to a boil. Add a little marinade, if desired. Serve the roast au jus, or thicken the gravy with 1 ½ tablespoons of cornstarch mixed with ¼ cup of cold water.

Howell Stake

One on my favorite dishes from Grandmother Wells.

1 large sirloin or top round steak
Salt
Thinly sliced onion

Thinly sliced lemon
Catsup
Parsley

In an iron frying pan sprinkle salt in the bottom and sear the steak. When brown, turn the steak over and arrange the thinly sliced onion and sliced lemon on top. Cover with catsup and sprinkle with parsley. Cook under the broiler until browned and done to the desired doneness.

Gang Plank Flank Steak

1 1 ½-pound beef flank steak
⅓ cup olive oil
⅓ cup lemon juice
6 jalapeño peppers, seeded and minced

1 tablespoon parsley, minced
1 teaspoon salt
1 teaspoon pepper
Salsa

Place the steak in a plastic bag. In a bowl combine the remaining ingredients except salsa. Pour the mixture over the meat. Close the bag securely and turn it to coat the steak well. Marinate overnight or for 6 to 8 hours.

Drain, reserving the marinade. Place the steak in a fish rack. Grill over medium coals for 10 to 15 minutes on each side, turning once. Test for doneness. Carve the steak across the grain into thin slices. Serve with salsa. Makes 6 servings.

———— " ————

I wouldn't say that, Skipper:

Skipper: Gilligan, I'm busy and I'm working up an appetite here. Now, what ever you've caught, I'll eat it.

Gilligan: O.K., Skipper. I sure hope you have a strong stomach.

(Gilligan caught a mine.)

———— " ————

The Tennessean

Hungry for a thick, juicy steak

Thurston's Little Chang Steak

Jim Backus did not know how to cook, and intended to keep it that way. Why not? He had me do it for him. The only reason this recipe is named for him is because whenever I made it, he hung around the kitchen and drooled. Once you have eaten this, you'll know why.

1 ½ teaspoons ginger
2 tablespoons Chinese bead molasses
3 tablespoons sherry
2 pounds sirloin steak, sliced
1 cup bouillon
1 14-ounce package frozen artichoke

hearts, defrosted and drained
1 8-ounce can water chestnuts, thinly sliced or diced
1 tablespoon cornstarch
1 cup frozen peas, thawed and warmed through

In a small bowl combine the ginger, molasses, and sherry. Marinate the steak in the mixture for 3 to 5 hours. In a pan or wok over high flame sauté the steak in the marinade to the desired doneness.

Add the bouillon, artichoke hearts, water chestnuts, and cornstarch, and stir until thick. Add the peas. Serve over rice with soy sauce, if desired. Makes 6 servings.

From Henny Backus.

Jim and Henny's Recipe for Disaster (recalled by Henny Backus)

One day our agent called us about doing the Joanne Carson cooking show. (Joanne was Johnny's second wife.) The producers requested that we "dress" for it, as this taping would be the deciding program for a possibile pickup, and the sponsors would be watching. Jim was his elegant self, and I wore a magnificent gold caftan.

Tape day arrived, and we were all in fine fettle. The show went steaming along. Now it was time for me to make a little something to titillate the palate. I had elected to make a low-calorie chocolate drink. The camera came in tight on the three of us—very close on me next to Joanne and Jim leaning over each shoulder.

I had put into the blender four tablespoons of cocoa, two packets of sweetener, a tumbler of ice cubes, two tumblers of water, a cap of vanilla, and three-quarters of a cup of powdered skim milk, when Joanne cried, "Oh, let *me* turn it on." Forgetting all about the lid, she reached over and pushed the button. We stood there with our mouths open in amazement as the chocolate mess flew up, went all over the set, and covered us three fools from head to foot with the best chocolate drink you ever tasted.

The audience howled as we tried to get all of that thick brown mess out of our hair, our eyes, and our clothes—all as the cameras rolled on and on and on. There was no need for retakes. The sponsors loved it, and the show was picked up.

Jim and Henny Backus were a wonderful couple. She guest-starred in one episode (*Gilligan's Mother-In-Law*) as an island native. In 1968, Henny and Jim co-starred as Cora and J.C. Dithers in the CBS sitcom "Blondie."

Dawn Wells collection

Henny's Secret Agent Recipe

1 quart stock (can be vegetable)
½ pound hamburger
1 16-ounce can whole tomatoes
1 cup chopped cooked turkey, chicken, or veal
4 cups leftover salad (lettuce, cucumber with seasonings)
1 avocado, sliced
1 or more ¼-inch slices mozzarella cheese
2 to 3 medium carrots, sliced or diced
2 or 3 ribs celery, sliced diagonally
4 or 5 sliced mushrooms with stems,

marinated overnight in oil, vinegar, and seasonings
6 green onions (or shallots, a leek or two, or combination), in 1-inch pieces
Sliced radishes
Salt to taste
1 or 2 cloves garlic
1 teaspoon oregano
1 tablespoon sweet basil
1 16-ounce can garbanzo beans, drained
1 cup pasta, broken up
1 whole lemon, thinly sliced and then halved

In a crock pot combine all of the ingredients. Cook on high for 3 hours or more. At 3 hours all the things that should be cooked are well done, and the carrots are still a little crisp.

Serve with toasted French bread and Parmesan cheese. Makes about 6 servings.

Note: This recipe is an approximation. You can switch it around depending on what you have at hand. Great for leftovers. Just as good without meat for vegetarians. Just as good with sausages or anything. I made meatballs out of the hamburger and threw them in without browning. Great!

From Henny Backus.

Homeward looking angels

High Five Prime Rib

2 tablespoons Worcestershire sauce
1 teaspoon paprika
1 teaspoon MSG
Salt and pepper to taste

Choice prime or standing rib roast, ½
  pound per serving
Ice cream salt

In a small bowl combine the Worcestershire sauce, paprika, MSG, salt, and pepper. Rub the mixture into the roast. Line a heavy roasting pan with aluminum foil. Cover with a layer of ice cream salt. Dampen the salt lightly with water until just moist. Place the roast on the salt in standing rib position. Cover the roast completely with ice cream salt. Repeat the dampening procedure. Do not cover. Bake at 500° for 12 to 20 minutes per pound, depending on the degree of doneness desired.

Remove the roast from the oven. Crack the salt with a mallet. Pull the salt sections away from the meat. Brush all salt particles from the roast. Enjoy the prime rib!

From Harlem Globetrotter Geese Ausbie.

Producer's Dream Meat Loaf

3 tablespoons oil
1 cup chopped onions
1 cup chopped celery
2 eggs
1 cup herb-seasoned stuffing mix
Salt and pepper to taste
¼ cup chopped parsley

1 teaspoon thyme
Sage
½ cup seltzer
2 pounds ground meat
1 8-ounce can tomato sauce
2 tablespoons soy sauce
2 tablespoons brown sugar

In a skillet heat the oil and sauté the onions and celery until soft. In a large bowl combine the sautéed mixture, the eggs, stuffing, salt, pepper, parsley, thyme, sage, seltzer, and meat. Turn the mixture into a loaf pan.

In a small bowl combine the tomato sauce, soy sauce, and brown sugar, blending well. Spread half of the sauce over the meat loaf. Bake at 400° for 30 minutes.

Spread the remaining sauce over the meat loaf. Reduce the heat to 375° and bake for 30 minutes more. Makes 6 servings.

From Mildred and Sherwood Schwartz.

——————————— **"** ———————————

Mr. Howell: That makes 300,012 bananas that you owe me.
Gilligan: Well, you can subtract from the 960 mangos you owe me from playing gin.

——————————— **"** ———————————

Mr. Howell's Life of Leisure Meat Loaf

⅓ cup mayonnaise
⅓ cup mustard (prepared)
1 ½ pounds ground beef
¾ cup oats
¼ cup chopped onion

2 teaspoons garlic salt
¼ teaspoon pepper
1 6-ounce can tomato paste
1 egg, beaten
½ teaspoon oregano

In a small bowl combine the mayonnaise and mustard. Set the mixture aside. In a large bowl combine the remaining ingredients. Pack the mixture firmly in an ungreased 8 ½ x 4 ½-inch loaf pan. Spread the mayonnaise mixture over the loaf. Bake at 350° for 1 hour and 15 minutes. Let the loaf stand for 5 minutes. Makes 8 servings.

From Henny Backus.

Mom's Meat Loaf Ramoo

2 pounds ground chuck
2 teaspoons salt
½ teaspoon pepper
½ teaspoon curry powder
½ teaspoon garlic powder
2 eggs

2 tablespoons minced onion
2 large peeled and chopped Granny
   Smith apples
½ cup orange juice
⅓ cup chopped chutney

In a large bowl mix together all of the ingredients except the chutney. Line a shallow pan with foil. Shape the mixture into a loaf, place it in the pan, and chill. Bake at 350° for 1 hour.

Remove the meat loaf from the oven and spread with chutney. Return the meat loaf to the oven for 10 minutes. Makes 6 to 8 servings.

Mighty Sailor Man Meat Loaf

2 10-ounce packages frozen chopped
   spinach, thawed and well drained
1 cup dried bread crumbs
1 8-ounce package American cheese
   slices, diced
1 pound lean ground beef
1 medium onion, minced

2 eggs
1 ½ cups fresh bread crumbs
½ cup toasted wheat germ
¾ cup milk
1 ½ teaspoons salt
½ teaspoon seasoned pepper

In medium bowl combine the spinach, dried bread crumbs, and cheese. Set the mixture aside. Grease a 9 x 5-inch loaf pan and line the bottom with foil. In a medium bowl combine the remaining ingredients. Mix well. Pat half of the meat mixture into the bottom of the pan. Spread with spinach mixture. Then top with the remaining meat mixture. Bake at 350° for 1 ½ hours or until hot and bubbly.

Pour off the fat and invert the loaf onto a platter. Remove the foil. Makes 6 servings.

———————— 66 ————————

Skipper: I can hardly wait to get to my favorite restaurant and my favorite steak sandwich.
Gilligan: Your favorite steak sandwich?
Skipper: Yes, a filet between two sirloins.
Gilligan: Order my favorite too—a choccolate-covered hamburger.

———————— 99 ————————

Hmmm...My kingdom for a chocolate-covered hamburger

Giant Gilligan Burger

1 ½ pounds ground beef
1 ½ teaspoons salt
¼ to ½ teaspoon Italian herbs
3 ounces cream cheese

1 tablespoon prepared mustard
1 tablespoon horseradish, drained
1 1 ⅝-ounce can french fried onion rings

Mix the meat and salt, and divide the meat in half. Pat one half evenly in ungreased 8-inch pie pan. In a small bowl mix the Italian herbs, cream cheese, mustard, and horseradish. Spread the mixture over the meat in the pan. Shape the remaining meat into an 8-inch circle and place it on the cheese mixture. Pinch the edges together to seal. Bake at 350° for 45 minutes for medium, 55 minutes for well done.

Remove the meat loaf to a large serving plate, and place the onion rings around the meat. Makes 4 servings.

Topsy-turvy Beef and Polenta Torte

5 ½ cups water
1 teaspoon salt
1 ½ cups yellow cornmeal
½ cup grated Parmesan
2 tablespoons margarine
1 ½ pounds ground chuck

1 15-ounce jar spaghetti sauce with
  mushrooms
1 10-ounce package frozen chopped
  spinach
2 tablespoons seasoned bread crumbs

In a large pot bring the water and salt to a boil. Reduce the heat to medium and add the cornmeal slowly, stirring constantly. Cook over low heat until very thick, about 15 minutes. Stir in the Parmesan and margarine.

In a skillet cook the beef until brown. Skim the fat, and stir in the spaghetti sauce. Cook the spinach, drain well, and squeeze.

Grease an angel or loose-sided pan. Spread half of the polenta in the bottom. Sprinkle with meat, then spinach. Spoon the remaining polenta over the spinach, evenly spreading the polenta to cover the surface completely. Sprinkle with bread crumbs. Bake at 450° for 10 to 15 minutes, until heated through and the top is golden. Remove the torte from the pan, and cut into wedges. Makes 8 servings.

——————— ❝ ———————

More carrots than Bugs Bunny:

Mr. Howell: If you need a diamond to cut the cable, Mrs. Howell and I, I
    must say, have quite an assortment.

Mrs. Howell: Oh, yes, five carats and up.

Gilligan: Oh, I'd rather have a diamond. I don't think carrots are hard
    enough.

——————— ❞ ———————

Millionaire's Meatballs

½ pound ground pork
½ pound ground beef
1 egg
½ cup water
3 tablespoons all-purpose flour
1 tablespoon beef base
3 heaping tablespoons dried onions
1 tablespoon brown sugar

1 tablespoon MSG
1 teaspoon salt
Dash allspice
Dash coriander
Dash nutmeg
Dash ginger
Dash white pepper
Dash rosemary

In a large bowl combine all of the ingredients. Shape into balls. To hold their shape, drop the meatballs into boiling water for 5 minutes. Drain. In a frying pan brown the meatballs well. These meatballs can be served hot with gravy, or sliced cold for sandwiches. The spice amounts may be adjusted. Makes 4 servings.

King Kaliwani Burger Topping

¼ cup dairy sour cream
¼ cup mayonnaise
¾ teaspoon curry powder
½ teaspoon onion salt

2 tablespoons raisins
2 tablespoons flaked coconut
2 tablespoons coarsely chopped peanuts

Combine the sour cream, mayonnaise, curry powder, and onion salt. Chill the mixture for 1 hour.

Stir in the raisins. Spoon the topping on burgers and sprinkle with coconut and peanuts. Makes 1 ½ cups.

--- **"** ---

The men fend for themselves:
Mr. Howell: Excuse me, gentlemen. Did you want your dinner well done?
Skipper: That's fine, Mr. Howell.
Mr. Howell: I mean *very* well done.
Skipper: That's O.K. with me.
Mr. Howell: Very, *very* well done?
Gilligan: We don't care how well done, Mr. Howell.
Mr. Howell: Oh, good.
Gilligan: What are we having for dinner?
Mr. Howell: Ashes.
Skipper: I thought you said you were a good cook!
Mr. Howell: Well, I *am* a good cook when I have a chef working for me.

--- **"** ---

Ham Radio Cranberry Chops

6 pork chops
All-purpose flour
1 16-ounce can jellied cranberry sauce

1 teaspoon grated orange rind
½ cup crushed pineapple, drained
¼ cup water

Dredge the chops with flour. In a hot skillet brown the pork chops. In a bowl mix the remaining ingredients and pour the mixture over the chops in the skillet. Cover and simmer for 1 hour or until tender. Makes 6 servings.

Dawn Wells collection

Sugar and spice and everything nice.

Ginger and Mary Ann

The image Mary Ann has is open, confident, and kind—the girl you could take home to Mom. She is a wonderful example of what young boys dream of and what young girls dream of becoming. I believe that Mary Ann and Ginger became the Betty and Veronica of that generation. Mary Ann is the symbol of the young, wholesome girl next door, and Ginger is, of course, the glamorous sex symbol.

There was a Nike tennis shoe ad recently that says it all. The high-top black tennis shoe called "Ginger" is racy and aggressive. The high-top white tennis shoe, "Mary Ann," is sweet and wonderful.

When we began filming "Gilligan's Island," I was very new in the business. The first year was a learning experience, and Tina Louise was an actress who already had a name and was extremely beautiful.

I learned a great deal from her about makeup, camera angles, and what looked best on camera. We didn't pal around together off the set, but I still felt we were friends.

We weren't buddy-buddies but there was no animosity or jealousy or competition between us. We were two totally different people. It's funny, though—I do remember I wasn't allowed to wear my hair down and I wasn't allowed to wear bangs because Tina's character wore her hair down and had bangs. I thought that was the funniest thing because even if I tried to look exactly like Tina, there would be no way in the world we could be the same type. I don't know who made the rule about hairstyles.

The Mary Ann trademark turned out to be the two-ponytail hairdo, as well as the bare midriff. When I first tested for the part, I had a long braid down the back, but I insisted on wearing the ponytails because I felt it fit the character better than any other hairdo. I was right because the ponytails have become Mary Ann's symbol. So many little girls say, "See, I wear my hair like Mary Ann."

Mary Ann and Ginger's Sweet and Sour Pork

1 pound lean pork
1 cup orange juice
1 ¼ teaspoons soy sauce
¼ cup white vinegar
3 tablespoons sugar
1 tablespoon cornstarch
2 tablespoons peanut oil

¼ cup diced green pepper
¼ cup diced red pepper or pimiento
1 teaspoon minced garlic
2 teaspoons shredded ginger root
6 water chestnuts, diced
½ cup diced unpeeled orange

Cut the pork into ½-inch squares and set aside. In a small bowl combine the orange juice, soy sauce, vinegar, sugar, and cornstarch and set aside.

In a wok or skillet heat 1 tablespoon of oil and stir-fry the pork until done, about 4 minutes. Add the remaining 1 tablespoon of oil, the peppers, garlic, and ginger root, and stir-fry for 1 minute. Add the orange juice mixture and cook, stirring constantly, until the sauce thickens. Add the water chestnuts and orange pieces, and stir constantly until heated through. Serve with rice. Makes 4 servings.

Trivia Quiz

Professor's Final Exam

1. What piece of "furniture" is located between the Howells' beds?

   A safe

2. What are the names of the four Mosquitos?

   Bingo, Bango, Bongo, and Irving

3. What is Mr. Howell's hat size?

   $6 \, {}^{7}/_{8}$

4. What is the name of Mrs. Howell's chauffeur?

   On the island, Gilligan; back home, Charles

5. What is the name of Gilligan's barber back home?

   Sam

Pirate Pork Chops

1 medium apple, cored and chopped
(about 1 cup)
1 cup unseasoned croutons
¾ cup apple juice

1 envelope onion soup mix (not instant)
1 teaspoon cinnamon
4 ¾-inch thick pork chops (about 1 ½
pounds)

In a medium bowl mix the apple, croutons, ½ cup apple juice, the onion-soup mix, and cinnamon. With a long sharp knife, cut a deep pocket in each chop, and fill with stuffing mixture. Arrange the chops in a single layer in a lightly greased shallow baking dish. Brush with some of the remaining apple juice. Bake at 400° for 35 minutes or until brown and tender, brushing with apple juice 2 or 3 times during cooking. Makes 4 servings.

El Presidente Pepper Pork Stew

¼ cup oil
2 pounds pork shoulder, trimmed, cut in
1-inch pieces
1 ½ cups chopped onion
2 teaspoons minced garlic
1 6-ounce can tomato paste
1 ½ cups water
¼ cup dry red wine
1 ½ teaspoons salt

¼ teaspoon cayenne pepper
¼ teaspoon cinnamon
⅛ teaspoon cloves
1 chicken bouillon cube
1 15 ¼-ounce can pineapple chunks,
juice reserved
2 green bananas, peeled and quartered
½ cup whipping cream

In heavy kettle heat the oil and brown the pork, onion, and garlic. Stir in the tomato paste, water, wine, salt, cayenne, cinnamon, cloves, bouillon cube, and juice from pineapple. Cover and simmer for 1 hour and 15 minutes. Add the pineapple chunks, bananas, and cream, and simmer for 15 more minutes. Makes 6 servings.

Skipper: My life is in that chest. That stuff is priceless.

Gilligan: A bottle cap?

Skipper: Singapore 1947—from the first bottle of beer I ever opened with my teeth.

Gilligan: What'd you want to do that for?

Skipper: I didn't want to, but some guy hit me in the mouth with a bottle.

Pork Chops Polynesian

6 pork chops ¾- to 1-inch thick	1 20-ounce can sliced pineapple
2 tablespoons shortening	¼ cup raisins
1 teaspoon salt	2 tablespoons brown sugar
Dash pepper	1 tablespoon grated orange peel

In a skillet brown the chops in the shortening. Pour off the drippings, leaving the chops in the skillet. Season the chops with salt and pepper. Drain the pineapple, reserving ¼ cup of syrup. Add the syrup to the skillet and place a pineapple slice on top of each chop. In a small bowl combine the raisins, brown sugar, and orange peel. Place about 1 teaspoon of raisin mixture in the center of each pineapple slice. Cover and cook over low heat for 45 minutes to 1 hour, or until the meat is tender. If gravy is desired, thicken the cooking liquid with flour. Makes 6 servings.

Dawn Wells collection

I love hats and must have worn at least a dozen different types during the run of the series. At the time, I didn't think to ask for any of them as souvenirs, but fortunately I did happen to keep this one as a memento.

Happy islander

Apricot Spear Ribs

3 tablespoons oil
3 ½ to 4 pounds English cut short ribs
2 16-ounce cans apricots in light syrup
½ cup dry red wine
Salt and pepper to taste

½ teaspoon thyme
4 to 5 carrots, cut in thirds
12 boiling onions
1 green pepper, cut in strips

In a Dutch oven heat the oil and brown the short ribs. Drain the syrup from the apricots and combine it with the wine, salt, pepper, and thyme. Set the apricots aside. Add the mixture to the short ribs. Cover the Dutch oven and bake at 325° for 1 ½ hours.

Add the carrots and bake 30 minutes longer.

Add the onions and green peppers, and bake for 15 minutes. Add the apricots and bake for 5 minutes. Serve over rice. Makes 4 to 6 servings.

Note: If desired, the sauce may be thickened by stirring in a paste made from 3 tablespoons each of flour and water.

🌴 Great Fire God Spare Ribs

5 pounds regular-style spare ribs (about
2 sides)
Water
1 teaspoon Italian seasoning (or ¼ teaspoon each marjoram, thyme,
oregano, and rosemary)
1 small onion, peeled

½ cup white wine vinegar
¼ cup soy sauce
½ cup firmly packed brown sugar
1 clove garlic, minced
¼ teaspoon ginger
½ cup pineapple juice
1 tablespoon cornstarch

In a large saucepan cover the spare ribs with water and add the Italian seasoning and onion. Bring the water to a boil and simmer for 1 hour. Drain. In a roasting pan place the ribs in a single layer. In a saucepan combine the vinegar, soy sauce, brown sugar, garlic, and ginger. In a small bowl mix the pineapple juice and the cornstarch, and add the mixture to the saucepan. Bring the sauce to a boil and cook, stirring constantly, until thickened. (The sauce and ribs may be prepared to this point a day in advance.) Pour the sauce over the ribs. Bake uncovered at 375° for 30 minutes (45 minutes if refrigerated), or until brown. Makes 6 to 8 servings.

🌴 Shoreline Short Ribs

3 tablespoons sesame seeds
4 pounds beef short ribs, cut in 2- to 3-
inch lengths
1 medium onion, sliced
½ cup soy sauce
¼ cup firmly packed brown sugar
1 large clove garlic, minced

¼ teaspoon ginger
¼ teaspoon pepper
2 small dried hot chile peppers, seeded
and crushed
1 ½ cups water
1 teaspoon cornstarch
1 teaspoon water

In a 4- or 5-quart kettle toast the sesame seeds over medium heat until lightly browned, shaking pan often to toast evenly. Remove the pan from the heat and arrange the ribs and onion on top of the seeds. In a medium bowl combine the soy sauce, brown sugar, garlic, ginger, pepper, chile peppers, and water. Pour the mixture over the meat. Cover and bake at 400° for 2 ½ hours, basting occasionally, or until the meat is tender when pierced.

Lift the meat to a warm serving platter, and keep warm. Skim the fat from the pan juices. In a small bowl combine the cornstarch and water, and stir the mixture into the juice. Cook, stirring constantly, until thickened. Pass the gravy in a bowl. Makes 4 to 6 servings.

Wrongway Feldman's Pork Turnover

1 16-ounce loaf frozen bread dough
2 ½ pounds lean boneless pork
1 large onion, chopped
1 large Golden Delicious apple (peeled and cored)
1 16-ounce can sauerkraut, drained and

chopped
½ teaspoon caraway seeds
½ teaspoon cinnamon
Garlic salt
Pepper
Melted butter or margarine

Thaw the bread dough according to the package directions. Cut the meat into ½-inch cubes. In a large frying pan brown the pork on all sides over medium heat. Stir in the onion and cook until soft. Dice the apple, and add it to the meat with the sauerkraut, caraway seeds, and cinnamon. Season with garlic salt and pepper to taste.

On a lightly floured board roll the dough into a 15-inch circle. Spread the pork mixture evenly over half the dough to within 1 inch of the edge. Fold the remaining dough over the pork, pressing the edges together. Use 2 wide spatulas to transfer the turnover to a greased baking sheet with a rim. Slash the top several times, and brush with butter. Bake at 375° for 30 minutes or until browned. Makes 6 to 8 servings.

Dawn Wells collection

This is my mom, "Chef" Evelyn Wells, and me on Mother's Day 1992. The watercolor of me in the background was painted when I was three years old.

This is a rare shot of Gilligan in a tie. Actually, Bob and I were making a 1992 personal appearance together in Atlantic City.

Lamb Ho Stew

⅓ cup all-purpose flour
½ teaspoon sugar
½ teaspoon ginger
1 ½ teaspoons salt
2 ½ pounds boneless lamb stew meat
2 tablespoons butter or margarine
1 medium onion, chopped
1 cup dry white wine (or ¼ cup lemon

juice with ¾ cup water)
1 ½ cups boiling water
1 pound green beans, tips removed
6 whole Seckel pears, peeled (or 3 Bartletts, quartered; or 12 dried pear halves)
Salt and pepper to taste

In a plastic bag combine the flour, sugar, ginger, and salt. Add the meat and shake it with the seasoned flour. In a Dutch oven heat the butter and slowly brown the meat on all sides. Push the meat to one side and sauté the onion until limp. Add the wine and boiling water, cover, and simmer gently for about 45 minutes.

Tie the beans into two bundles. Add the beans and pears to the stew and continue to simmer for 1 hour, or until the meat and beans are tender. (If Bartletts are used, peel and add them to the stew about 20 minutes before it is done.) Add salt and pepper if needed. Arrange the meat, beans, and pears on a serving plate with a little gravy. Serve the remaining gravy in a bowl. Makes 6 servings.

Grandma's Ham Loaf

A family favorite.

1 pound ground ham
1 ½ pounds ground fresh pork
1 cup bread crumbs
1 cup milk
2 eggs, slightly beaten

1 cup brown sugar
½ teaspoon dry mustard
½ cup vinegar (diluted with water)
Crumbled potato chips

In a large bowl mix together the ham, pork, and bread crumbs, and moisten with the milk and eggs. Shape the mixture into a loaf and place it in a loaf pan. In a separate bowl combine the brown sugar, dry mustard, and diluted vinegar. Pour some of the sauce over the loaf. Bake at 350° for 1 ½ hours. Baste frequently with sauce.

A few minutes before serving, crumble a few potato chips over the top and continue to bake until slightly brown. Makes 6 servings.

Dawn Wells collection

This shot is from the Cinderella episode, one of my favorites and one of Natalie's best. Alan played a court knave as well as the wicked stepmother, while Tina and I were really ugly stepsisters.

SOS Sausage and Apples

1 pound brown-and-serve sausage links
¼ cup butter or margarine
1 21-ounce can pie-sliced apples

Nutmeg
All-purpose flour

In a skillet cook the sausages until well browned. Remove the sausage and add the butter to the skillet. Sprinkle the apples with nutmeg and dredge with flour. Brown the apples on all sides and serve with sausage. Makes 4 servings.

Yummy Ham Mummy

1 5-pound pre-cooked ham shank
1 13 ¾-ounce package hot roll mix
¾ cup water

1 egg
1 teaspoon poultry seasoning

Remove the skin and trim off all fat covering the ham shank. Set the ham aside. Prepare the hot roll mix according to the package directions using the water, egg, and poultry seasoning. Cover and let the dough rise for 45 minutes.

Turn the dough onto a lightly floured board. Knead well. Roll out into a 12 x 8-inch rectangle. Place the ham in the center of the dough. Dampen all of the edges of the dough and bring the dough up to cover the ham completely and evenly. Press the seams well to seal. Place it on a shallow baking pan. Bake at 350° for 1 hour. Serve warm or cold. Makes 6 to 8 generous servings.

―――――― **"** ――――――

Gilligan: You know, if it weren't for those cannibals, we could have kind of a picnic.

Mr. Howell: Don't mention cannibals and picnic in the same breath. If they find this cave, we'll be the main course.

Mrs. Howell: Thurston.

Mr. Howell: I know—awfully vulgar.

Mrs. Howell: Well, at least let me think of myself as the dessert.

Gilligan: We could have a barbecue if we had hot dogs and hamburgers.

Mary Ann: Gilligan, stop the food talk.

Gilligan: But I'm hungry.

Ginger: Oh, we all are. We haven't eaten for ten hours.

Gilligan: Ten hours! I'm starved.

Mr. Howell: Don't mention food. It makes us hungrier.

Gilligan: All right, all right. I won't mention food again. I won't mention food even if you burn me at the stake. Steak?!

―――――― **"** ――――――

Burt Birdy's Black Cherry Chicken

2 2-pound broiler-fryers
½ cup all-purpose flour
1 teaspoon salt
⅛ teaspoon pepper
2 tablespoons butter or margarine
2 tablespoons oil
1 small onion, sliced

¼ cup port wine
1 16-ounce can pitted dark sweet cherries
¼ teaspoon allspice
1 tablespoon lemon juice
Lemon slices
Cooked rice

Cut the chicken into halves, quarters, or pieces. Cut out the backbones if using quarters. In a shallow dish mix the flour, salt, and pepper. Coat the chicken with the mixture. In a large skillet heat the butter. Add the chicken without crowding, and brown it on both sides.

Remove the chicken and pour off the excess fat. Add the oil, and sauté the onion until tender. Add the wine and bring it to a boil, stirring up the brown bits from the skillet. Return the chicken to the pan and add the cherry syrup, allspice, and lemon juice. Cover and simmer until the chicken is tender, 25 to 30 minutes. The chicken should be turned once or twice.

Add the cherries and heat for a few minutes. Taste and add more salt and pepper if needed. Garnish with lemon slices and serve with the hot rice. Makes 4 to 6 servings.

Bird of Paradise

2 tablespoons butter
2 whole chicken breasts, split (or 1 3-
  pound chicken, cut up)
1 20-ounce can sliced pineapple, syrup
  reserved
¼ cup dry sherry
3 tablespoons soy sauce
2 cloves garlic, pressed

2 tablespoons finely chopped candied
  ginger
½ teaspoon salt
1 red bell pepper
1 ½ cups sliced celery
½ cup sliced green onion
1 tablespoon cornstarch
½ cup cold water

In a skillet melt the butter and brown the chicken. Drain. In a small bowl combine the reserved syrup, sherry, soy sauce, garlic, ginger, and salt. Pour the mixture over the chicken. Cover and simmer for 30 minutes or until the chicken is done, turning once.

Remove the chicken and add the pineapple, pepper, celery, and green onion to the pan. In a small bowl dissolve the cornstarch in the cold water, and slowly stir the mixture into the pan. Bring the sauce to a boil and cook until thick. Pour the sauce over the chicken. Makes 4 servings.

Working on the episode *The Pigeon,* I met Sterling Holloway, the wonderful voice behind Winnie the Pooh and other Disney cartoon classics. He was such a joy to work with.

Henny's Party Henny

2 packages chipped beef
8 chicken breasts, split and boned (16 pieces)
1 pound sliced bacon
1 pint sour cream

3 10 ¾-ounce cans cream of mushroom soup
Pepper
Paprika

Grease a casserole and line it with the chipped beef. Wrap each chicken breast in one or two pieces of bacon and place the chicken on top of the beef. Combine the sour cream and soup and pour the mixture over the chicken. Add the pepper and paprika. Dish can be prepared to this point early in the day and refrigerated. Bake at 275° for 1 ½ hours. Makes 8 servings.
From Henny Backus.

Chicken Dijon Gillianna

2 tablespoons olive oil
4 boneless chicken breasts
2 chicken bouillon cubes
1 ½ cups heavy whipping cream

Cornstarch
2 tablespoons Dijon mustard (or to taste)
Cooked noodles

In a skillet heat the olive oil and brown both sides of the chicken. Cover and steam the chicken over low heat until done, about 40 minutes.
Remove the chicken from the skillet and mash the bouillon cubes in the skillet. Add 1 cup of whipping cream. To the reserved ½ cup, add cornstarch to thicken and stir it into the skillet. When the sauce has thickened, stir in the Dijon mustard. Pour the sauce over the chicken and noodles. Makes 4 servings.
From Dreama and Bob Denver.

A Spy Ring Ham

1 16-ounce package corn muffin mix
¼ cup chopped parsley
2 teaspoons chopped onion
2 eggs
⅔ cup milk
¼ cup butter or margarine
¼ cup all-purpose flour
1 ¾ cups milk

⅛ teaspoon pepper
½ teaspoon Worcestershire sauce
1 cup shredded cheddar cheese
1 cup cooked lima beans
2 cups cooked ham, cut in ½-inch thick
   strips
Fresh or canned drained fruit

In a large bowl combine the muffin mix, parsley, onion, eggs, and ⅔ cup of milk. Blend thoroughly. Pour the batter into a well-greased 5-cup ring mold. Bake at 375° for 25 to 30 minutes.

Meanwhile, prepare the filling. In a saucepan melt the butter. Blend in the flour. Slowly stir in 1 ¾ cups of milk. Cook, stirring constantly, over medium heat until thickened and smooth. Remove the pan from the heat. Add the pepper, Worcestershire sauce, cheese, lima beans, and ham strips. Reheat gently. Unmold the ring on a serving dish. Fill with the creamed ham. Arrange the fruit around the base of the ring. Makes 8 servings.

Dawn Wells collection

Dawn of today

Mrs. Howell's Orient Express Chicken

1 pound boneless chicken breasts
2 tablespoons corn oil
1 chopped onion
1 small red bell pepper
1 small green bell pepper
2 tablespoons cornstarch
1 cup chicken broth
¼ cup soy sauce

¼ cup dry sherry
½ cup apricot jam
½ teaspoon dried red pepper
½ teaspoon ginger
2 minced cloves garlic
1 cup halved mushrooms
Rice

Slice the chicken. In a skillet heat the oil and brown the chicken slices. Remove the chicken, then stir-fry the onion, red pepper, and green pepper.

In a medium bowl mix the cornstarch, chicken broth, soy sauce, sherry, apricot jam, red pepper, ginger, and garlic. Pour over the vegetables in the pan. Bring the mixture to a boil and cook, stirring constantly, for 1 or 2 minutes. Add the chicken and mushrooms. Serve over rice. Makes 4 servings.

From Natalie Schafer.

UFO Mustard Chicken

1 3 ½-pound broiler-fryer chicken, cut
   up (or 6 legs and thighs, joined; or 3
   whole chicken breasts, split)
2 cups water
2 chicken bouillon cubes
¼ cup butter or margarine
¼ cup all-purpose flour

1 cup milk or half and half
2 tablespoons Dijon mustard
½ teaspoon thyme leaves
Salt and pepper to taste
3 tablespoons chopped parsley
New potatoes, rice, or noodles

In a 4- to 5-quart Dutch oven arrange the chicken pieces. Add the water and bouillon cubes. Bring the water to a boil, and reduce the heat. Cover and simmer for 20 minutes. With a slotted spoon remove the chicken pieces from the broth and set them aside. Skim the fat from the broth, measure, and set aside 1 ¼ cups broth (use any extra broth for other purposes). In the Dutch oven melt the butter over medium heat. Add the flour and cook, stirring constantly, until bubbly but not browned. Remove the pan from the heat and gradually stir in the warm broth until blended. Stir in the milk and return the pan to the heat. Cook, stirring constantly, until it boils and thickens. Add the mustard, thyme, and salt and pepper to taste.

Remove the large pieces of skin from the chicken if desired, then return the chicken to the sauce. Continue simmering until the chicken is tender, about 12 to 15 minutes. To serve, lift the chicken from the sauce and arrange it on a rimmed serving dish. Skim the fat, if needed, then stir in the parsley. Pour the sauce over the chicken. Serve with potatoes, rice, or noodles. Makes 4 to 6 servings.

Ginger's Limelight Chicken

4 chicken breast halves
½ cup lime juice
½ cup olive oil

3 teaspoons fresh basil
3 minced cloves garlic
Salt and pepper to taste

Poke both sides of the chicken with a fork. Place the chicken in a plastic bag. In a small bowl combine the remaining ingredients. Pour the marinade over the chicken and seal the bag. Marinate for 1 hour at room temperature, turning frequently. Grill the chicken until no longer pink, brushing often with marinade. Makes 4 servings.

Mary Ann's Roast Turkey

1 whole turkey
Salt and pepper

Mayonnaise

Wash and clean the turkey. Pat to dry. Rub with salt and pepper, and coat with mayonnaise. Bake at 400° for 1 hour. Reduce heat to 350° and bake for 15 to 20 minutes per pound. Baste with drippings occasionally. Cover the wings and legs with foil if necessary to prevent drying.

Kansas Chicken and Dumplings

1 2 ½ to 3-pound fryer, cut up
4 cups water
1 cup chopped onion
2 cups sliced carrots
1 ½ cups sliced celery
5 chicken bouillon cubes

¼ teaspoon pepper
½ cup all-purpose flour
½ cup water
2 cups Bisquick
1 tablespoon chopped parsley
⅔ cup milk

In a stock pot combine the chicken, water, onion, carrots, celery, bouillon cubes, and pepper. Bring to a boil. Reduce the heat and simmer for 30 minutes, or until the chicken is done.

In a small bowl combine the flour and ½ cup of water. Blend until smooth. Stir in the celery. Add the flour mixture to the stock pot and cook, stirring constantly, until thick and smooth.

In a separate bowl combine the Bisquick, parsley, and milk until a soft dough forms. Do not overmix. Drop the dough by spoonfuls into the boiling broth. Cook uncovered over low heat for 10 minutes. Cover and cook for 10 minutes more. Makes 4 to 6 servings.

Mary Ann's Fried Chicken

Flour
Salt and pepper to taste
Herbs
Seasonings

1 3-pound fryer, cut up
Shortening
Butter

In a plastic bag combine flour, salt, and pepper, and any herbs or seasonings desired. Shake the chicken in the flour. In a heavy skillet melt equal parts shortening and butter. Have the pan hot, and brown the chicken well, turning often. Cover the pan tightly, reduce the heat, and cook until tender. When done, uncover the pan and let the steam out. This is excellent picnic chicken. Makes 4 to 6 servings.

Plane Talk

One of my most special memories was the last public appearance with Bob and Russell and Alan and me together. Alan and I sat together on the long flight from Los Angeles to Chicago. I hadn't seen Alan in several months and noticed that he looked thin. He told me that he had had cancer for the last year and had been in and out of the hospital for treatments the past several months. He shared with me his optimism—and Alan was always the most positive person—and his courage. It was a very emotional and intimate moment for both of us. I felt very privileged that he shared that with me because he continued to keep his illness very quiet.

On a more upbeat note, it turned out that Magic Johnson was on the same flight to Chicago. I had been tempted to go over and speak to him the whole flight. Finally, right before we landed, I couldn't resist it anymore. I went over to say hello and tell him I was a real fan. He said the same and then he got up—and up and up and up—to shake my hand. He was the tallest man I'd ever seen. And a delightful person. That also made that flight special. I've since appeared at several benefits for him, and he always remembers.

Lemon Chicken From Mars

2 ½ to 3 pounds chicken pieces
¼ cup melted butter
1 teaspoon lemon pepper

1 teaspoon lemon juice
Oregano

Arrange the chicken in a baking pan. In a small bowl combine the butter, lemon pepper, and lemon juice. Brush both sides of the chicken with seasoned butter. Sprinkle with oregano. Bake at 350° for 50 to 55 minutes, or until done. Makes 4 to 6 servings.

Skipper's Simple Chicken

Oil
4 chicken thighs
4 chicken breasts (or a combination)
2 10 ¾-ounce cans cream of celery soup

2 10 ¾-ounce cans cream of chicken
soup
Cooked rice (see note, below)

In a skillet heat a small amount of oil and brown the chicken. Reduce the heat to medium and precook for about 15 to 20 minutes. Add the undiluted soup to the chicken. Simmer for 45 minutes.

Serve with rice. Makes 4 servings.

Note: Substitute orange juice, pineapple juice, or cranberry juice for half of the liquid in making rice. Pretty color, great taste!

Dawn Wells collection

Fur and Away—After twenty-five years, Mary Ann, the Skipper, Gilligan, and the Professor finally got to say how they really felt about life on Gilligan's Island when they visited ALF.

🌴 Eye of the Idol Chicken

2 large whole chicken breasts, split
Salt and pepper to taste
¼ cup margarine
½ cup water
1 teaspoon salt
½ teaspoon pepper
1 6-ounce can frozen orange juice con-

centrate, thawed
1 bay leaf
Juice of 1 small lime
2 firm ripe bananas, thinly sliced
½ cup salted peanuts, finely chopped

Season the chicken with salt and pepper. In a skillet melt the margarine and brown the chicken on both sides over medium heat. Reduce the heat to low and add the water, salt, pepper, orange juice concentrate, and bay leaf. Bring the sauce to a boil, cover, and simmer for 20 minutes, turning once, or until the chicken is done.

Remove the chicken and keep it warm. Cook the liquid over high heat, stirring constantly, for about 5 minutes. Stir in the lime juice, add the banana slices, and heat gently. Remove the bay leaf. Arrange the chicken on a serving dish, sprinkle with peanuts, and pour the sauce over the top. Makes 4 servings.

"

Gilligan: If I get killed, I'm not talking to either one of you two, as long as I live.

"

🌴 Witch Doctor Chicken

1 2 ½- to 3-pound broiler-fryer
Salt
Pepper
¼ cup butter or margarine, melted
1 20-ounce can crushed pineapple

2 tablespoons lemon juice
3 tablespoons Chinese plum sauce
1 tablespoon cornstarch
¼ cup shredded coconut
2 tablespoons chopped almonds

Cut the chicken into pieces, quarters, or halves. Sprinkle with salt and pepper and place it in a shallow baking dish. Brush the chicken with butter. Bake at 350° for 45 to 50 minutes, or until the chicken is tender.

Meanwhile, drain the pineapple and reserve the syrup. Add water to the syrup to make 1 cup. In a saucepan combine the liquid, lemon juice, and plum sauce. In a small bowl mix the cornstarch with a little water to make a smooth paste and stir it into the pineapple liquid. Cook, stirring constantly, until thickened and clear. Spoon the sauce over the chicken and bake 10 minutes longer. Sprinkle with coconut and almonds. Makes 4 servings.

Watubi Chicken and Yams

2/3 cup salted peanuts
2 cloves garlic
1 teaspoon coriander
1 teaspoon grated lemon peel
1/2 teaspoon crushed red pepper
2 tablespoons salad oil
3 to 3 1/2 pounds whole chicken breasts,
split and boned
3/4 cup chopped green onion
1 8-ounce can sweetened coconut juice
1 tablespoon soy sauce
2 16-ounce cans yams, drained
Salt

In a blender combine 1/3 cup of peanuts, the garlic, coriander, lemon peel, and red pepper. Whirl until the nuts are finely chopped. Set the mixture aside.

In a large frying pan heat the oil over medium heat. Brown the chicken well on all sides. Discard the fat. Add the nut mixture, about half of the onions, the coconut juice, and soy sauce. Cover and simmer for 20 minutes or until the chicken is no longer pink when slashed. Add the yams, cover, and simmer until heated. Transfer the chicken and yams to a platter, and keep warm. Skim the fat and season the juices to taste with salt. Pour the sauce over the chicken, and garnish with the remaining onions and nuts. Makes 4 to 6 servings.

---- **``** ----

Mr. Howell: They're fattening you up like a turkey, and tomorrow is Thanksgiving.

---- **''** ----

A Howell's Pheasant Under Glass

3 tablespoons all-purpose flour
1/4 pound thin sliced mushrooms
1 10 3/4-ounce can cream of mushroom soup
1 10 3/4-ounce can cream of chicken soup
1/2 cup apple cider
1 tablespoon Worcestershire sauce
1/2 finely chopped onion
3 cloves minced garlic
3/4 teaspoon paprika
1 2 1/2-pound pheasant, cut into quarters

In a 2 1/2-quart casserole stir together the flour, mushrooms, soups, cider, Worcestershire sauce, onion, garlic, and paprika. Rinse and pat the pheasant dry. Push the pheasant into the sauce, and pour some of the sauce over the top. Cover and bake at 350° for 1 hour.

Uncover and bake for 35 to 40 minutes or until the thigh is tender to a fork. Baste frequently. Makes 4 servings.

"

Sweet dream for a dieting Skipper.

Gilligan: Goodnight, Skipper. Sleep tight.

Skipper: Sleep tight? That's all right for you to say that because you're not starving to death.

Gilligan: Just forget about it and go to sleep.

Skipper: Oh, I've tried to go to sleep. I've tried counting sheep, but they all turn into lamb chops. Phooey!

Gilligan: Skipper, we've got to get your mind off food. Let's talk about getting rescued.

Skipper: Good idea.

Gilligan: Yeah, It's a good thing we got the professor. He's one smart cookie.

Skipper: Cookie?!

Gilligan: I mean, I mean he knows his onions.

Skipper: Oh, Gilligan! If you don't shut up, I'm going to bend you like a pretzel. Now see what you've done! You've got me doing it to me!

Gilligan: I'm sorry, Skipper. Every time I try to help, I end up a dead duck.

"

Eva's Duckling

A favorite of my dad, the hunter.

1 ½ pounds wild mallard
½ teaspoon salt
⅛ teaspoon pepper
1 small orange, cut up and peeled
3 ¼-inch onion slices

1 celery stalk
1 medium carrot
2 bacon slices
Chicken broth

Rinse the duck well, and pat dry with paper towels. Sprinkle the cavity and surface with salt and pepper. Stuff the duck with the orange, onion, celery, and carrot. Fasten the skin of the neck to the back with a poultry pin. Fold the wing tips under the body to secure the wings close to it. Close the cavity with poultry pins. Lace with twine. Tie the ends of the legs together. Place the duck on a rack in a shallow roasting pan, and secure bacon slices across the top. Roast the duck at 450° for 30 minutes, basting frequently with chicken broth. Roast longer if a well-done duck is desired.

Serve with Mamasita Howell's Famous Duck Gravy (see recipe, page 171). Makes 2 servings.

Chief's Curried Fruit with Chicken

2 cups Coconut Cream (see recipe below)	1 cup diced avocado
4 cups chicken stock	2 bananas, sliced
Cornflour	1 cup diced papaya
1 teaspoon salt	1 cup diced pineapple
1 ½ teaspoons curry powder	1 cup diced mango
½ cup water	3 cups diced cooked chicken
Squeeze of lime juice	1 pound rice

In a saucepan bring the Coconut Cream and 1 ½ cups of chicken stock to a boil. In a small bowl mix the cornflour, salt, and curry powder with the water. Pour the cornflour mixture into the liquids and stir until thick. Allow the mixture to cool. Sprinkle lime juice over the avocado and banana. Toss the avocado and banana with the papaya, pineapple, mango, and the chicken. Cook the rice in the remainder of the chicken stock. In a large bowl combine the fruit, rice, and sauce mixture. Chill. Makes 6 to 8 servings.

Dawn Wells collection

Here I am a true Solomon Islands girl just waiting to be rescued. Notice the trees and bushes in the background are not too different from our set back in Hollywood.

Coconut Cream

Coconut Cream is the base for many Melanesian recipes. To make it, grate a dry coconut into a bowl, add some water, and knead. Take a handful of the kneaded coconut and wring the "cream" from it through a large strainer directly into the cooking pot.

The traditional "oven" used for baking in the South Pacific is the stone oven, known by various names. Motu is the common Melanesian name. Fist-sized river stones are heated on an open wood fire. The very hot stones are placed with bamboo tongs over and around the food (wrapped in leaves) to be cooked. The mound of hot stones is covered with large leaves such as banana leaves to keep in the heat, and left for several hours.

Fish Cooked in Taro Leaves

Whole fish
Taro leaves
Salt

Onion, finely chopped
2 cups Coconut Cream (at left)

Cut the fish into 2-inch cubes. Prepare clean, medium young taro leaves. Put a piece of fish on each leaf, and sprinkle with salt and 1 teaspoon of finely chopped onion. Wrap up the fish and if necessary fasten the leaves with toothpicks. Arrange the bundles in a pan. Pour the Coconut Cream over the leaves. Cover and bake at 300° for 45 minutes or until the fish is soft.

Touring the Real South Pacific

I once traveled to the Solomon Islands with the president of, and some wonderful friends from, Stephens College. We went into the islands and traveled from island to island by canoe. We slept on grass mats on the floors of huts, and there was no running water or electricity—no modern civilization as we know it.

On the island of Sulufu in the middle of the Pacific, nineteen generations of chiefs have come from the family of current chief, Nathan Watte.

Talk about recognizability—as we arrived on the island and walked into Chief Watte's hut, his wife, Janet, looked at me and said, "Oh, I know you. I went to nursing school in Honiara on Guadalcanal Island in the seventies, and we used to come home after school and watch you on 'Gilligan's Island.'" There's truly no escape!

Dawn Wells collection

This is me and a group associated with Stephens College when we toured the Solomon Islands. (Back: Friendly island natives; Front left to right: Dr. Patsy Sampson, Diane Skomars Magrath, Dawn, Jean Zunkel, and Mary Josie Blanchard.)

Baked Papaya

1 medium green papaya
½ pound ground beef
2 medium onions
4 cloves garlic

2 Tabasco chilies
2 tablespoons tomato paste
2 tablespoons vegetable oil
Salt to taste

Cut the papaya in half lengthwise and remove the seeds, then scoop out a little of the flesh of the papaya and set aside. In a skillet heat the oil and sauté the onions, garlic, and chilies. When the onions begin to brown add the meat, tomato paste, salt, and the papaya flesh. Mix well and simmer until the meat is cooked. Put the mixture in the papaya shells, and arrange the shells in a baking dish. Add a little boiling water to the dish. Bake at 300° for about 30 minutes. Makes 2 servings.

Dawn Wells collection

Real island cooks prepare sautéed lobster on one of the Solomon Islands. Believe it or not, even here I was recognized as Mary Ann from "Gilligan's Island."

Hibiscus Jelly

4 cups boiling water
20 red hibiscus flowers

¼ cup sugar
1 ounce gelatin

Pour all but about ½ cup of the boiling water over the hibiscus flowers, and add the sugar. Allow the mixture to steep for 5 to 10 minutes.

In a cup combine the remaining water and the gelatin, and stir until the gelatin is dissolved. Strain the water off the hibiscus. Add the strained liquid to the gelatin, and pour the mixture into a jelly mold. Cool, then refrigerate until the jelly is set. Makes about 6 servings.

———— " ————

Skipper's insomnia:

Gilligan: How about a nice warm cup of coconut milk to make you sleep?

Skipper: I've had thirty-four cups of that already. I never want to see another coconut or lamb chop.

Gilligan: Lamp chop?

Skipper: I also counted 19,000 sheep today.

———— " ————

Dawn Wells collection

Skipper Sipper— Alan Hale and Dawn draw straws as part of an ad campaign in 1990

The Skipper

Alan Hale was always a joy to be with. He reminded me of my dad. They both were about the same size. Every time I was with Alan, he would pick me up and hug me. It was like getting a hug from my father.

Alan had a wonderful disposition. I never saw him angry or hurt, and I never went anywhere that people's faces didn't light up when they saw him. He had a special way of making you feel he was so happy to see you.

Alan and I shared a lot of heart-to-heart talks, a lot of fun, and a lot of conversation about food. He was a good cook. He had this great chicken and rice recipe (Skipper's Simple Chicken) that was so easy to make. Many a night after working late on the set, I'd use this recipe for dinner.

His dear and wonderful wife, Trinket, was the joy of his life, along with his marvelous kids (Brian, Chris, Lana, and Dorian.) When he died, Alan was buried at sea and his ashes scattered on the Pacific Ocean. About twenty of us went out with the Neptune Society to share that final moment with Alan. I think he knew we were all there and that we loved him. It was a great honor to be invited, and I'll always be thankful to Trinket for including me. And it was also very special to see his children all grown up. I remember Lane as a little girl so well and of course the boys—are all men now.

Vandenberg Air Force Basil Shrimp

2 to 3 pounds shrimp
Oil
Lemon juice
Basil

Dill
Pepper
Parsley
Mayonnaise

Remove the heads from the shrimp and split the backs open. Wash the shrimp thoroughly. In a small bowl combine some oil with lemon juice, basil, dill, pepper, and parsley. Marinate the shrimp in the mixture overnight.

Remove the shrimp from the marinade. Broil until done. Combine enough basil and mayonnaise to make a dip. Serve unshelled. Makes 4 to 6 servings.

Fathom Fried Fish

1 pound fish fillets
3 tablespoons light mayonnaise
1 tablespoon lemon juice
5 tablespoons plain or seasoned bread
   crumbs
Salt

Celery salt
Pepper
Cayenne
Paprika
Cooking spray

Place the fish in a plastic bag. Add the mayonnaise and lemon juice, and shake to coat evenly. Sprinkle the bread crumbs on a shallow dish, and season to taste with salt or celery salt, pepper, cayenne, and paprika. Press the fish into the crumbs, coating both sides. Spray a shallow nonstick pan liberally with cooking spray and arrange the fish in a single layer. Bake uncovered at 475° for 8 to 10 minutes without turning, until fish is crisp and golden. Makes 4 servings.

Simple Salmon

2 tablespoons olive oil
4 whole green onions
2 salmon fillets

Salt and pepper to taste
Fresh dill or dried
Lemon wedges

In a skillet heat the oil over medium heat. Wash and trim the onions, and add them to the pan. Season the salmon with salt and pepper, and add it to the pan. Fry until crusty. The onions will be brown and taste good. Sprinkle with dill and lemon. Check for doneness by inserting a small knife in the center. The flesh should change from dark pink to pale pink. Makes 2 servings.

Mr. Howell: What did you ever cook?

Mrs. Howell: Well, I visited the kitchen in some of the homes we used to own.

"

Rudders and Spudders

1 12-ounce package frozen hash-brown
   potatoes, thawed
4 eggs, beaten
2 cups milk
1 teaspoon minced onion

1 ¼ teaspoons seasoned salt
⅛ teaspoon pepper
1 teaspoon dried dillweed (or fresh)
1 cup shredded sharp cheddar cheese
1 14-ounce package frozen fish sticks (16)

Break up the potatoes. In a large bowl combine the eggs, milk, onion, salt, pepper, and dillweed. Stir in the potatoes and cheese. Turn the mixture into a buttered 12 x 7-inch baking dish. Arrange the fish sticks on top. Bake at 350° for 55 to 60 minutes, or until the center is nearly set. Let the dish stand for 10 minutes before serving. Makes 6 servings.

Dawn Wells collection

Where were these guys when we needed them?

The Tennessean

This pose is from one of my favorite episodes, *Forget Me Not,* where Bob and I played Japanese soldiers. I started my acting career playing a four-teen-year-old boy in a melodrama at the Pink Garden Theatre in Jackson Hole, Wyoming. Here I go again.

🌴 Don't Rock the Boat Rockfish

½ cup sweetened shredded dried coconut
1 tablespoon minced or pressed garlic
¾ cup sliced green onions
2 ½ tablespoons olive oil
2 ¾ cups (1 pound) freshly cut or frozen corn
1 cup minced red bell pepper
1 2 ¼-ounce can sliced black olives,

drained
2 tablespoons water
¼ cup chopped parsley
1 ½ pounds rockfish fillets, about ½-inch thick, cut into 4 to 6 portions
2 tablespoons lemon juice
Lemon wedges
Parsley sprigs
Salt and pepper

In a 3- to 4-quart pan toast the coconut over medium heat until golden, 3 to 5 minutes. Remove the coconut from the pan and set aside.

Add the garlic, onions, and 1 tablespoon of oil to the pan; stir often over medium heat for 3 to 5 minutes, until the onions are limp. Add the corn, bell pepper, olives, and 2 tablespoons of water. Cover and cook until the corn is tender to bite, about 5 minutes. Mix in the chopped parsley, and keep the relish warm.

Rinse the fish and pat dry. Rub the fillets with lemon juice and the remaining 1 ½ tablespoons of oil. Arrange the fish in a single layer in a 12 x 17-inch broiler pan without a rack. Broil about 3 inches from the heat for 3 minutes. Turn the fish over and broil until opaque but still moist-looking in the center of the thickest part (cut to test), 2 to 3 minutes longer.

Spoon the corn relish onto a platter and place the fish on the relish. Sprinkle coconut over the fish. Garnish with lemon wedges and parsley sprigs. Season the fish with lemon and salt and pepper to taste. Makes 4 to 6 servings.

---------------- `` ----------------

Wrongway: What's for supper?

Mary Ann: Oh, soup and salad, fish. Oh yes, and Ginger made one of her delicious desserts.

Wrongway: Oh great, 'cause I'm almost starved.

Mary Ann: Oh-h. Too bad you missed it.

---------------- `"` ----------------

 # Something Fishy

2 pounds fish fillets, 3/4- to 1-inch thick
Salt and pepper to taste
3/4 cup sour cream
1/4 cup fine bread crumbs
1/4 teaspoon garlic salt

1 1/2 tablespoons chopped chives
1/4 cup grated Parmesan
1 teaspoon paprika
Chopped parsley
Lemon wedges

Preheat a large shallow baking pan at 400°. Wipe the fish with a damp cloth, and cut it into 3 x 5-inch serving-size pieces. Remove the pan from the oven, grease it, and arrange the fish pieces in a single layer. Sprinkle with salt and pepper. Mix together the sour cream, bread crumbs, garlic salt, and chives. Spread the mixture over the fish, and sprinkle with cheese and paprika. Bake uncovered at 400° until the fish flakes. Serve with parsley and lemon. Makes about 4 servings.

Skipper Baked Snapper

1 1 1/2- to 2-pound snapper
Olive oil
4 sprigs fresh rosemary
1 clove garlic, crushed
1/4 cup chopped parsley
1 tablespoon olive oil

1 tablespoon chopped fresh oregano
1/2 teaspoon cayenne pepper
1 large tomato, quartered (or 1 cup
   crushed canned)
1 1/2 teaspoons wine vinegar
Salt and pepper to taste

Thoroughly clean the fish, rinsing inside and out. Rub the skin with olive oil, and fill the cavity with rosemary. Place the fish in a baking pan. Bake at 350° for 20 minutes.

In a blender combine the garlic, parsley, 1 tablespoon of olive oil, oregano, cayenne, tomato, and vinegar, blending until puréed. Add salt and pepper to taste. In a saucepan warm the sauce. Pour the sauce on the fish, and cook until done, about 5 to 10 minutes more. Makes 4 servings.

Mr. Howell: Gilligan, my boy, I've prepared a dish to titillate even your unsophisticated palate. Behold, the specialty de la maisontre.

Gilligan: What is it? It smells like fish stew.

Mr. Howell: Fish stew? It's the world-famous French recipe—bouillabaisse.

Gilligan: What does bouillabaisse mean in English?

Mr. Howell: Fish stew.

Billionaire Bouillabaisse

½ cup butter
1 cup minced white onion
½ cup chopped shallots
1 teaspoon minced garlic
1 cup peeled whole raw shrimp
2 dozen raw shelled oysters
½ cup cooked, chopped lobster meat
½ cup whole raw crayfish tails, peeled (crab may be substituted, but grill one minute on both sides)

1 tablespoon all-purpose flour
1 cup whole tomatoes, peeled (canned or fresh)
1 teaspoon salt
½ teaspoon cayenne pepper
2 cups fish stock (from redfish head and bones)
Pinch saffron
4 to 5 pounds redfish
1 lemon, sliced

In a large pan melt the butter and sauté the onion, shallots, and garlic until tender. Add the shrimp, oysters, lobster, and crayfish, and cook a few minutes more. Stir in the flour and cook for 3 to 5 minutes. Add the tomatoes, salt, cayenne, and fish stock, and cook slowly for 20 minutes. Add the saffron and cook for 5 more minutes. Remove the pan from the heat. Meanwhile, remove the bones, skin, and head from the redfish. Cut the fish into 4 pieces and place it in a baking pan. Bake the fish at 350° for 15 minutes or until done. Place the fish in 4 soup bowls and pour the sauce over it. Garnish with lemon slices. Makes 4 servings.

Mrs. Howell: How's the bouillabaisse coming, darling?

Mr. Howell: Darling, I've surprised even myself, don't you agree?

Mrs. Howell: M-m-m. An epicurean delight. A culinary masterpiece.

Mr. Howell (pouting): Darling, I thought you'd make a fuss over it.

Mrs. Howell: Aw, darling. Thurston, dear, why have you never made bouillabaisse at home?

Mr. Howell: Well, back home our house is so big I can't find the kitchen. When I find the kitchen, I can't find the stove.

🌴 Conch Fritters Gilligan

5 conchs
1 ½ cups all-purpose flour
1 teaspoon baking powder
½ teaspoon salt

1 egg, beaten
1 cup milk
Fat for frying

Clean and pound the conchs. Slice very thin, and measure enough to make 2 cups. In a medium bowl sift together the flour, baking powder, and salt. Make a well in the center and pour the egg into it. Gradually blend the flour and egg, adding milk to make a smooth batter. Dip the sliced conch in the batter and fry in deep fat. Makes about 4 to 6 servings.

——————— **"** ———————

Mary Ann's Mystery Meal:
Gilligan: Pretty good, what is it?
Mary Ann: Well, I mashed up some halibut, some flounder, and some tuna.
Gilligan: Fish mash!

——————— **"** ———————

Dawn Wells collection

Lord and Lady of the island

Mission Control Marinated Shrimp

1 pound shrimp, shelled and deveined
1 quart water
6 tablespoons olive or salad oil
6 tablespoons lemon juice
⅓ cup vinegar

1 garlic clove, crushed
1 teaspoon salt
1 bay leaf, crumbled
2 tablespoons chopped parsley
¼ teaspoon pepper

In a medium saucepan heat the shrimp and water to boiling. Cook for 4 minutes or until the shrimp are tender. Drain well.

Meanwhile, in a small saucepan combine the oil, lemon juice, vinegar, garlic, salt, and bay leaf. Heat to boiling. Pour the sauce over the shrimp, and add the parsley and pepper. Toss lightly and transfer into a bowl. Cover and marinate for at least 4 hours. Makes 4 servings.

Mrs. Howell: My compliments to the chef. That was a superb seafood salad.
Mary Ann: I hope the lobster wasn't too rich for you.
Mr. Howell: Well, if he was, he didn't get a chance to mention it.

🌴 Mata Hari Curried Shrimp

¼ cup butter
1 cup chopped onion
1 cup chopped, peeled apple
½ to 2 tablespoons curry powder
1 teaspoon grated ginger root
¼ cup all-purpose flour
3 cups chicken broth
1 tomato, peeled and chopped

1 teaspoon sugar
Salt and pepper to taste
3 bananas, peeled, cut in 1-inch slices
2 pounds raw shrimp, peeled and deveined
Cooked rice
Grated coconut

In a large saucepan heat the butter and sauté the onion and apple until tender. Stir in the curry powder, ginger root, and flour, and cook for 2 minutes, stirring constantly. Remove the pan from the heat and stir in the chicken broth. Return the pan to the heat and cook, stirring constantly, until the mixture boils and thickens. Add the tomato, sugar, and salt and pepper to taste. Cover and cook over low heat 30 minutes, stirring occasionally. Add the bananas and shrimp to the mixture. Bring the mixture to a boil, reduce the heat, and simmer for 8 to 10 minutes. Serve over hot cooked rice. Sprinkle grated coconut on top. Makes 4 to 6 servings.

Bali Bali Shrimp

1 20-ounce can pineapple chunks
2 tablespoons oil
1 cup diagonally cut celery
1 medium green bell pepper, sliced
1 pound cooked shrimp
½ cup chopped green onions

3 tablespoons soy sauce
2 tablespoons cornstarch
⅛ teaspoon ginger
1 teaspoon garlic salt
1 cup cherry tomatoes, halved

Drain the pineapple, reserving the syrup. In a heavy skillet heat the oil and sauté the celery and green pepper until the pepper turns bright green. Add the shrimp and toss with the vegetables until heated through. Add the pineapple and green onions. In a small bowl combine the syrup, soy sauce, cornstarch, ginger, and garlic salt. Add the sauce to the shrimp mixture, stirring constantly until thickened and bubbling. Add the tomatoes and serve at once. Makes 4 servings.

Skipper's catch of the day

 Island Fish

3 pounds thick fish fillets or steaks (hal-ibut, swordfish, or mahi mahi)
3 limes
1 tablespoon salt
1 teaspoon pepper
2 cloves garlic, crushed

6 tablespoons water
6 tablespoons oil
1 tablespoon butter or margarine
½ cup sliced almonds
Lime wedges

In a shallow baking dish arrange the fish fillets. Squeeze the lime juice generously over the fish and sprinkle with salt and pepper. Let the fish stand for about 30 minutes. In a small bowl beat together the garlic, water, and oil. Brush the mixture over the fish. Bake at 500° for 10 minutes. Reduce the heat to 425° and bake 15 to 20 minutes longer or until the fish flakes easily with a fork. Brush with pan drippings 4 times while baking.

Meanwhile, in a small skillet melt the butter and sauté the almonds in butter until golden brown. Place the fish on a warm platter and sprinkle with almonds. Garnish with lime wedges. Makes about 6 servings.

------------- **"** -------------

Skipper: You know what I'd love to have for breakfast?
Mary Ann: What?
Skipper: Some soft scrambled eggs and a nice thick slice of tinned ham.
Mary Ann: O-h-h, so would I! But all you're gonna get is a mackerel and sliced banana.
Skipper: Mackerel and sliced banana?! That sounds awful!
Mary Ann: Probably will be.
Skipper (to others): Come on! Breakfast is ready.
Mary Ann: There you go.
Skipper: Oh, that Gilligan never does anything right!
Mary Ann: What's he done now?
Skipper: Look at the way he washed this plate.
Mary Ann: It looks clean to me.
Skipper: Well, what's that spot here in the middle of it?
Mary Ann: *That's* your breakfast.
Skipper: You call that a banana?!
Mary Ann: No-no—I think that's the mackerel.

------------- **"** -------------

Hauntingly beautiful

🌴 Ginger's Well-Cast Sea Bass

Oil	1 teaspoon basil
1 onion, chopped	Pinch garlic powder
1 green bell pepper, chopped	1 pound sea bass filets
½ pound mushrooms, sliced	½ cup white wine
1 teaspoon dill	3 tablespoons teriyaki sauce

In a skillet heat a small amount of oil and sauté the onion, green pepper, and mushrooms. Add the dill, basil, and garlic powder. Place the fish on top and add the wine and teriyaki sauce. Cover and simmer for 15 to 20 minutes. Makes 2 servings.

Ginger: M'mm. What smells so good?
Mary Ann: Burned swordfish.
Ginger: Burn the other side. I think it might be better.

""

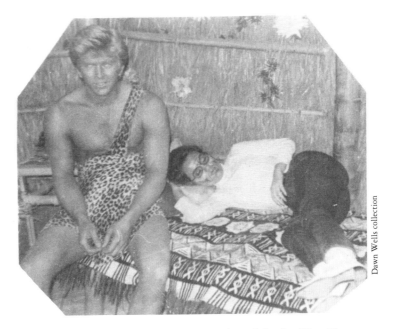

Here I am taking a little snooze between takes of the *Our Vines Have Tender Apes* episode. Tongo, the hunky ape-man beside me, was played by actor Denny Miller.

Dr. Jekyll and Mr. Hyde Casserole

8 slices bacon, diced
2 tablespoons butter or margarine
2 tablespoons all-purpose flour
1 cup milk
1 teaspoon Worcestershire sauce
½ teaspoon salt
½ teaspoon pepper
Dash garlic salt
3 hard-boiled eggs, sliced
4 ounces noodles, cooked
1 cup grated cheddar cheese

In a skillet fry the bacon until crisp. Drain. In the skillet melt the butter and blend in the flour. Stir in the milk, Worcestershire sauce, salt, pepper, and garlic salt. Cook over low heat, stirring constantly, until thickened. In a 2-quart casserole arrange half of the sliced eggs, noodles, cream sauce, and bacon. Repeat the layers, ending with bacon. Sprinkle the cheese over the casserole. Bake at 350° for 30 minutes. Makes 6 to 8 servings.

Luxury Liner Liver

My mother has been making this recipe since 1940.

1 ½ pounds sliced liver
¾ cup all-purpose flour
1 ½ teaspoons salt
¼ teaspoon pepper
2 tablespoons oil
2 medium onions, sliced

1 green pepper, cut in strips
1 tomato, cut in wedges
1 ½ cups water
1 teaspoon instant beef broth
Chopped parsley

Coat the liver with flour and seasonings. In a skillet heat the oil and sauté the liver for 4 minutes on each side.

Meanwhile, in a separate skillet heat a small amount of oil and sauté the onions and green pepper for 10 minutes or until soft. Stir in the tomato, and sauté for 2 more minutes. Arrange the onions, pepper, and tomato on top of the liver. Add the water and instant beef broth to the pan and simmer the mixture, scraping the browned bits loose from the bottom of the pan. Pour the liquid over the liver, and sprinkle with chopped parsley. Makes 4 servings.

Dawn Wells collection

Lovey Howell

Gilligan

Gilligan is everybody's little buddy. He remains as innocent on his tiny tropical island as he was on the rainy night he was born in a small town in Pennsylvania.

In a moment of exasperation, the Professor once said that the scientific term for Gilligan was "pest." But in their hearts, the Castaways all know Gilligan is about the most gentle and kind person they've ever met.

Blue-eyed Gilligan has all of the traits of a well-preserved and extended childhood. In fact, he still has his Boy Scout pocketknife (not to mention his copy of *A Boy Scout's Guide to New Jersey*) and his collection of Yogi Bear bottle caps.

Like most kids, Gilligan enjoys activities such as skateboarding, reading comic books, and playing baseball, plus tennis and hockey. He has fond memories of friends back home like Fatso Flannigan and Bobby McGuire.

Champion apple bobber Skinny Mulligan is probably his best pal from childhood.

It could be that Gilligan was seen as a leader among his cronies because he was elected president of the Eighth Grade Camera Club. Then again, that honor could have had something to do with the fact that he was the only one who had a camera.

Gilligan occasionally mentions his brother and sister, his grandfather Everett, and two uncles—John and Ramsey (a guide for the Lost Battalion in World War I). His barber back home is Sam.

But while Gilligan surely misses his old friends and family, no one seems more at home on the island than he does. As long as he has his lucky rabbit's foot and four-leaf clover charm, he can rest assured that all will be well. Lucky charms or not, the Skipper is always there to watch out for his little buddy.

And the other Castaways are reluctant to let Gilligan out of their sight either. For her part, Mary Ann does her best to make him easier to see by helping him maintain his 125-pound weight with a steady supply of coconut cream pies and other island treats.

Vegetables

Life Raft Rice

2 tablespoons butter
1 cup raw rice
1 4-ounce can sliced mushrooms
1 teaspoon seasoned salt

1 package Lawry's Cheese Italian
   Dressing Mix
Hot water

In a skillet melt the butter. Add the rice and stir until golden brown. Remove the pan from the heat. Drain the mushrooms and reserve the liquid. Add the mushrooms, seasoned salt, and dressing mix to the rice. Stir thoroughly. Add hot water to the reserved mushroom liquid to make 2 cups, and pour the liquid over the rice mixture. Bring to a boil. Pour into a buttered 1 ½-quart casserole. Bake at 350° for 25 to 30 minutes. Makes 6 servings.

Uncle Ramsey's Curried Rice and Raisins

2 ⅔ cups uncooked rice
½ cup raisins
1 teaspoon salt

2 tablespoons butter
1 tablespoon curry powder
2 tablespoons butter

In a large stock pot bring water to boil as directed on the rice package. Add the rice and return to a boil. Reduce the heat and add the raisins, salt, and 2 tablespoons of butter. Cover and cook according to the package directions. Fluff with a fork and add the curry and remaining butter. Makes 12 servings.

Longitude and Latitude Wild Rice

Prepare wild rice according to the package directions, substituting chicken broth for water. Chop some mushrooms and 1 medium onion. In a saucepan melt some butter and sauté the mushrooms and onions until tender. Stir the sautéed mixture into the cooked rice, and serve.

Serve with Mamasita Howell's Famous Duck Gravy (see recipe, page 171).

Roy Hinkley's Spanish Rice

2 cups brown Basmati rice
4 cups chicken broth
2-3 tablespoons olive oil
1 bunch green onions including tops, chopped
1 cup chopped parsley
1 green bell pepper, chopped

4 to 6 cloves garlic, crushed
¼ cup chili powder
1 teaspoon cumin
1 teaspoon oregano
1 16-ounce can tomatoes, crushed
2 7-ounce cans diced green chilies

In a large pot bring the rice and broth to a boil. Reduce the heat and cook for 45 minutes.

Meanwhile, heat the olive oil and sauté the green onions, parsley, green bell pepper, garlic, chili powder, cumin, and oregano for 4 to 5 minutes. Add the rice, tomatoes and diced green chilies. Mix well and transfer the mixture to a baking dish. Bake at 400° for 30 minutes. Serve with green salad. Makes 6 to 8 servings.

From Connie and Russell Johnson.

The Funny-Minded Professor

Russell Johnson is a funny, funny man. He had me in stitches the whole time we were working on "Gilligan's Island." He's also a terrific guy. He and I have remained close friends.

He now lives in the state of Washington with his second wife, Connie (whom I dearly love). Russell's love for his daughter Kim and his pride for his son David makes me appreciate him even more. They seem very happy, and they share each other's children and grandchildren and enjoy life a lot. He and Connie live in a magical spot and by living where they do have found a way to escape the pressures and stress of Southern California.

Russell used to tease me about "being put together" in the makeup room. I was always the focus of his good-natured ribbing because I was overhauled each morning (or so it seemed). It took a lot of makeup for the little farm girl since the show was done on film instead of videotape. Russell would continually poke fun at me because we could never show my belly button on TV (nervous censors, you know).

Russell is much funnier than the character of the Professor that he played, and if we could have captured that on camera, you would have seen another side of the serious professor.

I also think Russell is a very sexy man, handsome and talented, and he was a joy to work with. He was a stabilizing factor on the show, in addition to being wonderfully funny. I think Russell was sort of our Rock of Gibralter. Today Russell, Bob Denver, and I do personal appearances together. It's especially nice because it means we get to see each other fairly regularly, and I always look forward to it.

Regatta Risotto

5 cups chicken broth
¼ cup butter
2 cups uncooked white rice

2 tablespoons butter
Salt and pepper to taste
Parmesan cheese

In a saucepan bring the chicken broth to a simmer. In a large saucepan melt ¼ cup of butter and add the rice. Stir until the rice is coated. Reduce the heat and begin adding the broth a little at a time, stirring constantly, letting the rice absorb the liquid before adding more. This should take 20 to 25 minutes. When all of the liquid is used check for doneness, and add more broth if not done. Stir in 2 tablespoons butter, salt, pepper, and Parmesan cheese. Makes 8 servings.

Variations: Add ½ pound chopped cooked spinach. Add mushrooms, parsley, and herbs.

Richter Scale Green Chile Rice

1 cup uncooked rice
1 cup sour cream

½ pound cubed cheddar cheese
1 small can chopped green chilies

Cook the rice according to the package directions. Cool. In a medium bowl mix the rice with the sour cream. In the bottom of a buttered casserole spread half of the rice mixture and top with half of the cheese and chilies. Repeat the layers, ending with cheese. Bake at 350° for 30 to 40 minutes. Makes 4 to 6 servings.

Harold Hecuba's Hollywood Rice

1 cup uncooked white rice
½ cup chopped green onions
1 cup chopped celery
2 tablespoons chopped pimientos
1 clove chopped garlic
2 tablespoons butter
1 10-ounce package frozen chopped
  spinach, thawed and drained

1 teaspoon basil or 2 teaspoons fresh
1 teaspoon salt
¼ teaspoon pepper
1 ½ cups water
½ cup parsley
1 10 ¾-ounce can cream of mushroom
  soup

In a skillet sauté the rice, green onion, celery, pimientos, and garlic in butter. Add the spinach, basil, salt, pepper, and water. Transfer to a buttered casserole. Cover and bake at 350° for 35 minutes. Stir in the parsley and soup. Mix well. Let the casserole stand 5 minutes and serve. Makes 4 servings.

A pair of Gilligans—Bob Denver and son Patrick

Jack and the Beanstalk Bean Pot

1 pound pinto beans
Water
2 teaspoons salt
2 large onions, diced
4 cloves garlic, minced

1 7-ounce can green chilies, chopped
1 30-ounce can tomatoes
1 6-ounce can taco sauce
½ teaspoon cumin seed

Soak beans overnight in cold water to cover. Drain and rinse the beans, then cover them generously with fresh water. Add salt and cook over moderate heat for 1 hour, adding water if needed. Combine the onions, garlic, chilies, tomatoes, and taco sauce and stir the mixture into the beans. Stir in the cumin and simmer for 1 ½ hours. Makes 6 servings.

Note: Add 1 to 2 teaspoons chili powder for spicier beans. Add 2 pounds chopped beef sautéed with a chopped onion about an hour before serving, if desired.

Plan B Green Beans with Basil

This is from my Grandmother Rose.

3 cups fresh green beans (cut in 1-inch
   lengths)
2 to 3 tablespoons butter
½ cup chopped onion

¼ cup chopped celery
1 minced garlic clove
½ teaspoon dried rosemary
½ teaspoon dried basil

In a covered stock pot cook the beans for 10 minutes in boiling salted water. Drain. Stir in the remaining ingredients and replace the cover. Cook for 10 minutes or until tender. Makes 6 to 8 servings.

Note: If using fresh herbs use 2 teaspoons each.

Like Gilligan, Like Son

We shot one episode with Bob's son Patrick. It was the episode with the dream sequence about Jack and the Beanstalk (*'V' for Vitamins*). Alan played the giant and Patrick, who was then about five years old, portrayed a miniature Gilligan in the castle.

Patrick filmed with us all week and wore a little Gilligan costume. After the week's shoot, I asked Bob if Patrick could spend the weekend with me. He said, "sure," and I remember his final instructions to his son. He didn't say, "Be a good boy" or "Mind your manners" but instead, "Patrick, you give Mary Ann lots of love."

Patrick would not get out of the Gilligan costume that weekend. He even slept in it. One night he had gone to bed, but later there came the pitter-patter of tiny feet and then here came Patrick, just like a little Gilligan. He tugged on my arm and said, "Mary Ann, I'm scared. I'm having nightmares."

I went in the bedroom with him, and we sat on the edge of the bed and talked, and he seemed to calm down. When he was ready to go back to sleep, I said, "Now I'll leave the light on so you won't be afraid." He said, "Oh no, Mary Ann, it's best that I learn how to do this by myself. I'll sleep in the dark." It's a weekend I shall always remember.

All Bob's children (Kim, Patrick, Megan, Emily, and Colin) are special. Bob and his wife, Dreama, have the best marriage of any couple I know. They adore each other and spend days alone together enjoying Colin. Bob and Dreama seem to be two of the world's happiest people. Dreama is a wonderful actress and mom and is loving and supportive of Bob. I think Bob is so gifted. I've seen him on stage, and his versatility is unexpected and a joy to watch. Bob and Dreama seem to share the secret of a happy family. I envy that.

Island Madness—The Castaways manhandle mad scientist Boris Balinkoff (Vito Scotti)

Boris Balinkoff Baked Beans

1 pound dry navy beans, washed and sorted
8 cups water
1 cup chopped celery
1 cup diced carrot
2 beef bouillon cubes
1 teaspoon salt
Pepper

Giblets from poultry
½ pound bulk pork sausage
1 2 ½- to 3-pound broiler/fryer, cut up (or roasted duck, as the French do)
1 cup chopped onion
1 tablespoon Worcestershire sauce
1 ½ cups tomato juice
½ teaspoon paprika

In a large pot cover the beans with the water and bring to boiling. Boil for 2 minutes. Remove the pot from the heat, cover, and let the beans stand for 1 hour. Do not drain. Add the celery, carrot, bouillon cubes, salt, pepper, and giblets. Return to boiling. Reduce the heat, cover, and simmer for 1 hour.

Shape the sausage into small balls. In a large skillet brown the sausage. Remove the sausage from the pan, reserving the drippings. Sprinkle the chicken with salt and pepper, and brown it in the sausage drippings. Remove the chicken and set it aside. Cook the onion in the drippings until tender. Stir in the Worcestershire sauce and tomato juice. Drain the bean mixture, reserving the liquid. In a Dutch oven combine the bean mixture, sausage balls, and tomato juice mixture. Top with the chicken. Pour the reserved bean mixture liquid over the chicken. Sprinkle with paprika. Cover and bake at 325° for 1 hour, adding more bean liquid if necessary. Makes a full meal for 8.

Lovey's Sugar Beets

3 tablespoons sugar
1 ½ teaspoons cornstarch
1 teaspoon salt

½ cup orange juice
1 tablespoon butter
1 16-ounce can sliced beets, drained

In a saucepan combine the sugar, cornstarch, and salt. Slowly stir in the orange juice, cook, and stir until thick. Add the butter and beets. Heat well. Makes 4 servings.

Note: Use 1 ½ to 2 cups fresh beets.

Dawn Wells collection

Hat Tricks—Natalie Schafer with just a few of the hats Lovey brought with her on the three-hour cruise

Dow Jones Green Beans and Sour Cream

2 tablespoons fat
1 cup sliced mushrooms
4 cups cooked green beans

1 cup sour cream
¼ teaspoon salt
⅛ teaspoon pepper

In a skillet heat the fat and brown the mushrooms. Add the remaining ingredients and heat well. Makes 6 servings.

Dawn Wells collection

Hugs and kisses

Ginger's Hawaiian Ginger Beets

1 13 ½-ounce can pineapple tidbits
⅓ cup vinegar
⅓ cup water
⅓ cup sugar
4 teaspoons cornstarch
½ teaspoon salt

2 tablespoons butter or margarine
½ cup sliced onions
2 16-ounce jars small whole beets, drained
2 tablespoons chopped preserved ginger

Drain and reserve the syrup from the pineapple. In a bowl combine the pineapple syrup, vinegar, water, sugar, cornstarch, and salt. Blend well. In a skillet melt the butter and sauté the onion until tender. Add the syrup mixture and cook, stirring constantly, until thick and clear. Add the beets and ginger. Simmer to blend the flavors, about 15 minutes. Just before serving add the pineapple tidbits and heat through. Makes 6 servings.

Lovey's Broccoli Brooches

1 ½ to 2 pounds broccoli
½ teaspoon salt
Juice of 1 lemon
1 10 ½-ounce can cream of chicken soup
½ cup mayonnaise

¼ teaspoon curry powder
½ cup bread or cracker crumbs
2 tablespoons melted butter

Wash and split the broccoli stalks into halves or quarters almost to the blossom, or cut the stem into ¼-inch slices. Bring a large pot of salted water to a boil. Cook the sliced stems for 5 minutes before adding the flowerets. Cover and cook until tender crisp, about 8 to 10 minutes. Check for tenderness. Drain and turn into a 1 ½-quart casserole. Squeeze the lemon juice over the top.

In a medium bowl blend together the soup, mayonnaise, and curry powder. Pour the soup mixture over the broccoli. Top with bread crumbs and dribble with melted butter. Bake at 350° for 20 minutes or until bubbly. Makes 6 servings.

Note: To prepare ahead, do everything up to the point of putting it into the oven. Store the casserole in the refrigerator. Then allow more time in the oven.

————————— `"` —————————

Mrs. Howell: Well, you know, darling, there's only one honest way to influence anybody.

Mr. Howell: You're right! Bribery!

————————— `"` —————————

Balboa Broccoli Casserole

1 10-ounce package frozen broccoli
    spears (or equal amount of fresh broc-
    coli)
2 medium onions, quartered
2 tablespoons butter
2 tablespoons all-purpose flour
¼ teaspoon salt

Dash pepper
1 cup milk
1 3-ounce package cream cheese
Velveeta slices
5 to 6 slices of bread
½ cup melted butter

In a large pot cook the broccoli and onion together following the package directions.

In a skillet melt the butter and blend in the flour, salt, and pepper. Gradually add the milk stirring constantly, until thick and bubbly. Lower the heat and add the cream cheese. Stir until melted. Place the broccoli and onions in a 1 ½ to 2-quart casserole and cover with sauce. Top the entire casserole with Velveeta slices. Cover. Bake at 350° for 25 minutes. Meanwhile, cube the bread and toss it in the melted butter. Top the casserole with bread cubes and return it to the oven uncovered for 10 minutes. Makes 4 to 6 servings.

From Dreama and Bob Denver.

Kansas Fried Cabbage

Cabbage
Bacon drippings, margarine, or oil
Salt

Pepper
Caraway seeds
Water (if needed)

Shred the cabbage (not too fine). In a skillet heat a small amount of bacon drippings and lightly brown the cabbage until limp. Add the salt and pepper and a few caraway seeds. Add a little water if needed.

Lady in Red Cabbage

1 small red cabbage, shredded
2 large cooking apples, sliced
½ cup brown sugar

¼ teaspoon dry mustard
½ cup vinegar
¼ teaspoon salt

In a greased casserole layer the cabbage and apples. In a small bowl combine the brown sugar, dry mustard, vinegar, and salt. Pour the sugar mixture over the layers. Cover the dish. Bake at 400° for approximately 40 minutes. Makes about 4 servings.

Dawn Wells collection

If you don't eat your vegetables, Gilligan, you'll wind up like this. (From the episode *Up at Bat,* one of my favorite episodes.)

NASA-Kansas Carrots

2 cups sliced carrots
1 tablespoon cornstarch
1 tablespoon Tang instant drink
  (orange)

$\frac{1}{4}$ teaspoon salt
2 dashes nutmeg
1 tablespoon butter
Chopped parsley

In a saucepan cook the carrots in water until tender. Drain, reserving the liquid. Add cold water to make $\frac{3}{4}$ cup of liquid, if necessary. Pour the liquid into a saucepan. In a small bowl mix the cornstarch with the Tang, salt, and nutmeg. Stir this into the water. Add the butter and bring the liquid to a boil. Stir until thick, stirring constantly. Add the carrots and heat through. Sprinkle with parsley. Makes 4 servings.

————————— 66 —————————

Gilligan: Everybody knows carrots are good for your eyes.
Mary Ann: Certainly.
Gilligan: After all, did you ever see a rabbit wearing glasses?

————————— 99 —————————

Mary Ann's Carrots

5 cups carrots, peeled and quartered
1 $\frac{1}{2}$ cups beef bouillon
1 $\frac{1}{2}$ tablespoons butter
$\frac{1}{2}$ teaspoon salt

2 teaspoons lemon juice
2 tablespoons sugar
Salt and pepper to taste
Chopped parsley

In a 5-quart saucepan cover the carrots with the bouillon, butter, salt, lemon juice, and sugar. Cover and simmer until completely tender and the liquid is reduced to a syrup. Add salt if needed, and pepper. Before serving roll in the syrup and sprinkle with parsley. Makes about 8 servings.

Karate Pinky Carrots

2 (or more) tablespoons oil
6 carrots, shredded (not too fine)

Salt and pepper to taste

In a skillet heat the oil and sauté the shredded carrots over medium heat until the desired crispness, stirring constantly. Season with salt and pepper to taste. Makes about 4 servings.

Mayflower Cauliflower Casserole

2 10-ounce packages frozen cauliflower
1 tablespoon butter or margarine
1 tablespoon all-purpose flour
Dash salt
Dash pepper

½ cup milk
1 cup grated Swiss cheese
¼ cup cracker crumbs
1 tablespoon melted butter

Cook the cauliflower according to the package directions. Drain and place in a greased 1 ½-quart casserole.

In a skillet over low heat melt 1 tablespoon of butter or margarine. Add the flour, salt, and pepper. Cook, stirring constantly, until smooth. Gradually add the milk and stir constantly until the mixture thickens. Add the Swiss cheese, and stir until cheese melts. Spoon the sauce over the cauliflower.

In a small bowl combine the cracker crumbs and the melted butter. Sprinkle the mixture over the cauliflower. Bake at 325° for 20 minutes, or until thoroughly heated. Makes 4 to 6 servings.

Mr. Howell's Swiss Bank Chard

2 pounds Swiss chard
1 tablespoon butter
¼ cup whipping cream

¼ cup Roquefort cheese
Freshly ground pepper

Wash well and drain the chard. Cut the stems out of the leaves, and slice the stems crosswise into ¼-inch pieces. Slice the leaves into 1- to 2-inch widths. In a 5-quart pan melt the butter over medium heat. Add the stems and cook for 8 minutes. Add the leaves and cream. Cover and steam until wilted, about 3 minutes, stirring often. Uncover and add the cheese on high, stirring constantly, for about 3 minutes. Season with pepper. Makes 4 servings.

Cinderella Corn

4 slices bacon
1 medium green bell pepper, chopped
1 small onion, chopped
1 17-ounce can cream-style corn

1 teaspoon salt
⅛ teaspoon pepper
4 eggs, beaten

In a skillet fry the bacon until crisp. Remove the bacon and set it aside. Drain all but 3 tablespoons of drippings from the skillet. Sauté the pepper and onion in the drippings until the onion is tender. Add the remaining ingredients. Cook, stirring until the eggs are thickened throughout but still moist. Crumble the bacon and sprinkle it on the egg mixture. Makes 4 to 6 servings.

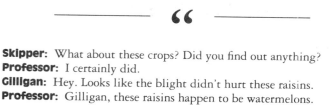

Skipper: What about these crops? Did you find out anything?
Professor: I certainly did.
Gilligan: Hey. Looks like the blight didn't hurt these raisins.
Professor: Gilligan, these raisins happen to be watermelons.

Spudnik Cucumber Surprise

1 pound potatoes, peeled and sliced
3 tablespoons olive oil
Salt and pepper to taste
1 sprig fresh basil

1 bay leaf
2 medium tomatoes, peeled and seeded
Water
2 chilled young cucumbers

In a skillet combine the potatoes, olive oil, salt, pepper, a sprig of fresh basil, a bay leaf, and tomatoes. Add water to just cover. Cover and cook for 20 minutes over medium high heat.

Peel the cucumbers and quarter each one lengthwise. Season with salt and pepper, and add them to the potatoes. Serve at once. The taste of the hot potatoes and the fresh, raw cucumbers together is a happy surprise. Makes 6 servings.

Ginger: I think the two things that I miss most are vegetables and dates.
Gilligan: We have plenty of dates here on the island.
Ginger: Not the kind I mean.

Cary Grant Eggplant

Eggplant
2 eggs
Water

All-purpose flour
Salt and pepper to taste
Olive oil

Slice the eggplant very thin. Soak the slices in salt water for 30 minutes. Peel. Beat the eggs with a small amount of water. In separate shallow bowl stir together the flour, salt, and pepper. Dip the eggplant slices in the egg, then in the flour mixture. Fry in olive oil until slightly brown. Turn over, and brown the other side. Stack on a plate and serve hot.

Mantis Cane Mushrooms

6 tablespoons butter or margarine
½ cup minced onion
2 cups minced fresh mushrooms
½ teaspoon salt

½ teaspoon hot pepper sauce
6 slices bread
12 eggs
¾ cup half and half

In a large skillet melt ¼ cup of butter and sauté the onion and mushrooms until tender. Add salt and pepper sauce. Turn the mushroom mixture into a small bowl. Cut the bread into 6 rounds and spread with remaining 2 tablespoons of butter. In the same skillet grill the bread. Grease 6 individual baking dishes and place a toast circle in each. Top with a layer of mushroom mixture. Carefully break 2 eggs into each baking dish. Top with 2 tablespoons of half and half. Bake at 350° for 15 to 20 minutes, until the eggs are set. Serve at once. Makes 6 servings.

The Howells make a discovery:
Mr. Howell: That does it, Lovey. A sturdy bit of construction, if I say so myself.
Mrs. Howell: Thurston, what on earth is that on your forehead?!
Mr. Howell (wipes brow): Huh. Looks like water. I wonder where it came from.
Mrs. Howell: Thurston, I know what it is. I used to see it on our gardener. It's perspiration!
Mr. Howell: It is?! What can I put it in? I've got to send it to Dad. He'd be fascinated.

Dawn Wells collection

It was great fun to be reunited with Bob Denver and the rest in our first "reunion" TV special. Here Gilligan and I are on the lam after the wedding party went haywire.

Mars Mushrooms

3 tablespoons butter or margarine
1 cup chopped onion
1 ¼ pound mushrooms, sliced ¼-inch thick
½ cup water

1 teaspoon salt
½ teaspoon pepper
1 teaspoon paprika
¼ cup chopped parsley
1 cup sour cream

In a skillet melt the butter and sauté the onion for 5 minutes, until golden. Add the mushrooms and water. Cook for 15 minutes or until tender, adding water if needed. Add salt, pepper, paprika, 2 tablespoons of the parsley, and the sour cream. Heat very slowly, stirring constantly, until very hot. Sprinkle with the remaining parsley. Makes 6 servings.

Mrs. Howell: Oh, Professor, it's wonderful having someone like you with us. You're absolutely marvelous.
Mr. Howell: If you were Republican, you'd be perfect.

Country Club Creamed Onions

2 15 ½-ounce cans small white onions
2 tablespoons butter
2 tablespoons all-purpose flour
1 ¼ cups milk

¼ teaspoon mace
½ teaspoon salt
Dash pepper
2 tablespoons dry bread crumbs

Drain the onions, reserving ½ cup of liquid. Melt the butter, and remove the pan from the heat. Add the flour, stirring constantly until smooth. Gradually add the onion liquid and milk, stirring until smooth. Bring to boiling, and boil gently for 1 minute. Add the onions, mace, salt, and pepper. Mix well, and pour into a greased 1-quart casserole. Sprinkle with bread crumbs and place under the broiler for 2 minutes, just to brown the top. Makes 6 to 8 servings.

Steve Cox collection

Natalie, Jim, Alan, and I celebrate with Sherwood Schwartz over the publication of Sherwood's autobiography, *Inside Gilligan's Island.*

New World Potatoes

2 ½ pounds small red-skinned new potatoes
1/4 cup fresh rosemary leaves (or 1 tablespoon dried)

2 cloves garlic, minced
2 tablespoons melted margarine
2 tablespoons olive oil
Salt and pepper

Scrub the new potatoes, and peel away a strip of skin around the center. Toss them with the rosemary leaves, minced garlic, margarine, and olive oil. Coat well. Place the potatoes in a medium baking pan. Bake at 375° for 35 to 45 minutes, until the potatoes are tender. Turn gently every 10 minutes. Season with salt and pepper. Makes 6 to 8 servings.

Dreamy Potato Dumplings

2 or 3 potatoes, boiled and grated
1 large egg

Salt
All-purpose flour

In a medium bowl combine the potato, egg, salt, and enough flour to make the mixture stiff. Turn onto a floured board and knead. Shape into balls. Cook the dumplings with pork roast and sauerkraut or pot roast. The leftovers may be diced and fried. Makes 4 to 6 servings.

Birds of a Feather

I remember the chicken people episode *(Smile, You're on Mars Camera)* oh so well. They painted us from head to toe with glue and then stuck feathers all over us. We had already shot the scene twice before and always at the end of the day. One Friday night a few weeks later, after shooting several other scenes, the bad news came: We needed to shoot the chicken people "just one more time." Out came the paintbrushes and glue, and we did the scene once again. Finally, the director yelled, "Cut! That's a wrap!" We were surely glad to hear that. What a mess and what a drive home—glue and feathers included. Yuck!

Chicken People Hash Browns

1 small potato
¼ cup butter or margarine
1 small onion, finely chopped
½ cup cubed cooked ham, beef, or pork
1 tablespoon chopped parsley
3 eggs

¼ teaspoon salt
Dash pepper
1 tablespoon milk
½ cup shredded cheddar or Monterey Jack cheese

Peel the potato and cut it into ½-inch cubes. This should make about ¾ cup. In a 10-inch frying pan melt 2 tablespoons of the butter. Add the potato, onion, and meat. Cover and cook over medium heat, stirring occasionally to brown evenly, until the potato is tender when pierced, about 15 minutes. Sprinkle with parsley, add remaining 2 tablespoons of butter, and reduce the heat to low.

Beat the eggs with salt, pepper, and milk until well blended. Pour the egg mixture into the pan and cook, lifting the set portion with a spatula so the uncooked egg can flow underneath. Cook until the eggs are almost completely set, sprinkle with cheese, and cover just until the cheese melts. Cut into wedges to serve. Makes 2 servings.

While filming at Zuma Beach once, somebody brought me a very small baby sparrow that had fallen out of a tree. I kept the bird in a shoebox. She had to be fed every few hours, so I had to bring the bird to work with me every day. I kept her in my dressing room, and all the prop men and everybody around would collect bugs for her. They took care of that little bird like I had brought my baby to the set. They chopped up bugs and fed her with tweezers. They gave her water with an eye-dropper. Even the big rough-and-tough guys would be in my trailer coaxing the little bird to open her mouth. We had a great crew.

I also had a kitten that was born backstage. We had a lot of wild cats on the set, and baby kittens were born back in that jungle all the time. Over the years, I brought two of them home from the set to raise as my own pets. It really was a jungle out there.

Mademoiselle Ginger's Mashed Potatoes

8 medium baking potatoes
2 teaspoons salt
Cold water
2 cups fresh basil leaves

½ cup Parmesan cheese
3 tablespoons olive oil
¼ teaspoon pepper
2 cups milk

In a large pot cover the potatoes with water, add 1 teaspoon of salt, and bring the water to a boil. Reduce the heat and simmer for 35 to 40 minutes, until tender.

In a blender combine the basil leaves, Parmesan, 2 tablespoons of olive oil, and pepper. Blend until well mixed.

Drain the potatoes and peel while still warm. Mash or put the potatoes through a ricer. Add 1 ½ cups of milk with a wooden spoon. Add ½ cup more milk, blending until soft enough. Add 1 teaspoon of salt and stir about 5 minutes. Add the basil purée and drizzle 1 tablespoon of olive oil on top. Makes 6 servings.

Potato Hut Puffs

1 8-ounce package cream cheese, softened
4 cups mashed potatoes
1 beaten egg

⅓ cup finely chopped onion
1 teaspoon salt
Dash pepper
¼ cup chopped pimiento

In a large bowl combine the cream cheese and potatoes, mixing well. Add the remaining ingredients and turn the mixture into a 1-quart casserole. Bake at 350° for 45 minutes. Makes 6 to 8 servings.

Minnow Mini-Quiz

1. Whose red shirt is Gilligan wearing?
   His brother's

2. What type of green bug bit Gilligan?
   Mantis cane

3. What kind of wristwatch does Gilligan wear?
   Manny Moose

4. What is the name of Gilligan's turtle?
   Herman

5. Whose nose does Gilligan wish he had?
   Richard Burton

Professor's Collegiate Colcannon

5 to 6 cups freshly mashed potatoes
Butter
Milk
Salt and pepper to taste
1/2 cup chopped green onion (tops
   included)

6 cups roughly chopped green cabbage
1 teaspoon caraway seeds (optional)
2 cups leftover ham, diced (or 1 pound
   bacon, cooked and crumbled)
Butter
Paprika

In a large bowl combine the mashed potatoes, butter, milk to taste, salt, pepper, and green onion.

In a steamer steam the cabbage and caraway seeds. Add the cabbage to the potato mixture. Add the ham. Turn the mixture into a shallow baking dish. Bake at 400° for 20 to 25 minutes or until the top browns lightly. Top with bits of butter and sprinkle paprika on top. Makes about 8 to 10 servings.

From Connie and Russell Johnson.

——— **❝** ———

Skipper: We're gonna grow some Idaho potatoes right here.
Gilligan: They're sure gonna have to have long roots.

——— **❞** ———

Compass Points Potato Casserole

6 large potatoes
1 cup sharp shredded cheddar cheese
1 pint sour cream
½ cup half and half

Salt and pepper to taste
¼ cup poppy seeds
1 bunch green onions, chopped

Boil the potatoes until tender. Refrigerate them until cold, peel, and grate. In a large bowl combine all of the ingredients. Place the mixture in a lightly buttered casserole dish. Cover and bake at 350° for 20 to 25 minutes. Uncover and bake 10 more minutes. Makes 8 servings.

Tina Louise with daughter Caprice

Dawn Wells collection

I Am What I Yams

4 sweet potatoes
3 ounces curaçao
2 tablespoons butter
½ teaspoon cinnamon

Salt and pepper to taste
6 oranges, halved, pulp removed

Bake the sweet potatoes until tender. Remove the pulp and mash. Add and blend the curaçao, butter, cinnamon, salt, and pepper. Remove the pulp from 3 halved oranges and fill the orange shells with the yam mixture. Bake at 400° for 15 minutes. Makes 4 to 6 servings.

Ginger's Sweet Potato Soufflé

5 eggplant-size yams (they are sweeter)
2 eggs, beaten
½ cup butter, melted
½ teaspoon cinnamon

¼ teaspoon nutmeg
¼ teaspoon ginger
½ teaspoon baking powder
Marshmallows

In a large pot boil the yams until the skin can be removed. Don't overcook. Remove the skin and place the yams in a large baking dish. Mash them down a bit with a large fork, then add the eggs and beat with an electric beater. Add the butter, cinnamon, nutmeg, ginger, and baking powder. Blend well.

Smooth out the top and add the marshmallows, as many as will fit. Sprinkle with a dash of cinnamon. Bake at 350° for 30 minutes. Makes 6 servings.

From Tina Louise.

Thanksgiving Dinner Dress Rehearsal

Tina Louise was just about to marry and had never before cooked Thanksgiving dinner. So she asked me if my mother and I would teach her how to cook one.

About a week before the big day, we went out and bought the turkey and all the trimmings. We made turkey and dressing, mashed potatoes, gravy, sweet potato pie, creamed onions, pumpkin pie, carrot pudding, and mince meat pie. My mother and I cooked the entire dinner, a dress rehearsal so to speak. While we cooked, Tina carefully wrote down what we were doing.

I often wondered whether Tina even remembered all that commotion. Then some years later I met her daughter Caprice when she was about twelve years old. Caprice told me that every Thanksgiving (or Christmas) her mom tells the story of how she got the recipes and how she learned to cook her first Thanksgiving dinner. Ginger's Sweet Potato Soufflé, provided by Tina, is one of those recipes.

I think it's wonderful that this little tradition has been passed on. Tina and I didn't always have many personal moments together away from the "Gilligan" set, but this occasion has turned out to be one of those especially nice memories.

Belly Dancer Breadfruit

6 large breadfruit or baking potatoes (3 ½ pounds), peeled and cut into small chunks

2 medium onions, cut into small chunks

5 eggs

2 teaspoons fresh lemon juice

¾ cup all-purpose flour

1 tablespoon salt

½ teaspoon freshly ground pepper

About 1 cup vegetable oil, for frying

Sour cream

In a food processor shred the breadfruit and onions. Transfer to a large strainer and squeeze out the excess moisture. In a large bowl beat the eggs. Stir in the lemon juice, squeezed onions, and breadfruit. Gradually stir in enough flour to make a thin batter. Season with the salt and pepper.

In a large heavy skillet heat ¼-inch of oil. Heat over moderately high heat until the oil begins to shimmer and a small spoonful of batter sizzles when added, about 5 minutes. Drop a heaping tablespoon of the batter into the hot oil and flatten it slightly with the back of a spoon. Form several more fritters in the pan without overcrowding. Fry until golden brown on one side, about 3 minutes. Flip and fry on the other side, about 2 minutes longer. Transfer to paper towels to drain. Stir the remaining batter well before making the next batch.

Serve the fritters hot from the pan or, if serving them all at once, keep warm in a 200° oven on a rack set over a baking sheet. Serve with sour cream. Makes about 45 fritters.

🌴 Seven Seas Peas and Rice

1 pound dried red beans or pigeon peas
2 tablespoons oil or lard
2 tablespoons diced ham
2 tablespoons diced salt pork
1 small onion, diced
1 clove garlic, crushed

1 green bell pepper, diced
1 pimiento, diced
1 ½ cups uncooked rice
4 cups water
2 teaspoons salt

Soak the beans overnight in water to cover generously. Bring the water to a boil, reduce the heat to low, and simmer for about 1 hour, until tender but not mushy. In a skillet heat the oil. Add the ham and salt pork, and cook until lightly browned. Add the onion, garlic, and green pepper, and cook until tender but not browned. Add the pimiento, rice, water, and salt. Drain and add the beans. Cover and bring the mixture to a boil. Reduce the heat to low and simmer until the rice is tender. Add water or bean liquid as needed. Makes 8 to 10 servings.

With Mom, "Chef" Evelyn Wells

🌴 Eva's Grubb

1 10-ounce package frozen peas
2 tablespoons butter
1 cup chopped Chinese cabbage

1 ½ cups cooked rice (add last)
1 teaspoon garlic powder
Salt and pepper to taste

Prepare the frozen peas. Drain. Add the butter and cabbage, and simmer until the cabbage is tender. When half-cooked, add the remaining ingredients, cover, and cook for 15 minutes. Makes about 4 servings.

Scarecrow Screamed Spinach

2 10-ounce packages frozen chopped
  spinach
3 strips bacon
1 clove garlic
1 medium onion

2 tablespoons butter
2 tablespoons all-purpose flour
1 cup milk
Salt and pepper to taste
Nutmeg (optional)

Cook the spinach according to the package directions just until it separates, then drain. In a food mill grind the bacon, garlic, and onion. In a skillet sauté the bacon mixture until the bacon starts to brown and the onion is tender. Pour off the fat.

In a skillet melt the butter and add the flour. Gradually add the milk, stirring constantly until smooth. Cook until thickened. Add the bacon mixture and spinach. Season to taste with salt, pepper, and a grating of nutmeg if desired. Bring the mixture to a boil slowly. Heat through and serve. Makes 6 to 8 servings.

Variation: Use 1 pound of fresh spinach cooked 4 minutes in boiling water. Drain thoroughly, and chop fine.

———————— " ————————

After three days, the radioactive seeds grow four-foot carrots and string beans, so the Castaways have a vegetable feast.
Gilligan: Skipper, pass the spinach, please.
Skipper: Gilligan, that's the fourth helping of spinach you've had.
Gilligan: Six, I snuck two.

———————— " ————————

Squish Squash Soufflé

4 eggs, separated
1 cup half and half
½ cup bread crumbs
Salt and pepper to taste

2 tablespoons finely chopped onion
½ clove garlic
½ cup grated Parmesan
2 cups mashed squash

Butter a soufflé dish. Beat the egg yolks slightly. Add the half and half, bread crumbs, salt, pepper, onion, garlic, and cheese. Add the mashed squash. Beat the egg whites and fold them into the squash mixture. Spoon into a soufflé dish. Bake at 350° for about 40 minutes. Makes 4 to 6 servings.

Variations: Use carrots or well-drained spinach. If using spinach, add a dash of nutmeg. If using carrots, leave out the cheese and garlic. Be sure to squeeze the vegetables dry after mashing.

Castaway Zucchini Casserole

Oil
1 clove garlic
½ small onion
4 cups shredded raw squash (or cooked spinach or carrots)

1 cup half and half
4 eggs, beaten
½ cup bread crumbs
½ cup Parmesan cheese

In a skillet heat a small amount of oil and sauté the garlic and onion until limp. Cool and add the sautéed mixture to the squash. Add the remaining ingredients. Mix well and pour into a buttered casserole. Bake at 350° for 45 minutes. Makes 6 to 8 servings.

Bikini Fried Zucchini

1 to 1 ½ pounds zucchini
Flour
1 egg
1 tablespoon water

½ teaspoon salt
Fine dry bread crumbs
Oil for frying

Cut the squash lengthwise into quarters or eighths. Roll in flour, then a mixture of slightly beaten egg, water, and salt. Coat in bread crumbs. In a skillet or deep-fryer heat oil. Fry the zucchini until golden. Makes about 4 servings.

Jungle Zoo-chini

3 medium zucchini
2 tablespoons butter
1 cup fresh mushrooms
2 tablespoons all-purpose flour
½ teaspoon fresh oregano
1 clove minced garlic

1 cup shredded Monterey Jack
2 tablespoons chopped pimientos
Italian herbs
¼ cup Parmesan cheese

In a large stock pot boil the zucchini in salted water for 10 minutes. Drain and cool. Cut in half lengthwise and cut off the ends. Scrape out the center, leaving ¼ inch of shell. Reserve the pulp. In a skillet melt the butter and sauté the mushrooms for about 3 minutes. Stir in the flour, oregano, and garlic. Remove the pan from the heat and add the pulp, cheese, pimientos, and herbs.

Preheat the broiler. Stuff the zucchini and sprinkle with the Parmesan. Broil for 3 to 5 minutes, until bubbly. Makes 6 servings.

Search Plane Succotash

1 10-ounce package frozen baby limas
1 16-ounce package frozen corn, thawed
1 small green bell pepper, finely
  chopped
1 small red bell pepper, finely chopped
½ cup heavy whipping cream

3 tablespoons butter or margarine,
  melted
½ teaspoon salt
¼ teaspoon pepper

In a medium pot cook the lima beans in boiling salted water to cover for 5 to 8 minutes or until the beans are just tender. Drain. Transfer the lima beans to a large skillet. Add the corn and remaining ingredients. Cook over medium heat for 20 to 25 minutes, or until the vegetables are tender, stirring occasionally. Makes 6 to 8 servings.

From Dreama and Bob Denver.

Professor: I think a signal fire's our best bet, Gilligan. Although, I don't know whether she'll [lady pilot circling the earth] be able to see it with all that nimbus cumuli.
Gilligan: Yeah. And all those clouds are in the way too.

Signal Fire Vegetables

½ cup butter
½ teaspoon thyme leaves
¼ teaspoon salt
¼ teaspoon pepper

3 cups cauliflower flowerets
2 cups broccoli flowerets
4 medium carrots, cut into strips
2 onions, quartered

In a 13 x 9-inch baking dish melt the butter in the oven. Stir in the thyme, salt, and pepper. Add the fresh vegetables and toss to coat. Cover with aluminum foil. Bake at 400° for 25 minutes or until the vegetables are crispy tender. Makes 8 servings.

From Dreama and Bob Denver.

True Grits Casserole

1 cup cooked grits
1 cup margarine
3 tablespoons milk
3 eggs, beaten one at a time

½ pound cheese, grated
1 teaspoon garlic salt
Dash salt

In a casserole dish combine all of the ingredients. Bake at 375° for 30 to 40 minutes. Makes about 6 servings.

Apricot Ahoy Casserole

1 4-ounce stack Ritz Crackers, crushed
⅔ cup firmly packed light brown sugar
5 17-ounce cans apricots, drained

½ cup butter, melted

Grease a casserole with butter. Place half of the apricots in the casserole dish. In a small bowl mix the brown sugar with the cracker crumbs. Sprinkle the apricots with half of the crumb mixture. Repeat the layers, ending with the cracker mixture. Pour melted butter over all. Bake at 350° for 30 to 40 minutes. Makes 8 to 10 servings.

 Curried Treasure Fruit

1 20-ounce can peach halves
1 20-ounce can pear halves
1 20-ounce can pineapple halves
5 maraschino cherries

½ cup butter
¾ cup light brown sugar
4 teaspoons of curry powder

Drain the fruit and dry it well on paper towels. Arrange all of the fruit in a 1 ½-quart casserole dish. Melt the butter and add the brown sugar. Add the curry powder. Spoon the mixture over the fruit. Bake uncovered at 325° for 1 hour. Serve with ham, lamb, or poultry. Makes 12 servings.

The Tennessean

Ginger

Movie star Ginger Grant's life as a Castaway is filled with dazzling drama. Many times, Ginger is the common link between the worlds of her fellow Castaways. After all, what could be more universal than movies. And when, for example, the Professor has a logical plan of action to be rescued, it's often Ginger who provides the personal touch for making the plan come together.

Ginger frequently calls upon her Hollywood experience and impressive array of movies to work to her advantage on the island. *The Hula Girl and the Fullback* is her most memorable film, but who could forget others like *Belly Dancers From Bali Bali* or *The Rain Dancers of Rango Rango*—not to mention *San Quentin Blues* and *Sing a Song of Sing Sing,* or the Indian astronaut movie, *Mohawk Over the Moon?*

The movies Ginger didn't get a role in sometimes sound as intriguing as the ones in which she did appear: *Standing Cow, Daughter of Sitting Bull* (Ginger couldn't shoot a gun) and *Land of the Vampires* (she had the wrong blood type).

In any case, Ginger has come a long way since her first job in show business when she worked for Merlin the Mindreader and Al Ben Casey, a phony sheik. Ginger was also voted Miss Hourglass because her sand was in all the right places. But any doubts of her seriousness about her craft are dismissed when she reveals her dreams of someday having a play on Broadway.

Still, even though she has her sights on the bright lights, Ginger can be very down to earth. She even has very practical training in first aid—especially mouth-to-mouth resuscitation. Of all the Castaways, however, she is the only one known to lack one very important skill that might ordinarily be considered crucial for someone shipwrecked on an island.

She can't swim.

Sauces

Gilligan Pesto Pasta Sauce

¼ cup olive oil
1 clove garlic, minced
2 tablespoons minced parsley
2 tablespoons grated Parmesan

Salt and pepper to taste
2 tablespoons pine nuts or walnuts, chopped
2 cups fresh basil, chopped

In a food processor or blender combine all of the ingredients. Mix until smooth and well-blended. This may be frozen in balls. Makes about 1 ½ cups.

"

Gilligan gives Mrs. Howell a choice of garden chores:
Gilligan: Dig, plant, water, fertilize, or pick?
Mrs. Howell: Eat.

"

Mary Ann's Machete Spaghetti Sauce

Oil
3 or 4 pounds chopped sirloin tip roast (or chuck or rump)
6 large onions, chopped
6 cloves garlic
1 32-ounce can crushed tomatoes
1 carrot, chopped
4 15-ounce cans tomato sauce
1 6-ounce can tomato paste

2 cups water
1 cup chopped dried mushrooms, soaked well and water reserved
Oregano
Rosemary
Thyme
Basil
1 tablespoon sugar
½ cup butter (when sauce is done)

In a large saucepan heat the oil and cook the meat until brown. Remove the meat and sauté the onions and garlic until tender. Add the remaining ingredients. Return the meat to the pan. Cook slowly for 4 or 5 hours. Season with salt and pepper to taste. Makes about 8 servings.

Gilligan comes across Mary Ann fanning a simmering kettle—and tries to make scents of it all:

Gilligan: That sure isn't paint thinner.

Mary Ann: Unh-unh. It's turtle soup—laced with clam sauce and shrimp.

Gilligan: Smells great. Can I help you fan it.

Mary Ann: Oh, I'm not trying to cool it off.

Gilligan: It sure looks that way.

Mary Ann: Oh, I'm just creating a breeze.

Gilligan: Why?

Mary Ann: Because we don't have a telephone.

Gilligan: Because we don't have a what?

Mary Ann: Gilligan, stand back, please. I can't get my message through.

Gilligan: I've heard of sending messages by drums and flags...but never by waving soup!

Mary Ann: Ah-hah—my message has been received and answered.

Island visitor Alexandri Gregov Dubov comes a-sniffing

Shark Repellant Mustard Sauce

½ cup dry mustard
¼ teaspoon turmeric

¼ cup water
1 tablespoon white wine vinegar

In a small bowl blend the mustard and turmeric. Stir in the water and vinegar until smooth. Serve as sauce for ham or pastrami sandwiches, or with boiled beef or tongue. Makes ½ cup sauce.

Ginger's Sweet Red Pepper Sauce

3 tablespoons olive oil
2 cloves garlic, finely chopped
1 medium onion, sliced
1 tablespoon dried oregano (or 2 tablespoons fresh)

3 red bell peppers, sliced
Salt and pepper to taste
3 tablespoons chopped parsley
2 tablespoons tomato paste
¼ cup water

In a saucepan heat the olive oil and sauté the garlic, onion, oregano, and peppers. Season with salt and pepper to taste. Cover and cook until soft, 10 to 15 minutes. Stir and add the parsley, tomato paste, and water. Cook for about 5 minutes. Makes 4 to 6 servings.

Wizard of Wall Street White Clam Sauce for Linguine

¼ cup corn oil
½ cup chopped onion
3 cloves garlic, minced
½ cup chopped parsley
½ cup dry white wine (or half and half)
2 6 ½-ounce cans minced or chopped clams

½ teaspoon salt
⅛ teaspoon pepper
Dash ground red pepper
1 teaspoon lemon juice
8 ounces linguine, cooked

In a saucepan heat the oil and sauté the onion and garlic for 1 minute, stirring constantly. Add the parsley and wine and cook for 1 minute, stirring constantly. Add the remaining ingredients except the linguine. Simmer for 5 minutes. Toss with linguine. Makes 4 servings.

Dawn Wells collection

Since leaving "Gilligan's Island" I have performed in a variety of plays across the country. One of my favorites was *Same Time Next Year*.

Cannibals Cranberry Salsa

1 6-ounce can orange juice concentrate, thawed
1 cup fresh cranberries, washed and picked
2 bell peppers, chopped (yellow and red)

1 red or yellow chile pepper, chopped and seeded (wear gloves)
1 red onion, chopped
½ cup cilantro or parsley
1 tablespoon cumin seeds

In a blender or food processor chop all of the ingredients together. Makes 3 ½ cups.

Lord Beasley's Blue Cheese Sauce

½ cup butter, melted
¼ cup crumbled blue cheese

1 tablespoon lemon juice
2 tablespoons chopped parsley or chives

In a small bowl mix together the melted butter and blue cheese. Add the lemon juice and parsley. Makes about ¾ cup.

Howell Chow Chow

4 quarts green tomatoes
6 large onions, sliced
2 red bell peppers, thinly sliced (for color)
2 cups firmly-packed brown sugar
1 tablespoon salt

1 tablespoon pepper
1 tablespoon allspice
1 tablespoon Coleman's dry mustard
1 ½ teaspoons cloves
1 pint vinegar (cider or white)

Slice the tomatoes without peeling them. In a kettle layer the tomatoes, onions, and red peppers. In a medium bowl mix together the brown sugar, salt, pepper, allspice, dry mustard, and cloves. Slowly add the vinegar, and stir well. Pour the mixture over the vegetables in the kettle and cook slowly until tender. Seal in sterilized jars while hot. Makes about 8 quarts.

———————— 66 ————————

Gilligan: Mr. Howell, you're not a mean, rotten, scary guy. You're a real nice guy.

Mr. Howell: Well, that's one flaw to an otherwise sterling character. If you dare breathe one word…

Gilligan: I won't.

Mr. Howell: I'll fry you in coconut oil and serve you with an apple in your mouth.

———————— 99 ————————

We all loved playing children in the dream sequence from *Forget Me Not.*

Mamasita Howell's Famous Duck Gravy

½ cup butter
1 12-ounce jar choke-cherry jelly (or currant jelly)
1 5-ounce bottle Worcestershire sauce

In a saucepan melt the butter and jelly over low heat. Add the Worcestershire sauce and simmer very slow. Use on game, chicken, or even pork or hamburgers.

Gilligan's Giblet Gravy

Giblets
Grease and scrapings from turkey roasting pan
¾ cup hot water

All-purpose flour
Cold water
Salt and pepper to taste

In a stock pot boil the giblets in salted water until tender. Use some of the water for basting the turkey, and the remainder for the gravy. Finely chop the giblets. After removing the turkey from the pan, remove some of the grease, scrape the bottom, and add the hot water. In a bowl mix some flour in cold water until smooth, and gradually add the paste into the roasting pan, stirring constantly. Season with salt and pepper, and add the giblets. Cook, stirring constantly, until thick enough and smooth.

Ripe Papaya Life Preserves

Use freshly picked, sound, firm, ripe papaya. Peel and cut in sizeable, uniform pieces. Remove seeds or not, as preferred. Weigh the pieces, and for every pound of papaya add 1 pound of sugar. In a saucepan or stock pot sprinkle the sugar over the fruit and allow it to stand for a few hours or until the sugar is dissolved. If enough liquid is not drawn from the fruit, add water to cover. Bring the papaya to a boil, and boil for 15 minutes or until the fruit is clear and transparent. Cover tightly and let the mixture stand overnight. Bring the papaya mixture again to a boil, and boil until the syrup is thick, stirring often. It is important that the fruit be kept well covered with syrup at all times. Pack the fruit in hot, sterile jars, and cover with hot syrup. Seal at once.

Note: Lime juice or other citrus juices may be added if desired, but many prefer only the mild, distinctive flavor of the papaya. The syrup left from the preserves is golden in color and most delicious in flavor. When heavy and rich it makes a fine accompaniment for ice cream and pudding or a delightful spread for hot cakes and waffles.

Alpha Centauri Cranberry Sauce

4 cups whole cranberries, washed and
  stems removed

1 navel orange, quartered
Approximately 1 ½ cups sugar

In a food processor or food mill grind the cranberries with the orange, rind and all. Add sugar to taste. This is a great relish for Thanksgiving and Christmas. Makes about 8 servings.

🌴 Gilligan's Island Guava Jelly

4 cups guava pulp (thoroughly ripe guava)
3 cups sugar

To prepare the guava pulp, peel the guavas and cover with water. Purée in a blender. In a saucepan mix the pulp and sugar together. Simmer for about 45 minutes or until the mixture thickens to a jelly consistency. Stir occasionally to prevent burning. Pour into hot, sterilized jars. Cool and seal with melted paraffin. Makes about 2 pints.

Nashville Banner

Pay Dirt—Old Prospector (Mr. Howell): "I haven't had a bath in twenty years." Marshal Gilligan: "We know, we know."

A birthday cake take on "Gilligan's Island" for Dawn from fans

🌴 Primitive As Can Be Papaya Butter

3 large ripe papayas
¼ cup lime juice

1 teaspoon grated lime peel
1 ½ cups sugar

Remove the peel and seeds from the papayas and cut into small chunks. In a blender combine part of the papaya and some of the lime juice. Blend until smooth, adding papaya and lime juice a little at a time. Pour the purée into a kettle. Stir in the lime peel and sugar. Bring the mixture to a boil, reduce the heat, and simmer uncovered for about 5 minutes, until thickened to the desired consistency. Cool. Store in the refrigerator for up to 3 weeks or freeze. Makes about 2 pints.

To can: Ladle the hot butter into sterile hot canning jars to within ¼ inch of the top. Wipe the rims. Top with scalded lids and ring bands. Place the jars in the rack in a canning kettle half-filled with hot water. Add more water if needed to cover the jars by 1 inch. Cover the kettle and bring to a simmer. Process for 10 minutes in simmering water. Remove the jars from the water and cool completely. Press the lids; if they stay down, they're sealed.

Coast Guard Curry Sauce

3 tablespoons butter
½ cup minced onion
3 tablespoons all-purpose flour
1 tablespoon curry powder
1 teaspoon salt

½ teaspoon sugar
¼ teaspoon ginger
1 cup coconut milk
1 cup milk
Shrimp, lobster, or crabmeat

In a skillet melt the butter and sauté the onion until tender. Add the flour, curry powder, salt, sugar, and ginger, and blend. Add the coconut and milk slowly to the above mixture and cook over low heat, stirring constantly, until smooth and thickened. Add shrimp, lobster, or crabmeat to the sauce. Makes about 2 ½ cups.

Swing Vote

I was recently filming with the Modernaires, singers for the Glenn Miller Band. They told me that a while back they had been discussing "Gilligan's Island" and debating the appeal of Ginger versus Mary Ann. They would periodically take informal votes among band members, and they would all chuckle and raise their hands to vote for Mary Ann.

Eventually, it got to where they would be on stage and a band member would simply call out, "Mary Ann," and the other band members would raise their hands.

Finally, during their last performance, the bandleader, while thanking the audience, casually slipped in a "Mary Ann," and the whole band's hands went up in unison. The audience responded with wild applause, but never knew why.

Community Hut Corn Sauce

1 cup sour cream
½ teaspoon salt

1 tablespoon fresh lemon juice
1 pimiento, diced

In a small bowl combine the ingredients and chill. Garnish with extra pimiento. Makes 1 cup.

Who needs to be rescued?

The First TV Movie

We had no trouble after twelve years away from the show with beginning again. It was almost as if we stopped on Friday and started again on Monday. It was a wonderful feeling because we really never had the chance to say good-bye when the original series ended. Sherwood Schwartz was terrific, and he got as many of the old crew together as possible to work on the movie. The rescue scene—coming into the marina with thousands of fans cheering us on from the docks—seemed almost real. We all got tears in our eyes. It was a truly wonderful moment.

Desserts

Mary Ann's Birthday Cake

2 ounces sweet chocolate
5 tablespoons boiling water
½ cup butter
1 ½ cups sugar
4 eggs, separated
½ cup milk
1 ¾ cups all-purpose flour, sifted
1 ½ teaspoons baking powder

¼ teaspoon vanilla extract
3 tablespoons unsalted butter
2 cups confectioners' sugar
2 egg yolks, beaten
½ cup black coffee
1 teaspoon vanilla extract
2 cups chopped walnuts

In a small bowl melt the chocolate in the boiling water. In a large bowl cream ½ cup of butter and sugar. Add the 4 egg yolks, milk, and dissolved chocolate. Stir together the flour and baking powder. Beat the egg whites until stiff peaks form. Gently fold the beaten whites and ¼ teaspoon of vanilla into the batter. Pour the batter into 2 layer cake pans. Bake at 350° for 25 to 30 minutes or until the center springs back when touched.

In a medium bowl cream 3 tablespoons of butter and the confectioners' sugar. Beat the remaining egg yolks well, and add them to the creamed mixture. Add the coffee drop by drop, then 1 teaspoon of vanilla and the nuts. Spread some of the frosting on one of the layers, and place the other layer on top. Frost the cake with the remaining frosting. Makes 10 to 12 servings.

"

Ginger: I've got samples of all of my cosmetics including one perfume guaranteed to drive any normal man wild.
Mary Ann: And to think I wasted all my time in Kansas putting honey behind each ear.
Ginger: Honey? Did you attract many boys that way?
Mary Ann: Not many boys but lots of flies.

"

Cleopatra's Chocolate Angel Cake

¾ cup sifted cake flour
¼ cup cocoa
¾ cup sugar
1 ½ cups egg whites
1 ½ teaspoons cream of tartar
¼ teaspoon salt

1 ½ teaspoons vanilla extract
¾ cup sugar
1 cup cream
Confectioners' sugar
1 banana, sliced
Frosting

In a medium bowl sift together the cake flour, cocoa, and ¾ cup of sugar. In a separate bowl beat the egg whites with the cream of tartar, salt, and vanilla until soft peaks form, but are still moist and glossy. Add ¾ cup of sugar, 2 tablespoons at a time, and continue to beat until the meringue holds stiff peaks. Sift about ¼ of the flour mixture over the whites, and gently fold it in. Fold in the remaining flour by fourths. Pour the batter into an ungreased 10-inch tube pan. Bake at 375° for 35 to 40 minutes. Invert the cake onto a rack to cool.

When the cake is cold, split it in half horizontally. Whip the cream with confectioners' sugar to make a spreadable consistency. Spread the mixture on half of the cake and arrange banana slices over it. Put the cake together, and frost with chocolate frosting, whipped cream, or white butter frosting. Makes 12 servings.

--- **``** ---

Ginger: Oh look, Mary Ann, a framed picture of my favorite movie star.
Mary Ann: Really! Who is it?
Ginger: Me.

--- **''** ---

Old Family Recipe Prune Cake

2 tablespoons butter
1 cup sugar
2 eggs
1 teaspoon baking soda
½ cup prune juice
1 ¼ cups all-purpose flour

1 teaspoon nutmeg
1 teaspoon allspice
1 teaspoon cinnamon
2 ounces unsweetened chocolate, melted
1 cup cooked chopped prunes, drained
    and juice reserved

In a large bowl cream the butter and sugar. Add the eggs one at a time. Dissolve the baking soda in the prune juice. In a separate bowl sift the flour with the spices, and add them to the creamed mixture alternately with the prune juice and chocolate. Beat the batter for about 3 minutes, adding the prunes after 2 minutes. Pour the batter into 2 layer cake pans or 1 square pan. Bake at 350° for 25 to 35 minutes.

Frost with confectioners' sugar frosting flavored with a teaspoon of vanilla extract and a dash of salt. Makes 10 to 12 servings.

Mary Ann's Mom's Chocolate Tater Cake

1 18 ¼-ounce package devil's food
  chocolate cake mix
¼ cup sugar
1 cup hot mashed potatoes (no milk,
  salt, or butter added)

1 teaspoon cinnamon
½ teaspoon cloves
½ teaspoon nutmeg
1 cup chopped walnuts

In a large bowl combine the cake mix, and sugar. Prepare the batter according to the package directions. Add the mashed potatoes, mixing until blended. Add the cinnamon, cloves, nutmeg, and walnuts. Pour the batter into an angel cake pan or a round loose-bottom pan. Bake at 350° for the time specified in the cake mix package directions. Makes 8 to 10 servings.

Note: The cake may be frosted with a powdered sugar, butter, milk, and cocoa frosting dribbled or frosted over the cake.

Periscope Persimmon Cake

4 to 6 very soft, ripe persimmons
1 teaspoon baking soda
½ cup butter or margarine
1 cup sugar
1 egg
1 ¾ cups all-purpose flour
2 teaspoons baking powder

1 teaspoon cinnamon
½ teaspoon nutmeg
½ teaspoon cloves
½ cup chopped almonds
1 teaspoon grated orange peel
1 teaspoon grated lemon peel

Scoop out the persimmon pulp and discard the skin, seeds, and stem. Whirl the pulp in a blender until smooth. Measure 1 ¼ cups. In a medium bowl blend together the persimmon purée and soda, and set the mixture aside.

In a large bowl beat the butter and sugar until fluffy. Add the egg and persimmon mixture. In a medium bowl stir together the flour, baking powder, cinnamon, nutmeg, and cloves. Add the dry ingredients to the butter mixture and blend well. Stir in the nuts and grated peels. Spoon the mixture into a greased 9-inch round cake pan. Bake at 350° for 40 minutes or until a wooden pick inserted in the center comes out clean. Cool the cake in the pan for 10 minutes before turning out onto a rack. Makes 6 to 8 servings.

Wrongway Feldman's Pineapple Upside-Down Cake

4 eggs, separated
½ cup butter
1 cup light brown sugar, firmly packed
1 20-ounce can sliced pineapple, drained
½ cup coarsely chopped pecans
16 maraschino cherries, drained and
    halved
1 cup sifted cake flour

1 teaspoon baking powder
¼ teaspoon salt
1 cup sugar
1 tablespoon butter, melted
1 teaspoon almond extract
¾ cup whipping cream
Sugar
Dash vanilla extract

Let the egg whites warm to room temperature, about 1 hour. In a heavy 10-inch skillet, melt ½ cup of butter over very low heat. Remove the pan from the heat. Sprinkle brown sugar over the butter, and arrange pineapple slices over the sugar to cover the bottom of the skillet. Place the pecans and cherries around the pineapple. Set the pan aside.

Sift the flour with the baking powder and salt. In a mixing bowl beat the egg whites with an electric mixer at high speed just until soft peaks form. Add the sugar gradually, beating after each addition until stiff peaks form. In a small bowl beat the egg yolks at high speed until thick and yellow. With a wire whisk or rubber scraper, using an under/over motion, gently fold the flour mixture and egg yolks into the egg whites. Fold in the butter and almond extract. Spread the batter evenly over the pineapple in the skillet. Bake at 375° for 30 to 35 minutes or until the top springs back when gently pressed with fingertips.

Loosen the edges of the cake, and let it stand for 5 minutes. Invert the cake onto a serving plate. Whip the cream with sugar to taste and vanilla until almost stiff. Serve warm with whipped cream. Makes 8 to 10 servings.

——————— 66 ———————

Gilligan: If I was going to spend all morning picking flowers for someone, I'd certainly pick those flowers for someone as sweet and nice as you are.
Mary Ann: Oh, that's an awfully sweet thing to say, Gilligan.
Gilligan: Well, that's an awfully sweet thing of you to think that.
Mary Ann: Not half as sweet as you.
Gilligan: Well, you're twice as sweet as me.

——————— 99 ———————

Coral Chocolate Sponge Cake

1 cup cake flour
½ cup cocoa
6 eggs
½ cup sugar
1 teaspoon vanilla extract
1 cup heavy cream

⅓ cup sour cream
2 tablespoons confectioners' sugar
1 tablespoon vanilla extract
¼ cup crystallized ginger, finely minced

Butter a 9-inch springform or loose-bottom cake pan and dust it with a little flour. In a medium bowl sift together the cake flour and cocoa three times. In the bowl of an electric mixer combine the eggs and sugar and beat at medium speed for 8 to 10 minutes, until thick and tripled in volume. Beat in the vanilla extract. Remove the bowl from the mixer and fold in the flour mixture with a rubber spatula ⅓ at a time, incorporating each addition well. Pour the batter into a prepared pan. Bake on the middle rack of a 350°oven for 20 to 25 minutes, until the cake tests done when a toothpick is inserted in the center. Do not over bake. Loosen the cake from the sides of the pan with a knife and remove the ring. Loosen the bottom with a spatula and slide the cake onto a cooling rack.

In a bowl combine the heavy cream and sour cream, and beat until it starts to thicken. Add the confectioners' sugar and beat again until soft peaks begin to form. Beat in the vanilla extract. Fold in the minced ginger.

When the cake has cooled, slice it horizontally into 2 layers. Spread ginger cream between the layers, then top generously with the remaining ginger cream. Makes 8 to 10 servings.

Sailor's Rum Cake

1 18-ounce package yellow cake mix
1 4-ounce package instant vanilla pudding mix
4 eggs

½ cup dark rum
½ cup cold water
½ cup oil

Grease and flour a tube pan. In a large bowl combine the cake mix, pudding mix, eggs, dark rum, cold water, and oil. Beat with an electric mixer on high speed for 2 minutes. Pour the batter in pans. Bake at 350° for 30 minutes, or until a toothpick inserted in the center comes out clean. Cool the cake on a wire rack for 10 minutes. Makes 10 to 12 servings.

Glaze

¼ cup rum
½ cup powdered sugar
½ teaspoon vanilla extract (warm)

Maraschino cherries
Whipped cream

In a small bowl combine the rum, powdered sugar, and vanilla. Poke holes in the cake and pour the glaze over the top. Decorate with maraschino cherries (and a ring of whipped cream if desired).

Uncharted Cherry Cake

1 package angel food cake mix
1 30-ounce can pitted Bing cherries,
  juice reserved
1 6-ounce package cherry-flavored
  gelatin
½ cup sherry

1 pint vanilla ice cream
Canned slivered almonds, toasted
2 tablespoons currant jelly
1 teaspoon lemon juice
1 cup heavy cream

Early in the day prepare the angel food cake according to the package directions, using a 10-inch tube pan.

Meanwhile, in a saucepan bring the reserved cherry juice to a boil. Stir in the cherry gelatin until dissolved. Remove the pan from the heat and stir in the sherry, then the ice cream until melted. Refrigerate until set.

When the cake has cooled level the top of the cake with a long, sharp knife. Invert the cake and cut a layer off the top of the cake and set it aside. With a fork hollow out the bottom layer of the cake, leaving a shell 1-inch wide at the sides and 1 ½ inches at the bottom.

When the gelatin mixture is set beat it with an electric mixer at medium speed until fluffy and smooth. Stir in ¼ cup of almonds and all but ½ cup of the drained cherries. Spoon the gelatin mixture into the cake shell and replace the reserved top layer. Refrigerate.

In a small saucepan combine the currant jelly and lemon juice. Stir in the remaining cherries until all are just coated. Cool.

In a large bowl whip the cream until stiff. Frost the cake, leaving the hole empty. Arrange almonds on the sides of the cake. Fill the hole with glazed cherries. Refrigerate until serving time. Makes 10 to 12 servings.

Clown Prince Pound Cake

2 cups butter
3 cups sugar
6 large eggs

4 cups all-purpose flour
1 cup milk
2 teaspoons flavoring (your choice)

In a large bowl cream the butter and sugar until light and fluffy. Add the eggs 1 or 2 at a time, beating well after each addition. Add the flour, milk, and flavoring. Pour the batter into a tube pan. Bake at 250° to 275° for 1 hour and 40 minutes. Increase the heat to 350° for the last 20 minutes. Makes 10 to 12 servings.

From Harlem Globetrotter Geese Ausbie.

Fudgy Cave Cake

1 ½ cups butter or margarine, softened
6 eggs
1 ½ cups sugar

2 cups all-purpose flour
3 ⅓ cups double Dutch frosting mix
2 cups chopped walnuts

In a large bowl cream the butter. Add the eggs one at a time, beating well after each addition. Gradually add the sugar, creaming until light and fluffy. Stir in the flour, dry frosting mix, and walnuts by hand until well blended. Turn the batter into a generously greased tube or 12-cup Bundt pan. Bake at 350° for 60 to 65 minutes. Cool the cake for 1 hour. Remove the cake from the pan and cool completely before glazing or serving. Makes 12 servings.

Glaze: Blend the remaining frosting mix and ¼ cup of water. If necessary, add a few drops water to make a glaze consistency. Spoon over the cooled cake. Store the cake under an airtight cover.

Grandma's Shortcake

2 cups sifted all-purpose flour
3 teaspoons baking powder
½ teaspoon salt

8 tablespoons shortening
About ⅔ cup milk

In a medium bowl sift the sifted flour with the baking powder and salt. Work in the shortening until the mixture resembles coarse meal. Add enough milk to make a soft dough. Turn the dough onto a lightly floured board, and knead for a few seconds. Divide the dough in half.

Pat half of the dough into a buttered 9-inch pie pan, and butter the top. Put the remaining half on top. Before baking cut in wedges with knife dipped in hot water and flour. Brush with melted butter. Bake at 450° for about 20 minutes. Pull the layers apart and spread the bottom layer with fruit. Turn the top layer upside down and top with more fruit. Makes 6 to 8 servings.

Note: To make individual shortcakes, roll the dough out ¼-inch thick, and cut circles of 2 sizes, butter the tops of the larger ones, and top with the smaller ones. Bake at 450° for about 15 minutes.

"

Skipper: Everything grows from seeds.

Gilligan: Not everything.

Skipper: Yes, Gilligan, everything. Orange trees grow from orange seeds, apple trees grow from apple seeds, watermelons grow from watermelon seeds.

Gilligan: Yeah, but birds don't grow from birdseeds.

"

Ginger: Oh, I can't believe it. Do I look like I have a vitamin deficiency?
Professor: Ginger, you don't look like you have a deficiency of anything.

Gorgeous Gingerbread and Banana Shortcake

1 14 ½-ounce package gingerbread mix
¼ cup chopped nuts
1 3 ¾-ounce package instant lemon pudding mix

1 ½ cups orange juice
2 medium-size bananas

Grease and flour 2 8-inch square pans. Prepare the gingerbread mix according to the package directions. Pour the batter into the prepared pans. Sprinkle the nuts evenly over the batter in each pan. Bake at 350° for 20 to 25 minutes, or until the cake tests done. Cool the cake for 10 minutes on a wire rack, then remove it from the pans.

In a small bowl combine the pudding mix and orange juice and beat the mixture slowly with a rotary beater for about 1 minute or until blended. Let the sauce mixture stand until thickened. Slice the bananas over 1 gingerbread layer. Spoon enough sauce over the bananas to cover. Top with the remaining cake layer. Serve with the remaining sauce. Makes 6 to 8 servings.

Wait and sea:
Mary Ann: Won't it be wonderful when those sailors pick us up, Ginger?
Ginger: It won't be the first time it's happened to me, Mary Ann.

Gingerbread

½ cup butter or shortening
½ cup sugar
1 egg, well-beaten
2 ½ cups all-purpose flour
½ teaspoon baking soda
1 teaspoon cinnamon

1 teaspoon ginger
½ teaspoon cloves
½ teaspoon salt
1 cup molasses
1 cup hot water
Applesauce or whipped cream

In a large bowl cream the butter. Add the sugar and beaten egg. In a separate bowl measure and sift together the flour, baking soda, cinnamon, ginger, cloves, and salt. Combine the molasses and hot water, and add it to the creamed mixture alternately with the flour mixture. Pour the batter into a greased and floured 13 x 9-inch pan. Bake at 350° for 45 minutes.

Serve warm with applesauce or whipped cream. Makes 12 servings.

What Ever Happened to Ginger?

The rest of the cast gets together a lot, but we have not seen much of Tina. I do see her from time to time, and we always have a pleasant visit. She lives on the East Coast and wasn't involved in the three specials we've done, and fans ask me a lot why she wasn't in them. Tina wanted me to help clear up that question.

She explained, saying that she was a dramatic actress before the comedy of "Gilligan's Island," and now she is again happily involved with her dramatic career. While she enjoyed her three years of "Gilligan's Island," she knows her real passion for acting is drama, and that is what she loves pursuing.

We very rarely get together as an entire cast. One of our happiest memories as an ensemble was when we all attended Tina's wedding in 1966. And we've all done a couple of appearances together in recent years. All of us were on a late-night show on Fox, but we have appeared in various combinations since then on other shows—mostly Bob, Russell, me, and Alan, before his death.

Lovey's Lady Baltimore Cake

6 egg whites (about ¾ cup)
3 ¾ cups sifted cake flour
4 ½ teaspoons baking powder
1 teaspoon salt
2 ¼ cups sugar
1 ¼ cups shortening
2 teaspoons vanilla extract
1 teaspoon almond extract

1 ⅔ cups milk
White Mountain Frosting (see recipe, p. 187)
¾ cup chopped pecans
¾ cup chopped raisins
½ cup finely chopped figs
2 teaspoons grated lemon peel
¼ cup orange juice or brandy

Let the egg whites warm to room temperature, about 1 hour. Grease and lightly flour 3 9-inch layer cake pans.

In a large bowl sift the flour with the baking powder and salt. In a large bowl beat the egg whites with an electric mixer at high speed just until foamy and soft peaks form. Add ¾ cup of sugar, 2 tablespoons at a time, beating after each addition. Continue beating until stiff peaks form.

In large bowl cream the shortening and the remaining 1 ½ cups of sugar with an electric mixer until light and fluffy. Beat in the vanilla and almond extracts at low speed. Beat in the flour mixture (in fourths) alternately with the milk (in thirds) beginning and ending with flour. Beat just until well combined, scraping down the beaters and sides of bowl. At very low speed, gently beat the egg white mixture into the cake batter. There should be no patches of egg white. Turn the batter into the prepared pans and spread evenly. Bake at 350° for 25 to 30 minutes, or just until the surface springs back. Cool on wire racks for 10 minutes.

Prepare White Mountain Frosting (see recipe, p. 187).

In a medium bowl combine the remaining ingredients. Cover the bowl and let the mixture stand overnight. Add the filling mixture to 1 ½ cups of White Mountain Frosting and spread the filling between the layers. Frost the top and sides with the remaining frosting. Makes 12 servings.

Dawn Wells collection

All-American girl

White Mountain Frosting

4 egg whites
1 cup sugar
⅓ cup light corn syrup
½ cup water

¼ teaspoon salt
1 teaspoon vanilla extract
½ teaspoon almond extract

In a large bowl let the egg whites warm to room temperature, about 1 hour. In a small saucepan combine the sugar, corn syrup, and water. Cook over medium heat until the sugar is dissolved. Continue cooking without stirring until the mixture reaches 244° on a candy thermometer, or until a small amount spins a thin thread 6 to 8 inches long when dropped from the tip of a spoon. Just before the mixture reaches the desired temperature, in a large bowl beat the egg whites with salt at medium speed just until soft peaks are formed. Do not over beat. In a thin stream slowly pour the hot syrup over egg whites, beating constantly at high speed. Add the vanilla and almond, beating until stiff peaks form. The frosting should be thick enough to spread and hold its shape. Makes about 5 cups.

Fireworks Celebration Cake

1 prepared 2-layer white cake
Blueberry jam

Raspberry jam

Frost the top of the bottom layer of cake with blueberry jam. Frost the top of the top layer with raspberry jam. On top of that, frost the entire cake with whipped cream and coconut or Seven-Minute Frosting and coconut.

Seven-Minute Frosting

2 egg whites
1 ½ cups sugar
1 tablespoon white corn syrup

⅓ cup water
1 teaspoon vanilla extract

In the top of a double boiler combine the egg whites, sugar, corn syrup, and water. Beat with an electric beater to combine. Cook over rapidly boiling water, beating for 7 minutes, or until stiff peaks form. Remove the pan from the water, and add the vanilla. Beat for about 2 minutes, or until thick enough to spread. Makes 12 servings.

Thurston's Lord Baltimore Cake

3 ¾ cups sifted cake flour
2 ¼ cups sugar
4 ½ teaspoons baking powder
1 teaspoon salt
¾ cup shortening, softened
1 ¾ cups milk
7 egg yolks (about ⅔ cup)
1 tablespoon grated orange peel

White Mountain Frosting (see recipe, p. 187)
¾ cup chopped walnuts
¾ cup chopped maraschino cherries
½ cup crumbled almond macaroons
2 teaspoons grated orange peel
2 tablespoons light corn syrup
2 tablespoons orange juice or sherry

Grease and flour 3 9-inch layer cake pans. In a large bowl sift together the flour with the sugar, baking powder, and salt. Add the shortening and ¼ cup of milk and beat with an electric mixer at low speed. Mix until well blended, then beat for 2 minutes at medium speed.

Add the egg yolks, orange peel, and the remaining 1 ½ cups of milk, and beat for 2 minutes longer. Pour the batter into the prepared pans. Bake at 350° for 25 to 30 minutes, until the surface springs back. Let the cake cool in the pans for 10 minutes, then remove the layers from the pans to a wire rack.

Prepare White Mountain Frosting (see recipe, p. 187).

In a medium bowl combine the remaining ingredients. Cover the bowl and let the mixture stand overnight. Add the filling mixture to 1 ½ cups of White Mountain Frosting and spread the filling between the layers. Frost the top and sides with the remaining frosting. Makes 12 servings.

Howell Sweet He Was

I always remember Jim Backus calling Henny, his wife, every night as he left for home. They once wrote in one of their books, "A good marriage cooks together."

Henny also appeared in the episode of "Gilligan's Island" titled *Gilligan's Mother-in-Law*, where she played a native girl's mother, all decked out in a grass skirt and beads—quite a different sight from the elegant caftans and turbans Henny normally wore. Henny and Jim had a lovely marriage and were so well suited as a couple.

Jim was a wonderful man to work with. He was generous with his comedy and advice on what was funny, which is rather rare with comedians, and he taught me so much. Among my favorite memories are the exit scenes with Thurston and Lovey. At first Jim did all the ad libs. Finally, fighting for survival, Natalie learned how to ad lib, too, and their exits are always a joy to watch.

Blueblood orange blues:
Mr. Howell: An orange, an orange! My kingdom for an orange.
Mrs. Howell: Kingdom? Oh, really, Thurston.
Mr. Howell: Would you believe half of my kingdom?

Mr. Howell's Wall Street Walnut Cake

2 cups cake flour
½ teaspoon salt
2 ½ teaspoons baking powder
½ cup shortening
1 ¼ cups sugar
2 eggs, separated

⅓ cup maraschino cherry juice
⅓ cup milk
1 teaspoon lemon juice
1 5-ounce bottle maraschino cherries
   (chop all but 5)
½ cup chopped walnuts

In a large bowl sift the flour with the salt and baking powder 2 times. In a separate bowl cream the shortening and sugar, and stir in the egg yolks. Add the liquids and dry ingredients alternately to the creamed mixture. Fold in the stiffly beaten egg whites. Divide the batter in half. Toss the chopped cherries in flour and add them to half of the batter. Add the chopped walnuts to the other half. Pour the batter into 2 greased and lightly floured 8-inch pans. Bake at 375° for about 25 minutes.

Frost with Boiled Frosting.

Boiled Frosting

2 cups sugar
¾ cup water
1 tablespoon light corn syrup
Dash salt
2 egg whites, stiffly beaten

1 teaspoon vanilla extract
½ cup candied cherries, chopped
Juice of 1 bottle maraschino cherries

In a saucepan combine the sugar, water, corn syrup, and salt. Cook over low heat until the sugar dissolves. Cover the pan and cook for 2 to 3 minutes to dissolve the crystals on the sides. Uncover and cook to the soft ball stage. Gradually add the hot mixture to the egg whites, beating constantly. Add the vanilla, blending well. Fold in the cherries and the maraschino cherry juice, and beat to a spreadable consistency.

🌴Appealing Banana Cupcakes

2 ¼ cups sifted all-purpose flour
1 ¼ cups sugar
2 ½ teaspoons baking powder
½ teaspoon baking soda
½ teaspoon salt

½ cup soft butter or margarine
1 ½ cups mashed ripe banana (about 4)
2 eggs
1 teaspoon vanilla extract

In a large bowl sift together the flour, sugar, baking powder, baking soda, and salt. Add the butter, banana, eggs, and vanilla, and beat at medium speed for 2 minutes, until the ingredients are blended and the mixture is smooth.

Fill cupcake liners or greased muffin cups ⅔ full. Bake at 375° for 20 minutes, until the cupcake is lightly browned and a toothpick inserted in the center comes out clean. Makes about 24 cupcakes.

— 66 —

Professor: Hello, Skipper. I hear you had dinner with the Howells last night.

Mr. Howell: Yes, a catered chuckwagon affair. All you could eat for $12 million.

— 99 —

Mad Desire Chocolate Cupcakes

3 cups all-purpose flour
2 cups sugar
½ cup cocoa
1 teaspoon salt
2 teaspoons baking soda
⅔ cup oil
2 cups water

2 tablespoons vinegar
2 teaspoons vanilla extract
1 8-ounce package cream cheese
1 egg
⅓ cup sugar
¼ teaspoon salt
1 6-ounce package chocolate chips

In a large bowl mix together the flour, 2 cups of sugar, cocoa, 1 teaspoon of salt, and the baking soda. Add the oil, water, vinegar, and vanilla. Fill cupcake papers ⅔ full of above mixture.

In a separate bowl combine the cream cheese, egg, ⅓ cup of sugar, and ¼ teaspoon of salt, and beat until fluffy. Add the chocolate chips. Drop 1 heaping teaspoon of cream cheese-chocolate chip mixture into each cupcake. Bake at 350° for 25 minutes. Frost when cooled, if desired. Makes about 18 cupcakes.

From Dreama and Bob Denver.

Tongo's Banana Frosting

2 egg whites
¼ teaspoon salt
¼ cup sugar

¾ cup light corn syrup
1 teaspoon vanilla extract
2 bananas, chopped

In a large bowl beat the egg whites with salt until foamy. Gradually add the sugar and continue to beat until the mixture is smooth and glossy. Add corn syrup, a little at a time, and beat until the frosting forms stiff peaks. Fold in the vanilla and bananas. Makes about 3 cups.

———— `` ————

The Skipper, the Professor, and Gilligan search for Mr. Howell.
Skipper: Professor, he must have been here. Look, here's a banana.
Gilligan: That doesn't mean he was here. An ape probably dropped it.
Skipper: Oh, Gilligan, does an ape use a napkin?
Gilligan: If he's neat.

———— '' ————

Captain Kidd's Chocolate Buttercream Frosting

4 ounces semisweet chocolate, coarsely
    chopped
2 tablespoons water
4 eggs

¾ cup sugar
1 cup plus 2 tablespoons unsalted but-
    ter, at room temperature

In a heavy saucepan combine the chocolate and water over low heat (if it gets too hot, the chocolate will separate). Stir constantly until melted and smooth. Remove the pan from the heat and set it aside.

In the top of a double boiler over simmering water combine the eggs and sugar, and beat with an electric mixer on high speed until thick enough to hold soft mounds, about 5 minutes. Remove the bowl from the water and continue beating until the mixture is cool. Beat in the butter 1 tablespoon at a time, blending well. Beat in the chocolate, 1 tablespoon at a time, blending well. Use the frosting or cover and chill for as long as 2 weeks. Let the frosting come to room temperature before using. Makes 4 cups.

The Honey Bees sing "You Need Us"—
Mary Ann: "You need me, you need
me/Like a baby needs a toy/Like an
Hawaiian needs his poi/Like a girl needs a
boy/You need me."

Honeybees Oatmeal Cake

1 cup oatmeal
1 ½ cups hot water
1 cup sugar
1 cup brown sugar
½ cup oil
2 eggs
1 ½ cups all-purpose flour
1 teaspoon baking soda

1 teaspoon cinnamon
Pinch salt
1 cup brown sugar
½ cup butter
1½ cup evaporated milk
Chopped nuts
½ cup coconut

In a medium bowl combine the oatmeal and hot water. In a separate bowl combine the sugar, 1 cup of brown sugar, oil, and eggs. Add the flour, baking soda, cinnamon, and salt, and mix well. Add the oatmeal and water, and mix again. Pour the batter into a 13 x 9-inch cake pan. Bake at 350° for 45 minutes.

In a small saucepan combine 1 cup of brown sugar, the butter, and evaporated milk and bring the mixture to a boil. Boil for 5 minutes. Remove the pan from the heat, and add the nuts and/or coconut. Pour the mixture over the hot cake. Makes 12 servings.

From Dreama and Bob Denver.

Cheery Cherry Cream Cheesecake

1 8-ounce package cream cheese, softened
1 15-ounce can sweetened condensed
  milk

⅓ cup fresh lemon juice
1 teaspoon vanilla extract
1 9-inch graham cracker crumb crust
1 21-ounce can cherry pie filling

Whip the cream cheese until fluffy. Gradually add the milk, continuing to beat until well blended. Add the lemon juice and vanilla, and blend well. Pour the filling into the crust. Chill for 2 to 3 hours. Top with cherry pie filling. Makes 6 servings.

King Kong Banana Cream Pie

1 recipe Mary Ann's Famous Coconut
  Cream Pie (see recipe, p. 217)

3 bananas, sliced
Meringue (see recipe, p. 194)

Follow the recipe for Mary Ann's Famous Coconut Cream Pie, omitting coconut. Slice the bananas in a baked pastry shell, and add the filling. Top with meringue or whipped cream. Makes 6 servings.

Going "ape" over Ginger

Mary Ann's Meringue for Pies

3 egg whites, at room temperature
¼ teaspoon cream of tartar

⅛ teaspoon salt
6 tablespoons sugar

In a mixing bowl beat the egg whites, cream of tartar, and salt with an electric mixer at high speed until frothy. Add the sugar gradually, beating well after each addition. Continue beating until the sugar disappears and the egg whites form stiff peaks. Top the pie with meringue, spreading to the edges of the crust. Bake at 350° for 12 to 15 minutes or until lightly browned. Makes meringue for 1 pie.

————————— **“** —————————

Gilligan: They're gonna break the world kissing record.

Mr. Howell: World kissing record?

Gilligan: Yeah, held by Skinny Mulligan and Florence Oppenheimer—6 hours, 12 minutes, and 13 seconds.

Mr. Howell: How could anyone possibly kiss that long?

Gilligan: Oh, it's easy. They were chewing bubble gum and their braces locked.

————————— **”** —————————

🌴 Gilligan's Island Best Key Lime Pie

4 egg whites, at room temperature
¼ teaspoon cream of tartar
Dash salt
¾ cup sugar
4 egg yolks
½ cup sugar

Dash salt
1 tablespoon grated key lime peel (or lemon)
3 tablespoons lime juice
1 cup whipping cream, whipped (with a little sugar added if wanted)

In a large bowl beat the egg whites, cream of tartar, and salt with an electric mixer until frothy. Gradually add ¾ cup of sugar, beating until the sugar disappears and the egg whites form stiff peaks, about 15 minutes. Spread the meringue in a well-buttered 9-inch pie pan. Spread the sides higher, leaving space for filling. Place the pan in a 450° oven, and turn off the heat. Let the meringue stand in the oven for 5 hours or overnight. Don't peek!

In the top of a double boiler over simmering water beat the egg yolks until thick and lemon-colored. Beat in ½ cup of sugar, salt, lime peel, and lime juice. Cook and stir until thick, about 5 minutes. Cool. Spread half of the whipped cream in the cold pie shell. Top with filling, then the remaining cream. Chill for 5 hours. Makes 8 servings.

Summers Sour Cream Apple (or Pineapple) Pie

2 tablespoons all-purpose flour
½ teaspoon salt
¾ cup sugar
1 egg
1 cup sour cream
1 teaspoon vanilla extract
¼ teaspoon nutmeg

2 cups diced apples (or well-drained pineapple)
1 uncooked 9-inch pie shell
⅓ cup sugar
⅓ cup flour
1 teaspoon cinnamon
¼ cup butter

In a large bowl mix together 2 tablespoons of flour, the salt, and ¾ cup of sugar. Add the egg, sour cream, vanilla, and nutmeg, and beat until smooth. Add the diced apples. Pour the filling into the shell. Bake at 400° for 15 minutes. Reduce the heat to 350° and bake for 30 minutes. Remove the pie from the oven. In a small bowl combine the remaining ingredients, mixing until crumbly. Sprinkle the topping over the pie. Return the pie to the oven and bake at 400° for 10 minutes. Serve with whipped cream. Makes 6 to 8 servings.

Indigo Mob Mocha Cheesecake

1 ¼ cups chocolate wafer cookie crumbs (about 24)
¼ cup sugar
¼ cup margarine, melted
1 8-ounce package cream cheese, softened

1 14-ounce can sweetened condensed milk
⅔ cup chocolate syrup
2 tablespoons instant coffee
1 teaspoon hot water
1 cup whipping cream, whipped

In a medium bowl combine the crumbs, sugar, and margarine. Press the mixture into the bottom and sides of a well-greased springform pan. In a large bowl beat the cheese until fluffy. Add the milk and chocolate syrup. Dissolve the coffee in the water and allow it to cool. Add the coffee to the filling mixture, mixing well. Fold in the whipped cream. Pour into shell. Cover, freeze 6 hours or until firm. Garnish with chocolate crumbs. Makes 6 servings.

 Double-Vision Banana Cream Pie

7 or 8 bananas, thinly sliced
2 tablespoons lemon juice
½ cup sugar
2 tablespoons all-purpose flour
½ teaspoon cinnamon

Pastry for 1 9-inch 2-crust pie
2 tablespoons butter
Nutmeg
Rum Sauce (below)
Lemon Sauce (below)

In a large bowl sprinkle the bananas with lemon juice. In a separate bowl mix the sugar with the flour and cinnamon. Carefully mix the sugar mixture with the bananas.

Line a 9-inch pie pan with half of the pastry. Fill with the banana filling. Dot the filling with butter and sprinkle lightly with nutmeg. Fit the top crust over the fruit, and seal the edges. Cut several slits in the top. Bake at 425° for 30 to 35 minutes or until brown. Serve warm or cool with Rum or Lemon Sauce. Makes 6 servings.

Rum Sauce

2 egg yolks
1 cup confectioners' sugar
6 tablespoons rum

1 teaspoon vanilla extract
1 cup whipping cream, whipped

Beat the egg yolks and add sugar, beating constantly. Slowly beat in the rum and vanilla until well blended. Fold in the whipped cream.

Lemon Sauce

3 tablespoons cornstarch
½ cup sugar
¼ teaspoon salt
2 cups water

⅓ cup butter
1 tablespoon lemon peel
3 tablespoons lemon juice

In a saucepan combine the cornstarch, sugar, and salt. Gradually stir in the water and butter, and bring the mixture to a boil. Stir constantly until the mixture thickens and clears. Stir in the lemon peel and juice.

Here's Mud in Our Eye

Tina and I had to do a mud bath as part of a scene. We weren't too eager to get dirty, but the prop men, who were always so creative and kind, were dear about keeping Tina and me as clean and comfortable as possible. The mud was sterile—made with clean dirt and hot water. I always get tickled thinking about the irony of that "clean dirt."

Mud Bog Pie

24 chocolate wafers, crushed
2 tablespoons butter or margarine, melted
1 ½ cups cold milk
1 envelope unflavored gelatin
½ cup sugar
⅛ teaspoon salt

4 eggs, separated
1 ½ ounces unsweetened chocolate, melted
1 teaspoon vanilla extract
1 tablespoon rum
½ cup heavy cream, whipped

In a medium bowl combine the chocolate wafers and melted butter. Pat the crumb mixture into a 9-inch pie pan. Bake at 350° for 8 to 10 minutes. Set aside.

Pour the milk into a saucepan and sprinkle in the gelatin. Allow the gelatin to soften for about 3 minutes. Stir in the sugar, salt, and egg yolks, and beat until blended thoroughly. Cook over moderate heat, stirring until thickened. Do not let the mixture boil. Remove the pan from the heat and divide the mixture in half. Add the melted chocolate and vanilla to one half, and the rum to the other half. Chill until the mixtures mound when dropped from a spoon.

Beat the egg whites until stiff but not dry. Divide the beaten whites in half. Fold half into the chocolate mixture, and the other half into the rum mixture. Spread the chocolate mixture over the crumb crust, then spread the rum mixture over the chocolate mixture. Spread the whipped cream over all. Refrigerate until ready to serve. Makes 6 servings.

Dawn Wells collection

Here I've just come back from a dip in the mud bath scene in the episode titled *High Man on the Totem Pole.*

Professor's Pecan Pie

3 eggs
½ cup light brown sugar
1 cup dark corn syrup
½ teaspoon salt

1 teaspoon vanilla extract
¼ cup melted butter
1 cup pecan halves
1 unbaked 9-inch pie shell

In a large bowl beat the eggs well. Add the sugar, syrup, salt, and vanilla. Beat until well blended. Stir in the butter and pecans. Pour the filling into the pie shell. Bake at 375° for 45 to 50 minutes, until the filling is set in the center when gently shaken. Makes 6 servings.

———— **"** ————

Mary Ann and Ginger hope to distract the Professor:
Mary Ann: You think you can handle it?
Ginger: Oh, believe me, for this kind of fishing, I've got the right kind of bait.

———— **"** ————

Rudder Peanut Butter Pie

½ cup crunchy peanut butter
1 cup confectioners' sugar
1 baked 9-inch pie shell
1 3-ounce package custard mix (or 2

cups homemade)
2 cups milk
1 cup whipping cream, whipped

In a large bowl mix the peanut butter and sugar until crumbly. Reserve ¼ cup to sprinkle on top of the pie. Sprinkle the remaining peanut butter mixture into the baked pie shell. Prepare the custard filling with the milk according to the package directions. Pour the filling into the shell. Chill until set.

Spread the cream on top of pie. Sprinkle with the reserved peanut butter mixture. Serve chilled. Makes 1 9-inch pie.

Easy Breezy Pumpkin Pie

1 16-ounce can pumpkin
1 14-ounce can sweetened condensed
  milk
2 eggs
1 teaspoon cinnamon
½ teaspoon salt

½ teaspoon ginger
½ teaspoon nutmeg
1 9-inch graham cracker crust
1 cup whipping cream
½ cup nuts

In a large bowl combine the pumpkin, milk, eggs, cinnamon, salt, ginger, and nutmeg. Mix well, and pour the filling into the shell. Bake at 425° for 15 minutes. Reduce the heat to 350° and bake for 25 to 30 minutes more, or until a silver knife inserted 1-inch from the edge comes out clean. Cool. Garnish with whipped cream and nuts. Refrigerate any leftovers. Makes 6 servings.

—————— **"** ——————

Mr. Howell: How can a skinny kid like you hold so much?
Gilligan: I don't know, Mr. Howell—not until I have dessert. Oh, Mr. Howell, Mary Ann's cooking my favorite—coconut, papaya, and tuna fish pie. Come on, Mr. Howell—especially when it's hot.
Mr. Howell: I feel like a beached whale.

—————— **"** ——————

Gilligan Screams for Ice Cream Pie

⅔ cup coconut bar cookie crumbs
2 tablespoons melted butter
16 coconut bar cookies
½ cup broken pecans

½ cup caramel ice cream topping
3 pints vanilla ice cream, softened
1 8 ¼-ounce can crushed pineapple,
  drained

In a small bowl combine the cookie crumbs and butter. Press the mixture evenly over the bottom of a buttered 9-inch pie plate. Stand whole cookies upright around the edge, trimming the cookies if too long. Chill. In a separate bowl combine the pecans and ice cream topping. Chill.

Spoon 1 pint of ice cream into the cookie shell. Top with ½ of the sauce and ½ of the crushed pineapple. Add an additional pint of ice cream, then the remaining sauce and pineapple. Top with the remaining ice cream. Freeze until serving time. Makes 6 servings.

Geiger Counter Berry Glacé

3 pints (about 6 cups) strawberries
1 cup sugar
2 ½ tablespoons cornstarch
½ cup water
1 tablespoon butter or margarine

2 tablespoons Cointreau or orange juice
1 9-inch baked pie shell, cold
Whipped cream
2 tablespoons confectioners' sugar

Wash the strawberries gently in cold water. Drain and hull. In a medium pan crush 2 cups of strawberries with a potato masher. In a small bowl combine the sugar and cornstarch, and stir the mixture into the crushed strawberries. Add the water. Over low heat bring the mixture to a boil, stirring constantly (it will burn easily). Cook until the mixture is thick and translucent. Strain, add the butter, and cool.

Measure 3 cups of strawberries and toss them with Cointreau or orange juice. Let the berries stand for 30 minutes. Arrange the berries in the pie shell. Pour the cooled glaze over the strawberries in the crust. Refrigerate the pie for 2 hours or so. Beat the whipped cream with the confectioners' sugar. Garnish the pie with the whipped cream and reserved strawberries. Makes 6 servings.

Variation: For Devonshire Glacé Pie, combine 3 ounces of softened cream cheese with 1 tablespoon of light cream. Spread the mixture over the bottom of the pie shell before adding the whole strawberries.

Gotcha! Japanese sailor (Vito Scotti) gets the drop on Gilligan.

Professor's Chess Pie

½ cup butter
1 teaspoon vanilla extract
1 cup sugar
1 egg white
3 egg yolks, beaten

1 cup chopped raisins
1 cup chopped nuts
1 unbaked 9-inch pastry shell or 10
  unbaked tart shells
Whipped cream

In a medium bowl cream the butter and vanilla. Gradually beat in the sugar until light and fluffy. Beat the egg white until stiff, and fold it into the egg yolks. Add the egg white mixture to the creamed mixture and blend well. Add the raisins and nuts. Pour the filling into the shell. Bake at 400° for 25 minutes. Serve topped with whipped cream. Makes 6 slices or 10 tarts.

──────── 66 ────────

Fruit of the loons:

Ginger: Blueberries for breakfast.

Mary Ann: I picked some blackberries too.

Skipper: Well, you're just in time. I was about to give Gilligan the raspberry

──────── 99 ────────

Popeye's Papaya Pie

½ cup sugar
1 ½ cups chopped ripe papaya
1 tablespoon unflavored gelatin
¼ cup cold water
½ cup boiling water
1 tablespoon lemon juice

Dash salt
1 cup heavy cream
1 baked 9-inch pie shell
1 tablespoon sugar
Mandarin orange sections
Mint leaves

In a medium bowl stir ½ cup of sugar into the papaya and let the mixture stand until the sugar is dissolved. Soften the gelatin in cold water, then dissolve in the boiling water. Cool. Add the papaya mixture, lemon juice, and salt. Chill until partially set.

Whip ½ cup of the cream and fold it into the gelatin mixture. Pour the filling into the pie shell and chill thoroughly.

Whip the remaining cream with 1 tablespoon of sugar and spread the mixture over the pie. Decorate with orange sections and mint leaves. Makes 6 servings.

Rolls Royce Raisin Pudding

2 cups milk
2 cups stale bread crumbs
½ cup brown sugar, firmly packed
¼ teaspoon salt
2 tablespoons butter or margarine, melted

1 teaspoon vanilla extract
2 egg yolks, beaten
2 cups seedless raisins
2 egg whites
¼ cup jelly

In a medium bowl pour the milk over the bread. Add ¼ cup of brown sugar, the salt, butter, vanilla, egg yolks, and raisins. Spread the mixture into a well-greased 8-inch square baking pan. Set the pan in a larger pan of hot water. Bake at 350° for 50 minutes.

In a separate bowl beat the egg whites until stiff. Add the remaining brown sugar gradually, beating constantly. Spread ⅓ of the meringue over the pudding. Break the jelly into small pieces with a fork. Carefully spread the jelly over the meringue. Heap the remaining meringue over the jelly. Return the pie to the oven for 15 minutes to brown the meringue. Makes 6 servings.

————————— " —————————

Ginger: You were right, Mary Ann. You have to feed a growing bird just like you would a baby.
Mary Ann: Well, when he finishes you can figure out how to burp him.

————————— " —————————

Redwood Rice Pudding

½ cup raw rice
3 cups milk
2 cardamom seeds
½ cup slivered almonds

½ cup pistachio halves
½ cup sugar or to taste
1 cup evaporated milk

In a small bowl soak the rice in 1 cup of milk for at least 2 hours. In a blender or food mill grind the rice well with the cardamom seeds. Bring the remaining 2 cups of milk to a soft boil and gradually stir in the rice mixture. Cook until thickened, about 8 to 10 minutes, stirring constantly.

Stir in the almonds, pistachios, sugar, and evaporated milk, and cook for 3 more minutes. Pour the pudding into individual serving dishes and sprinkle with more nuts, if desired. Cover and chill until serving time. Makes about 8 servings.

Grandma's Carrot Pudding

1 cup grated raw potatoes
1 teaspoon baking soda
1 cup grated raw carrots
1 cup all-purpose flour
1 cup sugar
1 scant cup suet
1 ½ cups currants and raisins
Pinch salt

½ teaspoon baking powder
1 teaspoon cinnamon
1 teaspoon nutmeg
½ teaspoon cloves
½ cup butter
2 cups confectioners' sugar
1 teaspoon vanilla extract
Bourbon or rum

In a large bowl combine the potatoes and baking soda. Add the carrots, flour, sugar, suet, currants and raisins, salt, baking powder, cinnamon, nutmeg, and cloves. Pack the mixture into greased pudding molds or small coffee cans. Place the molds in a large pan and add boiling water to the pan. Cover the pan and steam for 3 hours.

In a medium bowl cream the butter with the confectioners' sugar. Add the extract and bourbon, and beat until smooth. Serve the hard sauce with the pudding. Serves 8 to 10.

South Pacific Pineapple Pudding

3 ½ cups canned pineapple juice
3 envelopes unflavored gelatin
6 tablespoons sugar
⅛ teaspoon salt
2 teaspoons grated lemon rind
¼ cup lemon juice

1 ½ cups heavy cream
1 ½ cups flake coconut
4 cups halved fresh strawberries, (or 2
    10-ounce packages frozen, thawed)
4 canned pineapple slices, quartered

The day before, or early on the day: In a small bowl stir the gelatin into 1 cup of the pineapple juice. Add the sugar, and stir to dissolve. Let the mixture stand for 5 minutes. Set the bowl in boiling water, and stir until the gelatin is dissolved.

In a large bowl combine 2 ½ cups of pineapple juice, the salt, lemon rind, and lemon juice; then stir in the gelatin mixture. Refrigerate until the consistency of unbeaten egg white.

Beat the gelatin mixture with an electric mixer at high speed until fluffy. Whip the cream. Quickly fold the cream and ¼ cup of coconut into the gelatin. Pour the mixture into a 2-quart mold and refrigerate until set.

Just before serving unmold the pudding onto a large serving dish. Sprinkle the top with some coconut and strawberries. Arrange some quartered pineapple, strawberries, and the remaining coconut around the base. Pass the remaining pineapple and strawberries. Makes 8 servings.

Mary Ann's Favorite Butterscotch Tapioca Pudding

3 cups milk
1 cup brown sugar
¼ teaspoon salt
¼ cup tapioca (quick-cooking)
1 egg, beaten

1 tablespoon butter
¾ cup chopped dates
¼ teaspoon vanilla extract
¼ teaspoon orange extract

In the top of a double boiler over simmering water scald the milk. Add the sugar and salt, and heat until dissolved. Add the tapioca and cook until clear, stirring frequently. Pour some of the hot mixture into the egg, and return the egg mixture to the double boiler. Cook for 3 minutes. Remove the pan from the heat and add the butter, dates, and flavorings. Chill. Serve with custard sauce or whipped cream. Makes 8 servings.

———————— " ————————

Gilligan: I guess being married is O.K. for married people, but I'm single people.

———————— " ————————

Amalgamated Almond Pudding

½ pound blanched almonds
16 individual square saltine crackers
6 eggs
1 cup sugar
½ teaspoon nutmeg

1 teaspoon grated lemon peel
Confectioners' sugar
About 2 cups sliced strawberries or peaches sweetened to taste

Finely chop ⅓ cup of the almonds, and set them aside. Whirl the remaining almonds and crackers in a blender until very finely ground (almost to a powder). Separate 3 of the eggs. In a large bowl beat the 3 egg yolks with the remaining 3 whole eggs until frothy. Add the sugar gradually, beating until light and lemon-colored. Stir in the chopped and ground almonds, crumbs, nutmeg, and lemon peel. Beat the egg whites until distinct peaks form. Fold the whites into the almond mixture. Spoon the pudding into a well-greased and floured ring mold or other tube pan (6 ½ to 8-cup size). Bake at 275° for 1 hour and 10 minutes or until a wooden pick inserted in the center comes out clean.

Cool the pudding in the pan for 15 minutes. Turn out to cool completely. Dust with confectioners' sugar and serve with fruit. Makes 8 servings.

Twenty Trunk Chocolate Trifle

1 layer chocolate cake
¼ cup rum
½ cup cherry preserves (may use other preserves)

½ cup Custard Sauce (see below)
1 cup whipped cream
¼ cup toasted almonds

Cut the chocolate cake into ½-inch thick pieces. Put half of the cake pieces in a single layer in a dish. Add in order half of the rum, cherry preserves, and Custard Sauce (see below). Repeat the layers. Chill the trifle for 4 hours or overnight. Cover with the whipped cream and toasted almonds.

Custard Sauce

¼ cup cocoa
⅔ cup sugar
⅛ teaspoon salt

3 eggs
2 cups milk

In the top of a double boiler mix the cocoa, sugar, and salt. Beat in the eggs. Gradually stir in the milk. Stir constantly over simmering water for 15 minutes. Cool before using in the trifle. Makes 8 to 10 servings.

Java Gelatin

1 envelope unflavored gelatin
2 cups water
1 tablespoon instant coffee

¼ cup sugar
Whipped cream or packaged dessert topping

In a bowl soften the gelatin in ¼ cup of cold water. Bring the remaining 1 ¾ cups of water to a boil and stir in the coffee and sugar. Remove the mixture from the heat and add the softened gelatin, stirring until dissolved. Pour the pudding into a 1-pint mold and chill until set. Serve with whipped cream or dessert topping. Or mix with cream after partly set. Makes 4 to 6 servings.

Tiny Ship Chocolate Chip Cookies

⅛ teaspoon salt
2 egg whites
½ cup sugar
½ teaspoon vinegar

½ teaspoon vanilla extract
½ cup flaked coconut
¼ cup chopped walnuts
1 cup chocolate chips, melted

Add the salt to egg whites, and beat until foamy. Add sugar gradually, beating well each time. Continue beating until stiff peaks form. Add the vinegar and vanilla, and beat well. Fold in the coconut, walnuts, and melted chips. Drop by teaspoons onto a greased baking sheet. Bake at 350° for 10 minutes. Makes 2 ½ to 3 dozen.

Professor's Calculated Squares

½ cup shortening

1 cup sugar

2 eggs

½ teaspoon salt

½ teaspoon vanilla extract

1 ½ cups cake flour

1 teaspoon baking powder

1 cup brown sugar

1 beaten egg white

Chopped walnuts

In a large bowl cream together the shortening and sugar. Add the eggs, salt, vanilla, flour, and baking powder. Spread the batter thinly on a greased sheet. In a separate bowl combine the brown sugar and egg white. Spread over the batter. Sprinkle with chopped walnuts. Bake at 325° for 30 minutes. Cut in squares. Makes 12 bars.

Rescue from Gilligan's Island—"The smiles are on our faces because we know that after so many years marooned on the island, we are about to be rescued—at least temporarily."

Ginger Snaps

1 ½ cups sifted all-purpose flour

½ teaspoon baking soda

½ cup unsalted butter

¾ cup sugar

1 lightly beaten egg

1 tablespoon lemon juice

½ cup finely chopped candied ginger

In a medium bowl sift together the flour and baking soda. In a separate bowl beat the butter and sugar with an electric mixer for 4 to 5 minutes, until fluffy. Add the egg, and slowly beat for 3 to 4 minutes at very low speed. Gradually add the flour, then the lemon juice and ginger. Drop by teaspoonfuls onto a greased cookie sheet 1 ½ inches apart. Bake at 375° for 13 to 15 minutes, until golden. Cool on a rack. Makes 60 to 70 cookies.

Ginger's Star Sugar Cookies

½ cup butter
¾ cup sugar
1 egg or 2 yolks
½ teaspoon vanilla extract

1 tablespoon cream
1 ¼ cups all-purpose flour
¼ teaspoon salt
¼ teaspoon baking powder

In a large bowl cream the butter until light and fluffy. Beat in the sugar. Add the egg and vanilla, and beat thoroughly. Add the cream. Sift together the flour, salt, and baking powder. Stir the dry ingredients into the butter mixture and blend well. Drop by teaspoonfuls onto a greased cookie sheet 1 inch apart. Bake at 350° for about 8 minutes. Makes 50 to 60 cookies.

Variations: For Almond Cookies, add ⅓ cup blanched, finely chopped almonds and ½ teaspoon each of cinnamon, cloves, and nutmeg, and the grated rind of 1 lemon.

For Butterscotch Cookies, use brown sugar instead of white. In a saucepan melt the butter, add the sugar, and heat slowly until well blended. Continue as directed, and add ¼ cup of chopped black walnuts.

For Lemon-Sugar Cookies, omit the vanilla, and add ½ teaspoon of lemon extract and 2 teaspoons of grated lemon rind.

For Seedcakes, add 1 ½ tablespoons of caraway seeds.

 # Ginger's Spice Scones

3 cups all-purpose flour
⅓ cup sugar
2 ½ teaspoons baking powder
½ teaspoon salt
¾ cup butter or margarine
1 8-ounce can crushed pineapple in juice

Light cream or milk
3 tablespoons chopped macadamia nuts
   or almonds
1 tablespoon sugar
½ teaspoon cinnamon

In mixing bowl stir together flour, ⅓ cup of sugar, baking powder, and salt. Cut in the butter or margarine until the mixture resembles coarse crumbs. Make a well in the center and add the undrained pineapple, stirring until the dry ingredients are just moistened (the dough will be sticky). On a lightly floured surface knead gently for 10 to 12 strokes. Roll the dough to ¼-inch thickness. Cut with a floured 2 ½-inch biscuit cutter and place on an ungreased baking sheet. Brush the tops with cream or milk. For the topping, combine the nuts, 1 tablespoon of sugar, and cinnamon. Sprinkle about 1 teaspoon of the mixture over each scone. Bake at 425° for 15 minutes. Serve warm. Makes 21.

Peanut Butter Putters

¼ cup chunk-style peanut butter
¾ cup packed brown sugar
2 ¼ teaspoons corn syrup
2 ¼ teaspoons hot water
1 cup butter or margarine
¾ cup sugar

1 egg
1 teaspoon vanilla extract
2 ½ cups all-purpose flour, unsifted
½ teaspoon baking powder
½ teaspoon salt

Stir together the peanut butter, brown sugar, corn syrup, and water to make a thick paste. Cover and refrigerate. In a mixer bowl, beat the butter and sugar until well blended. Beat in the egg and vanilla. In a separate bowl stir together the flour, baking powder, and salt. Stir the dry ingredients into the butter mixture. Cover and chill for 2 hours.

Form the dough into 1-inch balls. Place about 2 inches apart on a greased baking sheet, and make a depression in the center of each ball. Bake at 400° for 6 minutes. Remove the cookies from the oven and place about ½ teaspoon of the peanut butter mixture in each depression. Continue baking until the topping is bubbly, about 5 minutes longer. Cool. Makes about 4 dozen cookies.

———————— **"** ————————

Professor prepares an anti-vampire potion:
Professor: Believe me, Gilligan. If you're a vampire, this potion will cure you.
Gilligan: Don't I get a cookie with it?

———————— **"** ————————

Pineapple Knockout Drop Cookies

1 cup light brown sugar
½ cup shortening and butter
1 unbeaten egg
1 teaspoon vanilla extract
¾ cup crushed pineapple
2 cups sifted all-purpose flour

1 teaspoon baking powder
½ teaspoon salt
½ teaspoon baking soda
½ cup raisins
¾ cup chopped walnuts

In a large bowl blend together the sugar, shortening, egg, and vanilla. Drain and add the pineapple. In a separate bowl sift together the flour, baking powder, salt, and baking soda. Stir the dry ingredients into the pineapple mixture. Add the raisins and walnuts. Drop by teaspoonfuls onto an ungreased cookie sheet. Bake at 375° for 12 minutes, until lightly browned. Makes 3 dozen.

Single Luxury Brownies

⅓ cup shortening
⅓ cup sugar
2 eggs, well-beaten
⅓ cup molasses

½ teaspoon vanilla extract
1 cup all-purpose flour
¼ teaspoon salt
1 cup chopped nuts

In a medium bowl cream the shortening and sugar. Add the eggs, molasses, vanilla, flour, salt, and nuts. Turn the batter into an 8-inch pan. Bake at 350° for about 30 minutes. Cut in squares. Makes about 9 squares.

Marooned Macaroons

⅔ cup sweetened condensed milk
1 cup coarsely chopped nuts
2 cups shredded coconut

1 teaspoon vanilla extract
¼ teaspoon almond extract

In a medium bowl mix together the milk, nuts, coconut, and flavorings. Drop by tablespoons onto a well-greased baking sheet 1 inch apart. Bake at 350° for 10 to 12 minutes, until dry around the edges. Remove the macaroons from the baking sheet immediately. Makes about 2 dozen.

Trivia Quiz

The Howells' Harvard Club Challenge

1. How many times do cosmonauts Ivan and Igor orbit the earth?
   679

2. Which three Castaways voted for Gilligan for President?
   Mary Ann, Mrs. Howell, and Gilligan

3. What was in the treasure chest that Gilligan dug up?
   Cannonballs

4. What is the mobster parrot's name?
   Sam

5. To whom back home does Mary Ann send notes in a bottle?
   Horace Higgenbotham

Chocolate-Banana Charms

¾ cup shortening
1 cup sugar
1 egg
1 teaspoon banana flavoring
2 cups sifted all-purpose flour
1 ½ teaspoons cinnamon

1 teaspoon baking soda
½ teaspoon salt
½ cup cocoa
1 cup mashed bananas
1 cup raisins
1 ½ cups chopped walnuts

In a large bowl cream together the shortening and sugar. Beat in the egg and flavoring. In a separate bowl combine the flour, cinnamon, soda, salt, and cocoa. Add the dry ingredients to the creamed mixture alternately with the mashed bananas. Stir in the raisins and walnuts. Drop by teaspoons on greased cookie sheet. Bake at 375° for 10 minutes. Makes 30 cookies.

Mr. Howell makes a hostile takeover.

Mr. Howell's Gold Bars

⅓ cup butter
1 cup brown sugar
1 egg
¾ cup sifted cake flour

1 teaspoon baking powder
¼ teaspoon salt
½ teaspoon vanilla extract
½ cup nuts and/or coconut (optional)

In a medium bowl combine all of the ingredients. Spread in a buttered 8 x 8-inch pan. Bake at 275° for 25 minutes. Cut in squares while warm. Makes 9 bars.

Mary Ann's Winfield Brownie Troops

¾ cup self-rising cornmeal
1 cup light brown sugar (firmly packed)
1 3 ½-ounce can flaked coconut
3 eggs

2 tablespoons melted butter
1 cup sour cream
1 6-ounce package chocolate chips
Confectioners' sugar

In a large bowl combine the cornmeal, brown sugar, and coconut. In a separate bowl beat the eggs, and mix with the melted butter. Stir in ½ cup of sour cream, and beat until smooth. Add the egg mixture all at once to the cornmeal mixture. Pour the batter into a 12 x 7 ½-inch baking dish. Sprinkle half of the chocolate chips over the batter. Bake at 350° for 25 to 30 minutes, until brown around the edges. Cool on a rack.

Mix the remaining chocolate chips, ½ cup of sour cream, and confectioners' sugar to make a frosting. Frost and cut into bars. Makes 20 bars.

Chocolate Manny Mousse

¾ cup half and half
6 ounces semisweet chocolate bits
2 eggs

2 tablespoons strong coffee
2 tablespoons Grand Marnier

Scald the half and half. In a blender combine the remaining ingredients, and pour the half and half into the blender. Cover and mix for 1 minute. Pour the mousse into 4 dessert glasses. Chill for several hours. Makes 4 servings.
From Natalie Schafer.

Semaphore Cinnamon Ice Cream

1 cinnamon stick
3 cups milk

1 cup sugar
1 cup heavy cream

Break the cinnamon stick into small pieces, and grind it to a powder. In a saucepan heat the milk. Add 1 teaspoon of the cinnamon and the sugar, and bring the mixture to a boil. Cool for 15 minutes. Add the cream. Pour the mixture into a freezer and prepare according to the manufacturer's directions. Makes 6 to 8 servings.

Gilligan: I wish I had a gallon of vanilla ice cream.
Mr. Howell: It isn't even raining vanilla, strawberry, or tutti-fruiti.

Lovey's Vanilla Ice Cream

3 eggs, separated
3 cups half and half
¾ cup sugar

1 tablespoon vanilla extract
¼ teaspoon salt
2 cups whipping cream

In the top of a double boiler combine the egg yolks, half and half, and sugar. Cook until the consistency of a soft custard that will coat a metal spoon. In a large bowl beat the egg whites until stiff, and slowly pour the custard into the whites. Add the vanilla and salt, blending well. In a separate bowl beat the whipping cream until thick. Fold the whipped cream into the custard. Refrigerate until chilled. Pour the mixture into a freezer and prepare according to the manufacturer's directions. Makes 10 to 12 servings.

The Tennessean

Ice cream fanatic

🌴 Rango Rango Mango Ice Cream

2 cups milk
2 cups mango pulp
Fresh lemon juice
¼ cup sugar
8 eggs

2 cups sugar
2 14-ounce cans sweetened condensed
   milk
Pinch salt
½ pint whipping cream

In the top of a double boiler over simmering water scald the milk. In a medium bowl blend together the mango pulp, lemon juice, and ¼ cup of sugar. In a mixing bowl beat the eggs with an electric mixer. Add 2 cups of sugar and beat until blended. Beat in the scalded milk, condensed milk, salt, mango mixture, and whipping cream. Pour into a 4-quart freezer and prepare according to the manufacturer's directions. Makes about 4 quarts.

Variation: For mango-pineapple ice cream use ½ cup of mango pulp and 1 cup of crushed pineapple.

Ice Cream Diet

Natalie's favorite thing was ice cream. Several times over the years, we went on her ice cream diet: two, two, two, and one. Two scoops for breakfast, two scoops for lunch, two scoops for dinner; and one scoop in between. We'd shop for flavors each day, and in a week we actually lost five pounds. It was about 900 calories a day—and what fun.

Natalie's favorite ice cream parlor, Baskin-Robbins, gave her a silver bowl full of ice cream for a public relations event. Natalie promptly made it into a bed for her little dog, Lovey. She had a little down pillow made, and from that day on Lovey slept on the pillow in the sterling silver "ice cream" bowl.

Thurston's Denver Mint Ice Cream

2 cups milk
¾ cup sugar
1 cup minced fresh mint leaves

2 large eggs
1 cup whipping cream
1 teaspoon vanilla extract

In a saucepan over medium heat stir the milk, sugar, and mint together until the mixture just comes to a boil. Remove the pan from the heat. In a medium bowl beat the eggs and cream. Whisk the beaten mixture slowly into the hot milk. Add the vanilla. Cover and chill for 2 hours or overnight. Strain the mixture into a freezer and prepare according to the manufacturer's directions. Makes 1 quart.

Ginger's Top Billing

1 cup heavy cream
⅓ cup sour cream
2 tablespoons confectioners' sugar

1 teaspoon vanilla extract
¼ cup crystallized ginger, finely minced

In a medium bowl combine the heavy cream and sour cream, and beat until the mixture starts to thicken. Add the confectioners' sugar, vanilla, and ginger, and beat until soft peaks form. Serve on warm waffles, cake, pudding, etc. Makes about 2 cups.

Operation Orchid Orange Dessert

4 oranges
1 cup ricotta or creamed cottage cheese
1 tablespoon sugar

1 teaspoon orange liqueur
Cinnamon

Cut a slice from top of each orange, then cut off the peel in strips from top to bottom, cutting deep enough to remove the white membrane. Or remove the peel in spiral fashion. Go over the fruit again to remove the remaining white membrane. Cut into crosswise slices.

In a small bowl mix the ricotta, sugar, and liqueur. To serve, arrange the orange slices on a platter and top with the ricotta mixture. Sprinkle with cinnamon. Makes 4 servings.

Gold Bullion Bananas Foster

2 tablespoons butter
3 tablespoons brown sugar
1 large ripe banana, peeled and sliced
   lengthwise
1 tablespoon lemon juice

⅛ tablespoon cinnamon
2 tablespoons banana liqueur
2 ounces white rum
Vanilla ice cream

In a skillet melt the butter and brown sugar. Sauté the banana in sugar and butter until tender. Sprinkle with lemon juice and dust with cinnamon. Add the banana liqueur and rum and flambé, basting until the flame dies. Spoon over vanilla ice cream. Makes 2 servings.

Professor's Apples Archimedes

6 to 8 tart apples (Granny Smith or
Pippin), peeled and sliced
Juice of ½ lemon
3 tablespoons dark brown sugar
1 tablespoon cinnamon
1 cup raisins

Hot water
2 cups any bran cereal or shredded
wheat
½ cup butter, melted
½ cup orange juice
Butter

In a large bowl combine the sliced apples, lemon juice, brown sugar, and cinnamon. In a small bowl soak the raisins until plump in hot water to cover. Drain and discard the water. Add the raisins and bran cereal to the apple mixture. Add the melted butter and mix. Pour the mixture into a buttered shallow baking dish, and pour the orange juice over all. Dot with butter. Cover the pan with foil. Bake at 400° for 40 minutes. Uncover and bake until brown on top, about 15 minutes. Makes 6 servings.

From Connie and Russell Johnson.

Name-Dropping

I have a lot of parents say to me, "I watched your show, and now my children watch you." I've had parents tell me they named their daughters after me, but my favorite was the family that said they named one daughter Ginger and another daughter Mary Ann. (Help!) I hope they grow up O.K. (Is there a Gilligan yet to come?)

Howell Doughnuts

2 cups Bisquick
1 egg
¼ cup sugar
1 teaspoon nutmeg
¼ teaspoon cinnamon

½ cup sour cream
½ cup sugar
1 teaspoon cinnamon
3 tablespoons melted butter
Frosting, if desired

In a large bowl combine the Bisquick, egg, ¼ cup sugar, nutmeg, ¼ teaspoon of cinnamon, and sour cream. Mix until a soft dough forms. On a floured surface smooth the dough gently into a ball, and knead 10 times. Roll the dough ½-inch thick, and cut with a floured cutter. Carefully lift the doughnuts with a spatula onto a cookie sheet, spacing the doughnuts 2 inches apart. Bake at 425° for 8 to 10 minutes, until golden brown.

In a small bowl mix together ½ cup of sugar and 1 teaspoon of cinnamon. Brush the doughnuts with melted butter and dip in the cinnamon-sugar mixture, coating all sides. Spread with frosting if desired. Makes about 8 to 10.

Mary Ann

Mary Ann Summers is the girl next hut for everyone on the island. The perky general store clerk from Winfield, Kansas, is almost always cheery and helpful. A conscientious worker, she's very likely the busiest Castaway, though the Professor seems rarely idle either.

Mary Ann's upbringing on a farm and her time spent in the Girl Scouts and 4-H make her well suited for handling most of the gardening and cooking on the island. The other Castaways are mighty thankful for that.

Back home, Mary Ann's family is hard working and probably of modest means — particularly after Randolph Blake forced her father into bankruptcy. But good fortune seems to follow Mary Ann like the sunshine. In fact, she won her cruise on the *S.S. Minnow* as part of a contest in Kansas.

It comes as no surprise that the pony-tailed farm girl is a fan of romance novels and that her favorite radio soap opera is "Blaze of Noon." One of her favorite island hobbies is butterfly collecting, yet farming and cooking are her true passions. You can't beat Mary Ann's pancakes, and she also comes up with some wonderfully imaginative dishes made from foods native to the island. But certainly none can top her most famous dish — everyone's favorite, her coconut cream pie.

Mary Ann is open and always honest. She is a good friend to all who know her, is always supportive of others, and is the kind of girl you could ask to the prom or take home to met mom. She's your best friend. Whether she's wearing her short-shorts or a gingham dress, it's Mary Ann's genuine homespun goodness that makes everyone comfortable around her. At one time or another, all of the Castaways find an understanding ear and an open heart with Mary Ann.

She dreams of living in London and on the Riviera, but Mary Ann also knows that when rescued, there'll be no place like home—back in Kansas.

Coconut Cream Pies

Mary Ann's Famous Coconut Cream Pie

3 egg yolks
Dash of salt
¾ cup sugar
3 cups milk
2 tablespoons butter
½ cup cornstarch

1 cup coconut
½ teaspoon vanilla extract
1 baked 9-inch pie shell
3 egg whites
Coconut for garnish

In the top of a double boiler over simmering water beat the egg yolks and salt. Add the sugar, milk, and butter. As soon as the bottom pot boils, mix the cornstarch with a small amount of water. Add it to the egg yolk mixture a little at a time. Cook until thick, stirring constantly with a wire whisk. Add the coconut and vanilla. Pour the filling into the baked pie shell. Beat the egg whites with a small amount of sugar and spread the meringue over the pie. Sprinkle coconut on top and toast in the oven. Makes 6 servings.

Cannibal Coconut Cream Pie

⅔ cup evaporated milk
⅓ cup water
½ cup coconut
2 tablespoons fine cracker meal
1 tablespoon butter

1 teaspoon vanilla extract
2 eggs, separated
1 unbaked 9-inch pie shell
2 tablespoons sugar
Coconut for garnish

In a saucepan combine the milk, water, and coconut, and cook for 10 minutes. Remove the pan from the heat and add the cracker meal, butter, and vanilla. When the mixture cools, add the beaten egg yolks. Pour the filling into the pie shell. Bake at 425° for 25 to 30 minutes or until set. Beat the egg whites with 2 tablespoons of sugar. Spread the meringue over the pie. Sprinkle with coconut, and toast in the oven. Makes 6 servings.

Gilligan's Favorite Coconut Cream Pie

1 ⅓ cup half-and-half
½ cup sugar
⅛ teaspoon salt
¼ cup all-purpose flour
3 eggs
½ teaspoon vanilla extract

3 cups shredded coconut
1 9-inch baked pie shell
3 tablespoons sugar
⅛ teaspoon salt
½ teaspoon vanilla extract

In the top of a double boiler over simmering water scald the half-and-half. Add ½ cup of sugar, ⅛ teaspoon of salt, and the flour, and stir until thick and smooth. Cover and cook for 15 to 20 minutes. Separate the eggs and beat the yolks. Remove the pan from the water and add the egg yolks gradually. Return the pan to the water and cook for 5 minutes. Remove the pan from the water again and add ½ teaspoon of vanilla and the coconut. Cool.

Pour the filling into the pie shell. Beat the egg whites with the remaining ingredients. Spread the meringue over the pie, and toast in the oven. Makes 6 servings.

Mrs. Howell's Favorite Coconut Custard Pie

4 eggs, slightly beaten
½ cup sugar
½ teaspoon salt
2 ½ cups milk

1 teaspoon vanilla extract
1 cup shredded coconut
1 9-inch unbaked pie shell
Nutmeg

In a large bowl beat the eggs slightly, and add the sugar and salt. Add milk and vanilla, and strain the custard. Add the coconut. Pour the filling into the pie shell. Sprinkle generously with nutmeg. Bake at 425° for 25 to 35 minutes or until a silver knife inserted in the center comes out clean. Makes 6 servings.

Ginger's Favorite Coconut Cream Pie

½ cup sugar
5 tablespoons all-purpose flour
⅛ teaspoon salt
¼ cup cold milk
1 ½ cups scalded milk

3 egg yolks, beaten
1 teaspoon vanilla extract
1 cup shredded coconut
1 9-inch baked pie shell
Meringue

In a saucepan blend together the sugar, flour, salt, and cold milk. Add the scalded milk gradually, stirring constantly. Cook over low heat until thick. Add the beaten egg yolks, then cook 2 minutes longer. Remove the pan from the heat and add the vanilla and coconut. Cool, then pour into the pie shell. Cover the top with meringue and toast in the oven. Makes 6 servings.

Mr. Howell's Favorite Coconut Custard Pie

⅔ cup sweetened condensed milk
2 cups hot water
3 eggs, slightly beaten
½ teaspoon salt

1 teaspoon vanilla or coconut extract
¼ cup shredded coconut
1 9-inch unbaked pie shell
Nutmeg

In a medium bowl combine the milk and water. In a separate bowl beat the eggs. Gradually stir the milk mixture into the eggs. Stir in the salt, vanilla, and coconut. Pour the filling into pie shell, and sprinkle the top with nutmeg. Bake at 400° for 10 minutes. Reduce the heat to 300° and bake 25 minutes longer, or until a knife blade inserted in the center comes out clean. Makes 6 servings.

Coconut cream what?

Dawn Wells collection

Skipper's Favorite Coconut Pie

1 envelope unflavored gelatin
½ cup sugar
¼ teaspoon salt
3 eggs, separated
1 ¼ cups milk

½ teaspoon almond extract
¾ cup shredded coconut, divided
1 9-inch graham cracker crust
¼ cup chopped toasted almonds

In the top of a double boiler combine the gelatin, sugar, and salt. Stir in the beaten egg yolks and milk. Cook over hot water, stirring constantly, until the mixture coats a silver spoon. Chill until the mixture is the consistency of unbeaten egg whites. Add the flavoring and ½ cup of the coconut. Beat the egg whites until stiff and fold them into the gelatin mixture. Pour the filling into the pie crust. Chill until firm. Combine the remaining coconut and almonds and sprinkle over the pie just before serving. Makes 6 servings.

""

Mary Ann bakes a special pie for the Skipper:

Skipper: Mary Ann just baked a coconut-pineapple pie, and I wanted to get the first piece before Gilligan finds out.

Professor: Coconut-pineapple pie? Mind if I join you?

Skipper: Oh, I've been smelling it all morning, just delicious, so creamy, so crunchy.

The pie is missing and all three think Gilligan took it, but Gilligan follows the trail of pie crusts and discovers his look-alike, a spy.

""

Professor's Favorite Coconut Cream Pie

¼ cup cornstarch
⅔ cup sugar
¼ teaspoon salt
2 cups milk
3 egg yolks, slightly beaten

1 cup flaked coconut
2 tablespoons butter or margarine
1 teaspoon vanilla extract
1 9-inch baked pastry shell
Meringue or whipped cream

In a saucepan combine the cornstarch, sugar, and salt. Gradually add the milk, and blend well. Cook over medium heat, stirring constantly, until thick. Blend a small amount of hot mixture into the egg yolks, then add the yolk mixture to the saucepan. Cook for 1 minute, stirring constantly. Add the coconut, butter, and vanilla, and blend well. Cover and cool to lukewarm, stirring occasionally. Pour the filling into the baked pastry shell. Top with meringue or whipped cream. Makes 6 servings.

Little Buddy Coconut Crunch Pie

1 4-ounce package butterscotch pudding
and pie filling
2 cups milk
1 8-inch baked pie shell

1 tablespoon butter
⅔ cup coconut
2 tablespoons firmly packed brown
sugar

In a saucepan combine the pudding mix and milk, and cook as directed on the package. Cool for 5 minutes, stirring once or twice. Pour the filling into the pie shell. Chill for about 30 minutes. In a skillet melt the butter and stir in the coconut and brown sugar. Blend well. Top the pie with this mixture. Broil about 3 inches from the heat until the coconut is golden brown and the sugar is melted, about 2 minutes. (Protect the rim of the pie shell with strips of aluminum foil.) Chill for 3 hours. Makes 6 servings.

Great Expectations—The Skipper knows Mary Ann has baked some coconut cream pies. Gilligan knows there aren't any left.

——————— **"** ———————

Skipper: Gilligan, you couldn't captain a toy ship in a rain barrel.

——————— **"** ———————

Island Native Coconut Pie

3 eggs
1 cup sugar
2 tablespoons butter

1 cup freshly grated coconut
1 9-inch unbaked pie shell

In a mixing bowl beat the eggs well with the sugar and butter. Add the coconut, and pour the filling into the pie shell. Bake at 350° until firm. Makes 6 servings.

Consolidated Chocolate Coconut Pie

1 ½ tablespoons butter or margarine, softened
1 ⅓ cup flaked coconut
3 eggs
½ cup sugar
1 8-ounce package cream cheese

1 12-ounce package sweet cooking chocolate broken into pieces
¼ cup milk
Whipped topping
Chocolate curls

Spread the butter evenly on the bottom and sides of a 9-inch pie pan. Press in the coconut to form a shell. In a blender combine the eggs, sugar, cream cheese, chocolate, and milk, and blend until smooth. Pour the filling into the shell. Bake at 350° for 30 minutes. Cool. Garnish with whipped topping and chocolate curls. Refrigerate any leftover pie. Makes 6 servings.

―― **"** ――

Skipper: If I only knew where I could get my hands on a two-inch T-bone steak.
Gilligan: I know.
Skipper: You do? Where?
Gilligan: Back there in Hawaii.

―― **"** ――

South Seas Coconut Pie

2 tablespoons melted butter
⅓ cup sugar
¼ teaspoon salt
3 eggs, slightly beaten
1 cup light corn syrup

1 teaspoon vanilla extract
½ teaspoon almond extract
⅔ cup finely grated coconut
1 9-inch unbaked pie shell

In a medium bowl blend the butter, sugar, and salt. Add the eggs, syrup, and extracts. Stir well. Sprinkle the coconut over the bottom of the pie shell. Pour the filling over the coconut. Bake at 375° for 45 to 50 minutes. Cool. Serve with whipped cream or ice cream. Makes 6 to 8 servings.

Trivia Quiz

Ginger's Teasers

1. Which two Castaways are you least likely to find wearing a hat?
   Ginger and the Professor

2. What is the rarest butterfly in the world?
   Pussycat swallowtail (according to Lord Beasley)

3. What were the names of the Castaways' two bands?
   The Honeybees and the Gnats

4. What is the name of Wrongway Feldman's plane?
   The Spirit of the Bronx

5. How many huts are on Gilligan's Island?
   Five

Fifi LaFrance's Coconut Pie

3 eggs
1 ¼ to 1 ½ cups sugar
¼ cup buttermilk

¼ cup melted butter or margarine
1 3 ½-ounce can flaked coconut
1 8-inch unbaked pastry shell

In a medium bowl beat the eggs slightly. Add the sugar, buttermilk, butter, and coconut. Mix well. Pour the mixture into an unbaked pastry shell. Bake at 350° for 35 to 45 minutes or until the coconut is golden brown. Makes 6 servings.

Mary Ann's Coconut Pie Crust

1 ½ cups coconut

2 tablespoons soft butter

Spread the butter evenly over the bottom and sides of a 9-inch pie pan. Press in the coconut to form a shell. Bake at 300° for 15 to 20 minutes, or until golden brown. Cool before filling. Makes 1 9-inch pie crust.

Maritime Meringue Pie Crust

2 egg whites
1 teaspoon vanilla extract
Dash salt

¼ teaspoon cream of tartar
1 cup sugar

In a large bowl beat the egg whites until frothy. Add the vanilla, salt, and cream of tartar, and blend. Add the sugar a small amount at a time, until stiff peaks form and the meringue is not grainy to touch. Spread into a well-buttered 9-inch pie pan, about ½-inch thick on the bottom and 1 ¾-inch thick on the sides. Make sort of a well in the center. Bake on the center rack at 275° for 1 hour.

Turn off the oven and let the meringue dry for 2 hours or longer. Do not open the oven door. Makes 1 9-inch pie crust.

Loco-Coco-Choco Fudge Pie Crust

2 1-ounce squares unsweetened choco-
**   late**
2 tablespoons butter

2 tablespoons hot milk or water
⅔ cup sifted confectioners' sugar
1 ½ cup coconut

In the top of a double boiler melt the chocolate and butter. Stir well. In a medium bowl combine the milk and sugar, and add the mixture to the chocolate. Add the coconut. Spread in the bottom of a greased 9-inch pie pan. Chill until firm. Makes 1 9-inch pie crust.

"Gilligan's Island" Episode Guide

1. *Two on a Raft.* After surviving the shipwreck of the *S.S. Minnow* and taking refuge on a deserted island, the Howells, Ginger, the Professor, and Mary Ann bid adieu and good luck to the Skipper and Gilligan as the duo sails for help on a raft.
2. *Home Sweet Hut.* The Castaways decide to build a large communal hut, but after disagreements, they begin constructing their own private huts.
3. *Voodoo Something to Me.* After a stranger raids the supply hut, the Castaways search for the thief, but the Skipper believes they're under a voodoo curse—especially when it appears Gilligan has been transformed into a chimp.
4. *Good Night Sweet Skipper.* The Castaways try to help the Skipper fall asleep, in order that he can dream about how to convert the radio into a transmitter.
5. *Wrongway Feldman.* The Castaways discover another inhabitant on the island, and he has an airplane.
6. *President Gilligan.* When the Castaways hold an election to select an island leader, Gilligan wins.
7. *Sound of Quacking.* As their food supply is dwindling, Gilligan catches a duck, which may be able to carry a message for help if it doesn't wind up as dinner first.
8. *Goodbye Island.* Gilligan discovers a sweet, sticky tree sap that appears to be strong enough to help patch up the Minnow and make it seaworthy.
9. *The Big Gold Strike.* Gilligan accidentally falls into a gold mine and strikes gold fever among the Castaways.
10. *Waiting for Watubi.* After unearthing a native idol, the Skipper believes he has been placed under an ancient curse.
11. *Angel on the Island.* Mr. Howell produces the play *Cleopatra* with Ginger in the lead role, but when Mrs. Howell gets jealous, he allows his wife a stab as the star.
12. *Birds Gotta Fly, Fish Gotta Talk.* On Christmas Eve, the Castaways recall their first day on the island when Gilligan tossed the transmitter into the ocean, and a fish swallowed it.
13. *Three Million Dollars More or Less.* Gilligan wins three million dollars from Mr. Howell on some golf bets, and the others all treat him differently because of his newfound wealth.
14. *Water Water Everywhere.* The Castaways run low on fresh water, and the Skipper turns to a divining rod in the quest for a new water supply.
15. *So Sorry, My Island Now.* Believing that World War II is still going on, a Japanese sailor in a submarine takes the Castaways captive.
16. *Plant You Now, Dig You Later.* The Castaways hold court to decide who gets possession of a treasure chest that Gilligan digs up while working for Mr. Howell.
17. *Little Island, Big Gun.* A bank robber with stolen loot takes refuge on the island.
18. *X Marks the Spot.* The Castaways await impending doom when they discover a Pentagon missile is zooming in on the island.
19. *Gilligan Meets Jungle Boy.* Gilligan makes friends with a jungle lad who is unable to speak English.

20. *St. Gilligan and the Dragon.* After the women become upset and retreat to the other side of the island, Gilligan and the Skipper disguise themselves as a dragon hoping to frighten them back.

21. *Big Man on a Little Stick.* A surfer hunk rides a long wave all the way to the island, where he then tries to make a splash with Ginger and Mary Ann.

22. *Diamonds Are an Ape's Best Friend.* A gorilla steals away Mrs. Howell for a girl-friend.

23. *How to Be a Hero.* Gilligan yearns to be a hero when a headhunter threatens the Castaways.

24. *The Return of Wrongway Feldman.* A woebegone pilot returns to the tropical island seeking relief from the burdens of civilization.

25. *The Matchmaker.* Mrs. Howell decides to make love blossom between Gilligan and Mary Ann.

26. *Music Hath Charm.* The Castaways create their own island orchestra, while natives from another island mount an offensive.

27. *New Neighbor Sam.* The Castaways overhear gangsters on the island at the same time they discover a talking parrot.

28. *They're Off and Running.* The Skipper bets Mr. Howell the services of Gilligan in a competition between racing turtles.

29. *Three To Get Ready.* Gilligan finds the Eye of the Idol, which the Skipper says is good for three wishes.

30. *Forget Me Not.* After a bump on the head and a dose of hypnotism, the Skipper imagines the other Castaways are Japanese soldiers.

31. *Diogenes, Won't You Please Go Home.* When the Castaways find out Gilligan has a secret diary, they all begin to pen their own versions of island heroics.

32. *Physical Fatness.* The Skipper goes on a diet to lose weight, while, at the same time, Gilligan gets fattened up.

33. *It's Magic.* When a crate filled with magician's props beaches in the lagoon, Ginger puts on a magic show and makes Gilligan disappear.

34. *Goodbye Old Paint.* The Castaways discover an artist is also living on their island.

35. *My Fair Gilligan.* The Howells adopt Gilligan and teach him the ways of fine society.

36. *A Nose by Any Other Name.* After Gilligan falls from a tree and busts his nose, the Professor agrees to perform surgery on his swollen proboscis.

37. *Gilligan's Mother-in-law.* A native chief and his family come to the island, and his homely daughter chooses Gilligan to be her husband.

38. *Beauty Is as Beauty Does.* Gilligan must cast the deciding vote in selecting which of the women will be named Miss Castaway.

39. *The Little Dictator.* A Latin American dictator is exiled upon the island with the Castaways.

40. *Smile, You're on Mars Camera.* The Castaways work to take advantage of a space satellite, equipped with a camera, which has dropped on the island.

41. *The Sweepstakes.* It appears that Gilligan has the winning ticket to a million-dollar sweepstakes.

42. *Quick Before It Sinks.* The Castaways try to build an ark after the Professor determines that the island is sinking into the ocean.

43. *Castaways Pictures Presents.* After salvaging movie-making equipment, the Castaways produce a silent movie telling the story of their plight.

44. *Agonized Labor.* The Howells attempt to learn a vocation after they find out their assets have been wiped out in a financial crisis.

45. *Nyet, Nyet—Not Yet.* The Castaways have high hopes of getting off the island after two Soviet cosmonauts accidentally land on the island.
46. *Hi-Fi Gilligan.* The Skipper accidentally raps Gilligan in the jaw, which causes his mouth to become a radio receiver.
47. *The Chain of Command.* The Skipper selects Gilligan to be next in charge, should the Skipper be incapacitated.
48. *Don't Bug the Mosquitoes.* A popular rock 'n' roll group drops in on the island to relax and practice their music.
49. *Gilligan Gets Bugged.* The Professor diagnoses that Gilligan has 24 hours to live after he is bitten by a deadly insect.
50. *Mine Hero.* A World War II mine floats into the lagoon, and Gilligan accidentally activates its timing mechanism.
51. *Erika Tiffany Smith to the Rescue.* A wealthy socialite comes to the island with plans of building an exotic resort and falls in love with the Professor.
52. *Not Guilty.* The Castaways find out a murder was committed the night before their ill-fated voyage, and they suspect one another as the culprit.
53. *You've Been Disconnected.* A telephone cable is washed ashore, and the Castaways try to make a call for help.
54. *The Postman Cometh.* Gilligan, the Skipper, and the Professor woo Mary Ann after she finds out her boyfriend back in Kansas has gotten married.
55. *Seer Gilligan.* Gilligan discovers that some wild sunflower seeds give him the ability to read other people's minds.
56. *Love Me, My Skipper.* The Howells decide to throw a big bash for the Castaways, but the Skipper never receives an invitation.
57. *Gilligan's Living Doll.* A robot parachutes to the island, and the Castaways hope to program it to send for help.
58. *Forward March.* The Castaways search for an unseen enemy that has been tossing grenades and firing bullets at them.
59. *Ship Ahoax.* Ginger appears to be able to read a crystal ball and predict the future.
60. *Feed the Kitty.* Gilligan practices being a lion tamer after the king of the jungle floats to the island on a raft.
61. *Operation: Steam Heat.* Gilligan discovers a hot water geyser, but the Professor realizes a volcano on the island is nearing the boiling point.
62. *Will the Real Mr. Howell Please Stand Up?* An imposter, a dead ringer for Mr. Howell, takes over Howell Industries and then is shipwrecked on the island.
63. *Ghost a Go-Go.* Gilligan finds a ghost has invaded the Castaways' island sanctuary.
64. *Allergy Time.* A sneezing fit seems to prove that the Skipper is allergic to Gilligan.
65. *The Friendly Physician.* A mad scientist takes the Castaways to his island laboratory where he is experimenting with brain swapping.
66. *"V" for Vitamins.* Because of a lack of vitamin C in their diet, the Castaways grow weary and attempt to plant orange seeds.
67. *Mr. and Mrs.?* Mr. and Mrs. Howell separate after finding out the minister who married them was a fraud.
68. *Meet the Meteor.* A meteorite falls to the island, and the Professor suspects it may cause them all to age much faster than normal.
69. *Up at Bat.* When a vampire bat bites Gilligan, he fears he is turning into a vampire.
70. *Gilligan vs. Gilligan.* A Russian spy, who exactly resembles Gilligan, investigates why the Castaways are on the island.

71. *Pass the Vegetables Please.* Gilligan discovers a crate of vegetable seeds, but, because they are radioactive, the fast-growing seeds produce unusual side effects.

72. *The Producer.* A Hollywood producer arrives on the island and directs the Castaways in a production of *Hamlet.*

73. *Voodoo.* A witch doctor comes to the island and wreaks havoc on the Castaways with his voodoo dolls.

74. *Where There's a Will.* Mr. Howell writes a new will and leaves a fortune to each of the Castaways, but then it appears one of them is trying to kill him.

75. *Man With a Net.* A butterfly collector alights on the island in search of a rare butterfly.

76. *Hair Today, Gone Tomorrow.* Gilligan's hair turns white, and then he goes bald.

77. *Ring Around Gilligan.* The mad scientist returns to the island and turns the Castaways into mind-controlled robots.

78. *Topsy-Turvy.* Gilligan has an accident that causes him to see everything upside down.

79. *The Invasion.* A lost U.S. government briefcase containing secret plans ends up handcuffed to Gilligan.

80. *The Kidnapper.* The Castaways attempt to reform an habitual kidnapper.

81. *And Then There Were None.* As the Castaways begin disappearing one by one, Gilligan starts to believe he is a Dr. Jekyll and Mr. Hyde clone.

82. *All About Eva.* Ginger tries to spice up the looks and personality of a homely librarian who has had no luck with romance.

83. *Gilligan Goes Gung Ho.* Gilligan takes his role as deputy a little too seriously and eventually locks all the Castaways in jail.

84. *Take a Dare.* A game show contestant is dropped on the island where he can win $10,000 if he can survive a week alone.

85. *Court Martial.* The Castaways recreate the wreck of the *S.S. Minnow* in order to convince the Skipper that he was not responsible for their misfortune.

86. *The Hunter.* A big-game hunter comes to the island and prepares for an exciting chase—to hunt down one of the Castaways.

87. *Lovey's Secret Admirer.* Mrs. Howell gets several anonymous love letters and then dreams that she is Cinderella.

88. *Our Vines Have Tender Apes.* An ape-man makes a nuisance of himself to the Castaways.

89. *Gilligan's Personal Magnetism.* Gilligan is struck by lightning while bowling, and the mishap leaves the bowling ball welded to his hand.

90. *Splashdown.* An unmanned space capsule lands in the lagoon and gives the Castaways hope for another chance of being rescued.

91. *High Man on the Totem Pole.* The Castaways discover a totem pole with a carved head atop that is the spitting image of Gilligan.

92. *The Second Ginger Grant.* Mary Ann suffers a concussion and awakens believing she is Ginger, so Ginger pretends to be Mary Ann.

93. *The Secret of Gilligan's Island.* The Castaways discover a jigsaw of stone tablets that may hold the key to getting off the island.

94. *Slave Girl.* When Gilligan saves the life of a native girl, she makes herself his servant forever.

95. *It's a Bird, It's a Plane, It's Gilligan.* The Air Force loses a jet pack, which gives Gilligan a chance to lose his head in the clouds.

96. *The Pigeon.* A homing pigeon flies to the island and provides the Castaways with a way to communicate with a birdman back in civilization.

97. *Bang! Bang! Bang!* Gilligan finds a crate of "Secret Material," which the Castaways use in a variety of ways—not realizing how explosive it is.
98. *Gilligan, the Goddess.* A native king comes to the island in search of a goddess wife.

The Gilligan TV Movies
1. *Rescue From Gilligan's Island* (1978). A tidal wave proves to be a godsend as the Castaways float to Hawaii in their huts and begin life anew back home after fourteen years of being marooned. They eventually realize that they miss one another's company.
2. *The Castaways on Gilligan's Island* (1979). When Mr. Howell builds a resort on Gilligan's Island, the others assist in the daily operation and help some of their guests solve their personal dilemmas.
3. *The Harlem Globetrotters on Gilligan's Island* (1981). The Globetrotters crash near the island and then compete in a basketball game against robots—with ownership of the island at stake.

Dawn Wells collection

Olé! —This is one of my favorite costumes from the run of the series. I wore it in *The Little Dictator* episode.

The Original "Gilligan's Island" Fan Club

At the helm of The Original Gilligan's Island Fan Club is Bob Rankin of Salt Lake City, Utah. He took over as president after somewhat of a low tide in the lagoon in 1991.

"The fan club originated in 1965 out of Hollywood from the efforts of a United Artists publicity agent who was working on the show," says Rankin. "The club continued for a few more years after the show went off CBS, then it slowly drifted apart.

"It started back in 1972 out of Las Vegas, and when the *Rescue From Gilligan's Island* movie was released in 1978, the club grew again and had thousands of members. Over the following few years it had slowly gone by the wayside, so, because I had always had an interest in the show, I decided to try to get it back up and running."

And that's just what Rankin, a club member since 1972, did. In 1978, he initiated a petition to have the Castaways rescued from Gilligan's Island by contacting NBC programming chief at the time, Fred Silverman. "He told me, 'You show me there's some interest and we'll do the show.'"

That's all Rankin, then in his late teens, needed to hear: "I got a list of names from all fifty states—more than 18,000 signatures on petitions in just a few weeks. We boxed them and sent them off to Silverman."

Today there are about 750 first mates listed on the club's log. Skipper Rankin says 1994, the thirtieth anniversary of "Gilligan's Island," is a watershed year for the show and the club. He hopes 1994 will be remembered as the Year of Gilligan.

How does Rankin explain the fascination for a television sitcom set on a desert island that's nearly thirty years old? "You always hear Sherwood Schwartz say it's because of the significance of the people and how it's a microcosm of society. But what it is, it's the show that so many people remember coming home to after school and having it give them a good feeling.

"Many fan club members are between the ages of 28 and 40 and are raising kids themselves, and they're looking at the influence TV has on kids," Rankin says. "They'd much rather have their kids sitting in front of 'Gilligan's Island' because it's sort of a safety zone for them; it's harmless and enjoyable. It's a safe show for parents."

Membership in The Original Gilligan's Island Fan Club entitles all its little buddies to a quarterly, sixteen-page newsletter, a T-shirt that says "Stuck on Gilligan's Island" and a 4x6-inch color photo of the seven Castaways—all for $15 dues ($20 overseas.) Fifty cents of each initiation fee goes to the Make a Wish Foundation.

The club will forward fan mail to cast members of the show, and it also offers "Gilligan" memorabilia for sale. To join The Original Gilligan's Island Fan Club, ship your message in a bottle to P.O. Box 25311, Salt Lake City, UT, 84125-0311. Enclose a self-addressed, stamped envelope for a response to make sure your letter doesn't get lost at sea.

The Dawn Wells Fan Club

By the time Dawn began her role on "Gilligan's Island" in 1964, she already had made a number of appearances on some of the most popular television shows of the sixties. It's therefore no surprise that Dawn already had her own fan club when she auditioned for the role of Mary Ann and that she generally received the most fan mail of the seven Castaways when the show was in its original run. Her first fan club president was Pam Payne, followed by Brian Panette. They are all still friends.

Today, Dawn still receives letters from all over the world. "Many of the letters are from fans who want to tell Dawn how much the laughter she has given has helped them through some painful time in their lives," says Bill Graff who now runs the fan club.

"Young girls often write to express their admiration of her as a role model, while boys write to propose marriage!" Graff adds. "Some of the nicest letters, though, come from adults who grew up watching 'Gilligan's Island,' and now watch with their own children."

The club publishes *The Masthead,* a four-page quarterly newsletter dedicated to Dawn and her career. It gives the latest news about her stage and television performances, her public appearances, and other activities. The newsletter also includes trivia, Dawn's answers to questions from fans, and behind-the-scenes stories about "Gilligan's Island."

The annual membership of $14 includes a personalized membership card, subscription to the newsletter, a personally autographed picture of Dawn, and a photograph of the whole cast of "Gilligan's Island." Also offered are some T-shirts and memorabilia for sale.

For more information or to join The Dawn Wells Fan Club, write to P.O. Box 291817, Los Angeles, CA 90029. In the meantime, Dawn wishes you well!

Making a Lasting Impression—Here I am signing my name in cement in the Cowboy Hall of Fame in Oklahoma City.

Dawn Wells collection

Dawn Wells Biography

Dawn Wells has fans running from eight to eighty years of age and all because "Gilligan's Island" is never ending.

Although Dawn thought she had escaped the island many years ago, she never counted on the show's being seen in syndication—often two or three times daily—for three decades.

Meanwhile, she has run the gamut of the entertainment business—working in television, feature films, and theater—and even teaching drama as artist-in-residence at Purdue University and her alma mater, Stephens College.

Dawn, who has made guest appearances on more than 100 television shows and starred in several motion pictures, is a fourth-generation Nevadan. She was born and raised in Reno and competed as Miss Nevada in the Miss America pageant.

Attending Stephens, a women's college in Missouri, she earned her A.A. degree after switching her major from chemistry to acting. She then received a B.A. in drama at the University of Washington. Dawn credits Stephens for giving her self-confidence and the ability to think for herself—qualities she considers an advantage in acting. She feels so strongly about her alma mater that she returns occasionally as an artist-in-residence, performing on campus and teaching an advanced acting class. She serves on the school's advisory boards for radio and television and was past chairman of the Development Board, and she currently serves on the Board of Trustees .

In addition to television and film, Dawn has done over sixty stage productions. She adores theater and has enjoyed a versatility of starring roles in such plays as *Steel Magnolias, Night of the Iguana, Playing Our Song, Chapter Two, Romantic Comedy, Private Lives,* and *The Effect of Gamma Rays on Man in the Moon Marigolds,* to name just a few. She played opposite John Lawlor in *Same Time, Next Year* and with Marcia Wallace in the female version of *The Odd Couple.*

Dawn has performed throughout the United States and Canada—including Toronto, where she originated the role of Blair, opposite Ken Howard, in Bernard Slade's *Fatal Attraction.*

The other side of Dawn reflects her many interests. She's been actively involved with the Children's Miracle Network Telethon for many years. She has co-hosted and co-produced the event for mid-Missouri since 1985, and she serves on the University of Missouri's Children's Hospital advisory board.

Dawn has been honored with the Alumna of the Year Award from Stephens College, the Volunteer of the Year Award by the Council for the Advancement and Support of Education (CASE), and the National Civic Leadership Award from Alpha Chi Omega. She also serves on the board of directors for Artsgenesis, a national arts-and-education, not-for-profit organization in New York that brings professional artists into the schools for performances, workshops, and teacher training.

Additionally, Dawn is a businesswoman: She has created a fashionable, specialized clothing line, Wishing Wells Collections. She believes in preserving the quality of life and providing beauty and individuality for those who have difficulty in dressing themselves. She was inspired to design the collection because of an ill grandmother and as a result of the quick costume changes she has so often experienced backstage.

Dawn's private life is as busy as her business life. She is a true adventurer. She has traveled much of the world—from Rwanda with its mountain gorillas to the primitive islands of the Solomons. Dawn loves to learn about other lands, cultures, and peoples. She wants to see what there is to see, do what there is to do, and be all she can be.

Natalie and I were very close friends. Here she is helping me by posing with my "Wishing Wells Collections" line of clothing.

Acknowledgments ("...and the Rest")

There are so many people that Ken, Jim, and I would like to thank for their recipes, encouragement, photos, and just plain hard work. We're grateful to them all for making this launch a smooth sail, and a dream come true for me.

For the recipes, thanks to my mother first and foremost, and to my ancestors for handing down such sumptuous dishes—my Grammie Rose, Grandmother Wells, Great-Aunt Louise, and my Great-Grandmother Wells. Others who contributed recipes are cousins Ruth and Jim Thomson; friends Lucy Kohn, Diane Skomars Magrath, Angie Berg, Mary Jane Kaufman, Carole Britton, Barbara Hales, Marcia Moussa's mom, Marion, and Michael and Annie McCoy from the Solomon Islands.

Our heartfelt gratitude goes to "Gilligan" creator Sherwood Schwartz and to Mildred Schwartz, as well as to my fellow Castaways and their spouses: Bob and Dreama Denver; Russ and Connie Johnson; Alan and Trinket Hale; Jim and Henny Backus; Tina Louise; Natalie Schafer and her dear friend Maury Hill; and Globetrotting friend Geese Ausbie. I'd especially like to thank Bob Denver for his lovely foreword.

For the photos and general encouragement, we're most grateful to James Tobin; Dr. Patsy Sampson; Bob Rankin; Steve Cox; Frank Sutherland and Sandy Smith at *The Tennessean;* Pat Embry and Mike McGehee at the *Nashville Banner;* Turner Entertainment; Kevin Marhanka; Brent Baldwin; Ron Turner; and everyone else who has sent me photos over the years.

Our deepest appreciation goes to all of those who helped tremendously throughout the process of putting this book together: Mickey Freeman, Bill Birnes, Bill Graff, Max Smith, Jim Mancuso, and Jamie Lafer. And special thanks to Larry Rosen for helping me land the role of Mary Ann in the first place. Ken has particular thanks for his wife Wendy, daughter Kylie, and son Cole, and Jim is grateful to his wife, Mary, for not sending out the search planes while their two little buddies were stranded with me on Gilligan's Island.

And finally, we'd like to thank all the folks at Rutledge Hill Press: Larry Stone and Ron Pitkin for making all the pieces fit together; Julie Pitkin for her savvy and patient editing; designer Harriette Bateman; marketing director Bryan Curtis; and the rest of the hard-working Rutledge Hill crew that helped make this book a reality.

Thank you all so much.

Index